WHAT TO COOK

When You Think There's Nothing in the House to Eat

MORE THAN 175 RECIPES AND MEAL IDEAS

by Arthur Schwartz

HarperPerennial

A Division of HarperCollinsPublishers

HarperCollins books may be purchased for educational, business, or sales promotional use. For information, please call or write: Special Markets Department, HarperCollins Publishers, 10 East 53rd Street, New York, NY 10022. Telephone: (212) 207-7528; Fax: (212) 207-7222.

FIRST EDITION

Designed by Charles Kreloff

LIBRARY OF CONGRESS CATALOG CARD NUMBER
91-55141

ISBN 0-06-055326-X
ISBN 0-06-096432-4 (pbk.)

92 93 94 95 96 DT / RRD 10 9 8 7 6 5 4 3 2 1
92 93 94 95 96 DT / RRD 10 9 8 7 6 5 4 3 2   (pbk.)

In memory of my dear parents, Sydell and Larry

Contents

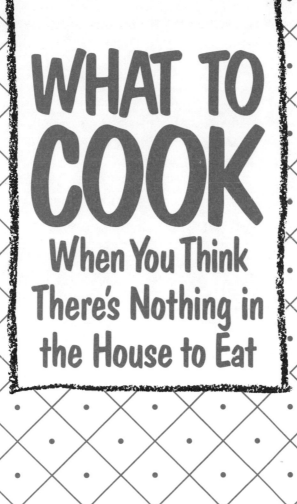

WHAT TO COOK

When You Think There's Nothing in the House to Eat

Introduction

Holly Golightly types will have no use for this book. Those who keep only champagne and shoes in the refrigerator must suffer with no supper at all. At least Holly could breakfast at Tiffany's.

On the other hand, Boy Scouts and Girl Scouts, those who feel more secure knowing they're always prepared to cook a little meal for themselves, family, and friends should find this book invaluable. It proves that by strategically stocking the cupboard, refrigerator, and freezer, what is quaintly called "the larder," it is always possible to make something simple, quick, delicious, and nutritious to eat.

This is not a fancy food cookbook. It's an everyday food book with mostly traditional, mostly basic recipes, mainly updated working-class and farm food from many different cultures and for the new working class—those singles, couples, and young families that often do not have time to shop for dinner. It is not for hobbyist cooks who like to spend hours in the kitchen, nor for those who would just as soon microwave a frozen dinner as boil up some spaghetti or prepare a little pot of hot soup. It is meant for those who have only elementary cooking skills, as well as ingredients, but still think something cooked from scratch at home—no matter how basic—is more rewarding to eat than something picked up from the frozen food case or a takeout shop. Still, I hope the serious cook with a midnight appetite, an unexpected guest, or any other last-minute or emergency situation can also find inspiration and guidance for taking kitchen staples and turning them into a comforting and tasty plate of food.

Because of their peasant background, many of the world's most noble and sustaining dishes are made with the most mundane ingredients, many storable for longer periods than most people believe.

Did you know, for instance, that a box of spaghetti lasts longer than the average marriage? Add olive oil (which, even in the typically overheated American cupboard, will keep for at least a year), some garlic (a two-month life at room temperature, if it's really fresh when bought), a pinch of hot pepper (my three-year-old Abruzzese *peperoncino* is still perfectly peppery), and you've got a dish—*spaghetti aglio e olio*—that every Italian, from the boot's heel to the hip, will applaud.

There are many pasta dishes here, and other one-bowl or -plate dishes that can be considered a meal unto themselves—rice recipes, a potato casserole, many soups, and some bean dishes—most of them are proportioned to serve two or three. In fact, there are few recipes that serve more than four, under the assumption that if you need to cook for a greater number than that, you would certainly be prepared.

In addition, there are many appetizers and snacks for when someone drops by for a drink or you simply need to fulfill a craving. There are quick desserts—some cooked in the microwave oven—and baking recipes that take a conventional amount of time, for days when you're stuck at home with nothing but sweets on your mind.

How to Use This Book

This book is organized alphabetically by ingredient. Each entry offers tips for selecting and purchasing the ingredient, where and how long it can be kept on hand, under what conditions, plus recipes in which that ingredient is the main feature.

If you actually had every ingredient in the book, you probably wouldn't need the book, but if, for instance, you have not much more than a can of tomatoes on hand, look under Tomatoes for a recipe in which you will need little else. At the end of that entry, there are suggestions for variations, substitutions, and "fresh touches"—additions of fresh ingredients. There is also a list of recipes that secondarily feature tomatoes and that can be found elsewhere in the book.

If you are interested in a recipe to fit a specific occasion—a one-bowl meal for a simple supper, a recipe for brunch, a soup or a pasta recipe, a rice dish, or a side dish to go with some fresh fish, meat, or poultry that you have managed to pick up at the market, see the recipe indexes at the back of the book.

About Storage Conditions

The optimum refrigerator temperature is 40 degrees, though most people keep it slightly higher and, within each unit, the temperature varies from top to bottom. In a model with separate top freezer, the top shelf is usually the coldest, as cold as vegetable storage bins at the bottom. The center shelves are the point where the temperature is measured.

For optimum storage time, the temperature in your freezer should be 0 degrees or less.

Room temperature is about 70 degrees, which is pretty warm. It makes for rapid deterioration of food. Colder household temperatures will result in a longer shelf life for foods kept in the cupboard. For example, foods kept in a weekend home will last longer than the times cited in most entries because the temperature is kept to a minimum—50 or 55 degrees—most of the week in the winter.

About Storage Containers

Air, heat, light, and insects are the enemies of food, so it makes sense to store foods that are sold in boxes or bags—such as rice, beans, grains (including flour), and sugar—in glass jars with screw tops, rubber-sealed canning jars, plastic storage containers, or kitchen canisters designed for the purpose. At garage sales and flea markets I've collected numerous old jars with ground glass stoppers—like apothecary jars—to display foods that do not deteriorate with some exposure to light, such as beans and wild rice. They are attractive kitchen decor at the same time that they are a reminder that there is always something in the house to eat. Foods that are affected by light should be kept in a dark cupboard. Specifics are mentioned in each ingredient entry.

About Cans

Canned foods are among the longest-lived in the larder, but they do spoil. Do not purchase or use cans with rust spots. Dented cans should be used as soon as possible; they are the most susceptible to air penetration and quick deterioration. Beware of bloated cans or lids, even those on jars of refrigerated products; throw them out. In fact, it's wise to observe this rule in general: When in doubt, throw it out.

About Kitchen Equipment

As most of the recipes in this book call for only basic ingredients, they also call only for basic pots, pans, and other equipment. A food processor or blender will be handy for some recipes, but necessary in very few. There are microwave directions for some recipes, and some have been developed specifically for the micro-wave oven. However, you can prepare almost all the recipes in the book with equipment that is basic to any kitchen: A small (about 1 quart) saucepan, a medium (2½- to 3-quart) saucepan, a pot for boiling pasta (at least 5 quarts), a small (about 7-inch) skillet, a medium (about 10-inch) skillet, an 8- or 9-inch round and 8- or 9-inch square baking pan, a four-sided grater, a strainer, a colander, some wooden spoons, a set of measuring spoons, a set of dry ingredient mixing cups, a 2-cup and 4-cup Pyrex measuring cup, a few mixing bowls, and rubber spatulas.

The Top Ten Ingredients and Other Pantry Staples

Think of making something from nothing as a game, an ingredient anagram. The goal is to put your food stores together in as many combinations and permutations as possible. Admittedly, cooking meals in a kitchen with only these top ten ingredients would become dreary in a short time, but with them on hand you could prepare, at the very least, spaghetti with onions, spaghetti with onions and tuna, spaghetti with butter and cheese, spaghetti with butter alone or oil alone. And, in any of those combinations, you could substitute rice for the pasta. You could also prepare a tuna-noodle casserole, a cheese omelet, an onion omelet, scones, biscuits, rice pudding, salad dressing, and eggnog.

It was extremely difficult to narrow down the essential ingredients to merely ten. For example, I'd hate to be without garlic. One might want to substitute potatoes for rice. And I find canned tomatoes, cans of chicken and beef broth, fresh carrots, and canned and dried beans absolutely invaluable.

The Top Ten Ingredients

(Aside from salt, pepper, sugar, and water)

1. **Spaghetti or Macaroni** (see page 198)

2. **Milk**

"Bevete piu latte," "Drink more milk," sang a billboard-sized Anita Ekberg in the 1962 Italian film *Boccaccio 70*. Her famous endowment made the innocent jingle a joke, but drinking more milk is no longer a

laughing matter. For the same high-fat, high-cholesterol reasons that Americans now eschew eggs, we now drink mainly skimmed or low-fat milk. All the recipes in this book, including baked goods, have been tested with 1 percent milk, the same milk I use in coffee and therefore always have (I wish) in the refrigerator.

Unfortunately, and though it sounds like the opposite of what should be true, low-fat milk (1 percent, 2 percent, and skim, at under 0.5 percent) spoils more quickly than whole milk (with from 3 to 3.8 percent fat). A last date of sale marked on the milk carton is the consumer's only freshness authority, which is why so many municipalities and states require them. Find out what the regulations are in your area, and figure that after the last date of sale, the milk has another 3 days to a week.

Keep it refrigerated, pour off the amount needed, then return the rest to the refrigerator immediately, and don't pour back any unused milk; store it separately and covered. (This is a very good excuse for collecting creamers and little pitchers.)

For when all else fails, there's nothing like the security of a packet of nonfat dry milk, a product that the processors say will keep a year on a relatively cool and very dry shelf, but which I have pressed into service significantly after that time. It may not be a particularly nutritious food by then—the proteins become denatured or something—but it will serve a cooking purpose. In a pinch, reconstituted nonfat dry milk can replace fresh milk in most baked goods, batters, and white sauces. It is a more significant compromise as a beverage. You don't want to drink it when it is just prepared. It tastes much better if made ahead and well chilled for at least 8 hours.

3. Eggs (see page 125)

4. Onions (see page 190)

5. Tuna (see page 254)

6. Olive Oil (see page 182) **or Butter or Vegetable Oil**

Contemporary concerns about cholesterol may have turned real creamery butter into a "bad guy" food, but I find its unique flavor and texture irresistible and indispensable. Though I cook more frequently with olive oil, I always have at least one stick of butter in the freezer because there are some things I cannot imagine wanting to eat without it: Risotto, any variety of cornmeal mush, most baked goods, and that other cholesterol powerhouse, eggs.

Butter and eggs seem to have been made for each other. Even egg noodles are better with butter than olive oil. One of the most heavenly smells (and tastes) on earth is onions frying in butter. Margarine or oil, though perhaps acceptable for baking, leaves cookies and cakes lacking.

Butter easily picks up refrigerator odors, and most refrigerator butter storage dishes don't protect it enough. Wrap opened sticks of butter closely in plastic. How long it will stay fresh depends on how often it goes in and out of the refrigerator, and how long it stays out each time. Don't worry: Rancid butter, which you should not eat, is easily detectable by its smell.

Unwrapped sticks of butter in wax paper will keep in the refrigerator for about 3 months, even longer if wrapped in foil, as some brands are. To be safe, however, keep butter in the freezer, where it will remain fresh for up to a year.

What is sold generically as "vegetable oil" is usually soybean oil or a blend of oil containing mostly soybean oil. However, corn oil, peanut oil, safflower oil, sunflower oil, canola (rape seed) oil and grape seed oil are also known collectively as vegetable oils. They are, in varying degrees, low in saturated fats and high in polyunsaturated and monounsaturated fats, nearly tasteless or with a light taste, and they all have a light texture and a high smoking point, making them the right oils for some sautéing and almost all frying. Even when sautéing or frying with butter, a little vegetable oil added to the pan will prevent the butter from burning easily.

Light-colored, light-flavored virgin olive oil can also be lumped with these vegetable oils, even more so the new "lite" light olive oils. Fruity virgin and extra-virgin olive oils (see page 182) are technically vegetable oils, too, but their flavor is too aggressive for general use.

Air, light, and heat are the enemies of oil. An unopened bottle of vegetable oil will keep a maximum of a year on a dark, typically overheated cupboard shelf. An opened, optimally fresh bottle will keep about 6 months or so. Between store turnover, buying and opening dates, and kitchen temperatures, there are so many variables determining oil freshness that it is always best to check for deterioration before pouring any oil into a skillet. Rancid oil is dark, and it smells. If in doubt, taste some.

7. Vinegar

In a sense, vinegar is the result of something—specifically a sweet liquid—having spoiled twice. Grape juice ferments and becomes wine; wine turns to wine vinegar. Malted barley ferments and becomes beer, then micro-organisms turn beer into malt vinegar. Apple juice becomes cider; cider becomes cider vinegar. Rice ferments to rice "wine"—though it is technically a beer because it is made from a grain, not fruit—and faintly sweet rice wine, what the Japanese call *sake*, becomes rice vinegar.

In all cases, the first "spoilage" takes place when yeasts metabolize sugar into alcohol. The second transformation takes place when certain bacteria metabolize the alcohol into acetic acid. This may be oversimplifying, but you get the point: Vinegar has spoiled so much that it will never spoil again. It will keep, at room temperature, in a closed bottle indefinitely; that is, until it evaporates. Sometimes, however, after very long storage with slight exposure to air, wine vinegar will become cloudy, or develop a scum or sticky sediment that is, in fact, a new colony of vinegar-producing bacteria. This is called the "mother of vinegar." Cherish it; use it to transform leftover wine into more vinegar.

As must also be clear, vinegar comes in natural flavors that reflect the source of the vinegar. Cider vinegar has an unmistakable apple aroma. Rice vinegar smells like the Orient. Malt vinegar has the right taste to sprinkle on fish and chips. Red wine vinegar can be dark and fruity, sharp and austere, mellow and subtle. Sherry vinegar, produced from the Spanish fortified wine, has its own special vinous flavor and aroma. Unflavored white wine vinegar is hard to find these days but a really good one should be soft and almost butter flavored.

Balsamic vinegar from Modena, Italy, is a rich, rather sweet vinegar that has become somewhat overexposed in the last decade. Authentic, traditionally made balsamic vinegar —which takes generations to mature and requires micro-organisms particular to a small northern Italian eco-system—is an elixir that's doled out by the teaspoon. More medicine (balsam) than food, it was never meant to be tossed on every salad, stirred into any sauce, or sprinkled anywhere a little cachet is needed. The vast majority of balsamic vinegars available here are factory made, relatively inexpensive, and though an excellent product, should still be used with restraint.

White vinegar is a colorless, relatively characterless product of grain alcohol, and though it is good for household cleaning, and is the preferred vinegar for making pickles, it is the least interesting for seasoning food.

To that end, an enormous number of flavored vinegars are now on the market—tarragon vinegar, basil vinegar, berry vinegars, vinegars with mixed herbs, vinegars with flower petals, and vinegars with mixed herbs and flower petals.

8. **Flour** (see page 131)

9. **Cheese** of some kind (see page 81)

10. **Rice** (see page 218)

Other Pantry Staples

Herbs, Spices, and Extracts

Now that American home cooks have discovered the vibrant flavors of fresh herbs, and fresh herbs have become more widely available in supermarkets (at luxury prices I must add), cooking teachers and cookbook writers are trying to discourage the use of all dried herbs. I was shocked to hear a popular TV cooking personality denounce them soundly. It is true that dried herbs are often second best, and in a few cases (dried basil and parsley) they can indeed ruin a dish rather than enhance it. But there are some common herbs that are just as flavorful in their dried state as when they are fresh—thyme, tarragon, and rosemary, for instance. And a few dried herbs can, because they have a more potent flavor than their fresh counterparts, be preferable in some recipes—oregano and mint, to name the most dramatic examples.

Herbs are the leaves (and sometimes stems) of plants. What we call spices are usually the seeds, berries, barks, and roots of plants. In the case of herbs, buy the most whole form available. They will last longer—usually about a year. Rosemary leaves, for example, remain potent a good 18 months, while ground rosemary becomes as tasty as dust almost as soon as the jar is opened. The more delicate the herb, the shorter its shelf life in the dried form. Dill probably has the shortest, and, after rosemary, oregano is the next longest keeping. To increase the flavoring power of whole-leaf herbs—particularly those that have faded—put the measured amount of dried herb in the palm of one hand and rub with the heel of the other.

As is unquestionably the case with black and white pepper, some spices are also better bought in their whole form. For instance, freshly grated whole nutmeg has far more flavor and aroma than the preground nutmeg available in bottles, and small, easy-to-use nutmeg graters are available in any kitchen shop. On the other hand, though cumin seeds and allspice berries keep years longer than their ground counterparts, it can be quite inconvenient to have to grind cumin or allspice every time you want to add a little to a recipe.

Different brands of herbs and spices vary dramatically in quality, and most of the processors now have two qualities—the lesser most often sold in tins, the premium in bottles. From considerable experience and experimenting, I would say it definitely pays to buy the most expensive —so long as the store turns its stock over regularly. In particular, Spice Island products are not only superior in vibrancy and flavor to start, but remain viable longer than any other brand. Incidentally, some spice companies now sell small jars of herbs on the theory that consumers would rather buy a small amount than throw away half of the larger jar because it wasn't used quickly enough. However, the considerably higher unit cost of the small packages does not make them an economical purchase. When herbs and spices lose their power, put them on the hot coals of the barbecue right before the food goes on the grill. They'll scent the smoke and flavor the food faintly.

The worst place to keep herbs and spices is over the stove, as so many people do. The second worst place is on a spice rack hung on a kitchen wall, under a cabinet, or placed on the counter, unless the rack is designed to keep light from the jars. The best place to keep herbs and spices is on the same dark, dry shelf on which other foods are kept. As herbs and spices age, use more of them to keep the flavor level the same. The only way to know how far gone they are is to smell them or taste them. Also remember that herbs and spices added at the beginning of cooking marry into food and taste less dominant. If a more pronounced flavor is desired, add them toward the end of cooking.

Extracts are alcohol-based flavorings, mainly for cakes and desserts. Vanilla and almond extracts are the two most commonly used. Purchase pure extracts, not vanillin or imitation products. They keep indefinitely.

Honey

Honey has the reputation of being healthier than white sugar, but most nutrition experts now agree that it is only marginally superior. In any case, it is tricky substituting honey for sugar in recipes, especially baked goods, and the flavor of most honey is so aggressive that, unlike sugar, it tends to dominate desserts to which it is added. If you like the flavor of honey, however, it makes a fine ice cream topping, sweetener for hot or cold cereal, or dip for fresh fruits, particularly apples and pears.

Keep jars or pots of honey tightly closed on a dry, dark shelf. If the honey crystallizes or becomes cloudy, it can be restored to a clear liquid by placing the jar in a pan of very hot, but not boiling water. Heating gently in a microwave oven (on LOW) will also do the job. Do not allow honey to heat beyond 160 degrees or its flavor will change.

Jams, Jellies, and Preserves

After my father died, my sister and I wondered what my mother ate when she was alone for dinner. Most nights she went out to a restaurant with friends, but because she had never been much of an eater (and cooked only when she absolutely had to) we thought she might be eating nothing when she wasn't socializing.

"You don't have to worry," she told me. "I have jam and crackers." And I can guarantee, she didn't say that to invoke any pity or guilt. To her, jam and crackers, plus a couple of cups of black coffee (always in china, never pottery) was a very fine supper. At the time she had a stock of Fauchon strawberry preserves that we had bought in Paris together several months before, and I'm sure she felt quite luxurious eating what she liked best, in a tiny amount, with no one around to urge her to eat more, and with nothing but a little plate, a knife, and a mug to wash afterward.

It's nice to be so easily satisfied.

For those many of us to whom ice cream is more comforting than crackers, jams and preserves are useful as a topping—straight from the jar or heated and thinned with an appropriate liqueur or spirit. And for those of us who will go so far as to cook for comfort, jams, jellies, and preserves make good fillings for crêpes (see page 137), omelets, and cream puff shells (see page 140).

Unopened jars of jelly (clear), jam (jelly with fruit pulp), preserves (a less gelatinized product with distinguishable pieces of fruit), marmalade (made with citrus peel), and conserves (jams or preserves with more than one fruit, and sometimes nuts) usually keep about a year on a relatively cool, dry shelf. Discoloration is an indication that the product is oxidizing and has changed flavor. Opened jars should be kept refrigerated and will hold up about 6 months. If mold forms on the top of the product, spoon it off and use the remainder as soon as possible.

Leavenings

Baking soda and baking powder are a boon to busy cooks; they're stable chemicals that can be left indefinitely in a kitchen cupboard, always handy for rising pancakes, quick breads, cookies, biscuits, and muffins.

Dry yeast, which is used for leavening breads and some cakes, has a long but limited shelf life, and an expiration date is always marked on the package. (Fresh yeast, which is a live microorganism and deteriorates within a week, is not used in any recipes in this book.)

Maple Syrup

Pure maple syrup is an incomparable product, a rare, uniquely North American delicacy. It is the sap of sugar maple trees that has been painstakingly reduced from 40 to 50 gallons to 1 gallon over a gas or wood fire, at which point it becomes this viscous elixir. It is, therefore, very expensive. You don't need to buy the highest grade of syrup, however. Depending on where it comes from—New York State, Vermont, Connecticut, Massachusetts, Canada, etc.—the highest grade (the lightest, most delicate syrup) is graded AAA or called "light amber." Lesser letter grades or the words "medium amber" or "dark amber" are used for the heavier, thicker syrup which, to many people, including me, is at least as good if not preferable.

Unopened cans or jugs of maple syrup can be kept on a dry shelf for about 2 years. Once opened, they should be refrigerated. Maple syrup does turn sour on occasion, but more frequently mold is its spoiler. Sour syrup should be dumped. The mold should be skimmed off the syrup—it will probably be necessary to pour the syrup into a bowl to do so—then boiled and skimmed again. Repack the syrup into a sterilized jar and continue to store in the refrigerator.

For the sake of keeping pancakes, waffles, and French toast hot, warm syrup that has been kept refrigerated. Pour off as much as will be served into a jar or cup, then place the jar or cup in a pot of barely simmering water until heated through.

Maple syrup is a fabulous ice cream topping, flavoring for milk, topping for oatmeal (see page 177), and sweetener for fruit (see page 19).

Mustard

There are a bewildering number of mustards on the market today, though there seems to be little gastronomic reason for most of them. I have yet to find a compatible food partner for raspberry mustard, zinfandel mustard, or tarragon mustard with orange rind. A tin of English dry mustard; a jar of normal, American brown deli-style mustard; one of strong Dijon-style, one of whole-grain mustard, and perhaps one of honey mustard is already a very complete mustard collection, offering even the most avid sandwich maker, salad tosser, and serious saucier more than enough mustard flavors. The only thing I'd add to this collection is Chinese mustard. I always seem to have some plastic tubes of it around from takeout Chinese dinners, and it often comes in handy to spike a sauce or a salad dressing. I have even gone so far as to use it,

without embellishment, as a cracker spread and as a dip for ziti. That was really making something from nothing.

Pickles, Chutney, and Condiments

I have to laugh when I read that pickles, relishes, chutneys, and other vinegar- or vinegar- and sugar-preserved condiments keep only several months in the refrigerator. I now have had a jar of French-style cornichons—tiny sour gherkins—in my refrigerator for over a year and it has developed neither the murkiness nor mold the storage charts say I should have noticed at least 6 months ago. However, I do see jars of faded green pickles on the supermarket shelf from time to time, and they should of course be avoided.

It's amazing how often a jar of pickles can come in handy to perk up an otherwise mundane meal or dish. Other than as a complement to sandwiches, I dice them into salad dressings (see page 156), cabbage slaws (see page 70), and love tuna salad spiked with the acid taste of a sour pickle (see page 255).

Chutney, which is a fruit-based pickle preserved with vinegar, sugar, and spices, is also a meal enhancer. Keep it on hand for dolling up a rice pilaf, a baked potato, a roasted onion, an omelet, or scrambled eggs. Blend a few tablespoons of chutney with 3½ to 4 ounces of cream cheese and you have a spicy-sweet spread for bread or crackers.

Sugar

It is fairly safe to say there may be no home in America without sugar. For the last 100 years, Americans have consumed between 90 to 100 pounds of refined sugar a year. The only foods we consume in near or greater quantity are red meats, milk, cream, and wheat flour. Not all of that sugar is sucrose in the form of white granulated or powdered sugar (also called confectioners' sugar) or brown sugar. Much of it is in the baked goods, candies, soft drinks, and processed cereals, processed meats, and other foods we buy. I'll still guarantee you have some sugar in the house.

Sugar keeps indefinitely, though it can clump and cake due to moisture or humidity. Brown sugar, which is merely white sugar covered with a film of highly refined, colored, molasses-flavored syrup, used to be a big problem in this regard; especially dark brown sugar, which has a greater quantity of the syrup. Once the box was opened it was sure to turn to stone in no time. Modern processing has remedied this to some extent. I now have a box of brown sugar on my shelf, protected only by the plastic insert bag and a twist tie, that has remained soft for a year. In case you buy a brand that is not so processed, or have a box that has been around so long it has, indeed, turned to stone, brown sugar can be softened very easily by heating it in a micro-wave or conventional oven. But use it immediately. It returns to stone quickly.

Anchovies

Few people are indifferent to anchovies. I love anchovies so much that I've become a proselytizer. To prove to an anchovy hater how subtle these little preserved fish can be, I soak the anchovies in water (or milk) to leach out the salt and temper their taste. Or, to demonstrate how anchovies can enhance other foods without taking over, I prepare a sauce or casserole (see Tomato Bulgur, page 65) in which the anchovies are a background flavor, a boost to other flavors.

I must point out, however, that there are vast differences in quality between brands of anchovy fillets in oil—whether canned or jarred—and between fillets in oil and those that come whole and preserved in salt.

Anchovies packed in oil should be firm and smooth, not falling apart or with a fuzzy surface. You should have good luck with any of the canned or jarred brands packed in Portugal, Spain, or Italy. I am suspicious of those without an identifying origin (the world's worst anchovies are used for chicken feed). Whole salted anchovies, which can be bought in Italian markets and other specialty stores, should look plump, not shriveled.

Whole salted anchovies will keep for several months in a covered jar or plastic container in the refrigerator. They are more perishable than anchovies in oil—which, until they are opened, last indefinitely—but once salted anchovies have been rinsed and filleted under cold running water they are actually less salty and have a milder flavor than canned ones.

An unfinished can or jar of anchovies in oil will keep for about 6 months in the refrigerator if you keep the unused portion covered with oil, then wrapped in plastic. Anchovy paste in tubes, which generally contains added oil and salt, keeps almost indefinitely.

Whole, salted anchovies are extremely easy to fillet; you don't even have to use a knife. Hold the anchovy under cold, running water and, using your thumbs at the belly, split it in half. The central bone usually lifts out in one piece. The skin, or most of it, will rub off by just stroking the fish while you hold it under the water. To rid them of salt, soak the fillets for 10 minutes in cold water or milk.

In the small amounts we eat anchovies, their nutritional content is beside the point, but anchovies are, on the negative side, high (for a fish) in cholesterol, and, on the positive side, high in calcium.

Anchovy Butter

In the days when canapés were a popular cocktail party form, caterers—or whoever else had the time and patience to fuss with bite-sized food—would make rolls of anchovy butter, chill them, and slice them to precisely fit each round of bread or melba toast. Today, it's better to pack the butter in a crock or ramekin and put it out with a knife and crackers. You might also try anchovy butter on a baked potato, a bowl of noodles, or macaroni or rice.

Makes a scant ¼ cup

1½ tablespoons anchovy paste, or
   6 anchovy fillets
3 tablespoons butter, softened
Few drops lemon juice or vinegar
   (optional)
Few drops Tabasco (optional)

1. In a small bowl, using a fork, blend the anchovies and butter together to form a relatively smooth paste.

2. Blend in the lemon juice or vinegar.

Variations: Add a very finely chopped or crushed clove of garlic to the paste, or up to 1 teaspoon Dijon mustard.

A Fresh Touch: Add up to a tablespoon of finely chopped parsley or basil to the paste.

Anchovy Toast

Because of their salt and oil content, anchovies, like olives and nuts, are a perfect foil for alcoholic drinks. During Prohibition and until World War II, the era in which cocktails came into their own, anchovy toast made with crustless white bread quarters was an elegant hors d'oeuvre. Contemporary tastes might better appreciate it made with ¼-inch slices of French or Italian bread—the denser the better—pita triangles, or, for very informal moments, anchovy-buttered English muffins. It really is good on white bread, too, but don't cut the crusts off —they give a crisp-fried texture.

Serves 6 as a snack

6 slices white bread, 12 rounds from a long loaf, or 3 pitas, quartered
4 tablespoons anchovy butter

1. Arrange the bread on a baking sheet and place in a 350-degree oven for 5 minutes.

2. Spread the anchovy butter on the untoasted underside of the bread and arrange back on the baking sheet buttered side up.

3. Just before serving, return the bread to the oven for another 5 minutes.

4. Serve immediately.

Spaghetti with Anchovies

As simple as it is, this is more than a dish for emergencies. For an anchovy lover it is supreme comfort food. I've given directions for cooking the anchovies in the microwave oven. It's fast, easy, you don't lose any anchovies or oil to the pot, and it means one less utensil to wash. The conventional method, however, is to combine the anchovies and oil in a small skillet or saucepan and cook over very low heat until the anchovies have melted.

Serves 2

5 or 6 canned or jarred anchovy
  fillets (one-half a 2-ounce can), or
  3 whole salted anchovies, filleted
  and soaked 10 minutes in cold
  water or milk
2 or 3 tablespoons olive oil
½ pound spaghetti or linguine
Freshly ground black pepper (or red
  pepper flakes)
Sautéed Bread Crumbs for Pasta (see
  page 55) (optional)

1. Combine the anchovies and olive oil in a microwave-safe bowl that can be used to toss and serve the spaghetti. Cook on LOW for 30 seconds.

2. With a fork, mash the anchovies into the oil. Cook on LOW 30 seconds more. Mash again. Set aside.

3. Cook the spaghetti in a large pot of boiling salted water until done to taste.

4. Meanwhile, if you are going to top the spaghetti with bread crumbs, cook them while the pasta cooks. They take about the same time, 8 to 10 minutes.

5. Drain the spaghetti well, and toss with the anchovy and oil mixture, as well as some black or red pepper.

6. Serve immediately, topped with sautéed bread crumbs, if desired.

Variations: The pure anchovy flavor is a nice change from garlic, but if you love to put garlic in everything, chop a small clove very finely and cook it along with the anchovies. Capers are also a good addition: Add brined capers straight from the jar. Soak and dry salted capers before adding them.

A Fresh Touch: If possible, add a tablespoon of finely chopped parsley for the last 30 seconds of cooking time.

Another recipe with anchovies
Sardine Tapenade (see page 229)

Apples

Because they are waxed to prevent dehydration, firm, blemish-free apples bought in the supermarket and kept in a refrigerator crisper drawer can often last from early fall through late winter. How they taste after such hibernation is another thing. They certainly won't be like crisp October apples bought at an orchard on a day trip to the country. On the other hand, they'll be no worse than the storage apples we purchase in spring or summer.

Red and Golden Delicious, McIntosh, and Granny Smith apples are the most popular in our markets, and among the best keepers. Of those, the Granny Smiths and Goldens keep their shape best when cooked. None are, strictly speaking, cooking apples, though should you choose to eat your apple a day in a form other than the way it grew, they all work fine in the following recipes.

Apple Canapés

Apple slices take the place of bread in this little snack, a classic combination of apples and cheese. Top round slices of peeled (or unpeeled) apple with crumbled blue cheese or shreds of Gruyère, Swiss, or cheddar, then place under the broiler or in a toaster oven to melt the cheese.

Baked Apples

I've never felt that the large Rome apples sold for baking, sometimes identified merely as "baking apples," are actually best for the purpose. They lack flavor and are mealy, and neither of these drawbacks are improved by cooking them. In any case, it is unlikely you'd have a Rome apple lurking in the refrigerator. Instead, bake a crisp Granny Smith, or a firm Golden Delicious. Both are available all year, excellent for eating out of hand, and make a fine baked dessert to end almost any meal or to eat as a fruit snack anytime.

Serves 1

Apples

For each apple

Lemon juice (optional)
1 tablespoon (or slightly more) brown sugar, white sugar, honey, or maple syrup
1 teaspoon butter
Cinnamon (optional)
Raisins and/or chopped nuts (optional)

1. Preheat the oven to 400 degrees.

2. Core the apple(s) and peel it (them) two-thirds down from the stem end. If desired, sprinkle on a few drops of lemon juice.

3. Into a small baking cup (or, if baking 2 or more apples, a small, shallow baking dish), pour the sugar, honey, or maple syrup.

4. Put the apple into the dish, peeled side down, and roll the apple around to coat the peeled portion with sweetening. Some sweetening will remain in the cup (or baking dish).

5. Dot with butter, or, if the butter is soft, spread it on the top of the apple. Sprinkle with cinnamon to taste, if desired. Stuff core hole with raisins and/or nuts, if desired.

6. Bake for 25 to 30 minutes.

7. Serve hot, warm, or at room temperature.

Sautéed Apple Slices

Put this on a piece of dry cake you need to moisten and embellish, on toast for breakfast or a snack, or on vanilla ice cream.

Serves 2

2 tablespoons butter
3 tablespoons sugar
2 apples, cored and cut into wedges

1. In a small skillet, heat the butter to sizzling.

2. Add the sugar. Stir over medium-high until syrup begins to turn golden.

3. Add the apples, toss with the syrup.

4. Serve on ice cream, pound cake, even toast, perhaps spread with apricot preserves.

Noodle Kugel with Apples and Raisins

Kugel is Yiddish for pudding, and I grew up eating a couple of kinds of kugel. My favorite was the "dairy pudding" made with sour cream, pot cheese, butter, and eggs, and seasoned with salt and pepper, which we always had as part of our Yom Kippur "break fast." It came out with a buttery crust of noodles on the sides and bottom and a soft, custardy interior. I can taste it as I'm writing about it. The other noodle pudding we ate was much more meager: simply noodles bound with egg and flavored with a little chicken fat, also seasoned with salt and pepper—lots of black pepper. It was the kugel that was a side dish to a meat meal—a roast chicken, for example. However, sweet noodle puddings were always something other families ate. Certainly no one related to me would put canned fruit cocktail in their kugel. The following is a sweet kugel I like a lot, though. I wouldn't eat it with a meal, but I could eat it *as* a meal. And, with a cup of coffee or tea, it's a great breakfast or afternoon snack.

Serves at least 4

½ pound egg noodles
2 eggs
4 tablespoons sugar
1 teaspoon ground cinnamon
1 cup coarsely grated apples
   (2 medium, peeled and cored)
½ cup raisins
5 tablespoons butter, melted
½ cup bread crumbs

1. Preheat the oven to 350 degrees.

2. Cook the noodles in boiling salted water until just tender, 5 or 6 minutes. Drain well.

3. Meanwhile, in a mixing bowl, beat the eggs with 2 tablespoons sugar and ½ teaspoon cinnamon until blended.

4. Stir in the apples, raisins, and 3 tablespoons melted butter.

5. Stir in the drained noodles, mixing well.

6. Pour into a buttered 8- or 9-inch-square baking pan and smooth out the top.

7. In a small bowl or cup, stir together the bread crumbs and remaining 2 tablespoons sugar and ½ teaspoon cinnamon.

8. Sprinkle the bread crumb mixture over the top of the noodles. Drizzle with remaining butter.

9. Bake for 35 minutes, until top is crisp and golden.

10. Serve warm, cut into squares.

Apple Crisp

As basic and American as apple pie but significantly less tricky to prepare.

Serves 4 to 6

2 to 2½ pounds apples (about 6), peeled, cored, and cut into thin wedges

2 tablespoons sugar
½ teaspoon ground cinnamon
1 tablespoon butter

For crumb topping

½ cup flour
½ cup oatmeal (regular or quick)
1 cup brown sugar
½ teaspoon ground cinnamon
⅛ teaspoon freshly ground nutmeg
Pinch of ground cloves (optional)
8 tablespoons (1 stick) butter, melted
½ cup coarsely chopped nuts,
  preferably walnuts or pecans

1. In a bowl, toss the apples with the 2 tablespoons sugar and ½ teaspoon cinnamon.

2. Preheat the oven to 375 degrees. Grease an 8- or 9-inch-square baking pan with 1 tablespoon butter. Arrange the apple mixture evenly in the pan.

3. In the same bowl, combine the flour, oats, brown sugar, cinnamon, nutmeg, and cloves. Blend well.

4. Stir in the melted butter and chopped nuts, until the mixture resembles coarse meal.

5. Sprinkle the topping evenly over the apples. (May be made ahead to this point, but, to prevent browning, the apples should be tossed with some lemon juice before the sugar and cinnamon.)

6. Bake for about 40 minutes, until the apples are tender and topping has browned. (Add 10 minutes if crisp was prepared ahead and refrigerated.)

Variations: You can really play with this recipe. To the apples you might add raisins or currants or chopped dried fruit (perhaps plumped in brandy, rum or whisky). Freshly ground black pepper is interesting with the apples, especially if you have no cinnamon. Instead of putting nuts in the topping, you can put them in the apples. Use half apples, half pears. Add a couple of tablespoons of cocoa to the crumb topping; use a pinch of allspice in addition to the other spices or instead of cloves.

Bacon

Think of bacon as a flavoring and a cooking fat, not as meat to be consumed in multi-strip portions, and most of the nutritional woes associated with it are reduced. Use it in small amounts, to season a bean soup (see page 51), a chowder (see page 104), an omelet filling, or a bowl of pasta (see the following recipes).

The paradox of bacon is that though it is cured (usually with nitrites, other salts, and sugar) and smoked, both processes meant to inhibit decay, it does not keep well for all that long. Because of health concerns, today's bacon is cured with fewer salts and smoked to a milder degree than it was in the days before refrigeration was so good and so common. Vacuum packaged sliced bacon is stamped with a last date of sale and, unopened, the package will keep in the refrigerator for only about one week beyond that date. Once the package has been opened, the bacon will not keep in the refrigerator for much more than a week. If the bacon gets slimy, throw it out.

The freezer will keep unopened packages of bacon for several months, but once the vacuum seal has been broken deterioration begins and, even very well wrapped in aluminum foil, freezer wrap or plastic, frozen sliced bacon will begin to turn rancid after about a month.

Spaghetti alla Carbonara

The essentials of carbonara are bacon, eggs and grated cheese. Nothing more. No cream. No prosciutto. No onion. Maybe some garlic; actually garlic makes it extra wonderful. Traditionally speaking, the bacon should be pancetta, the cured, unsmoked bacon from Italy. However, an excellent dish is possible with American bacon so long as it is not reeking of hickory. And if all you have is heavily hickoried bacon, cut the bacon as directed below, then put it in boiling water for a minute to rid it of the heavy smoke taste. Pat it dry on paper towels before proceeding. Carbonara is not a saucy dish. The egg and cheese and fat should merely coat the pasta, not drench it. One egg is barely enough for ½ pound of spaghetti. Two eggs make it rich. For a full pound of spaghetti, three eggs are just right.

Serves 2

3 or 4 slices bacon, cut into ¼-inch
 pieces
1 tablespoon butter or olive oil
1 lightly smashed large clove garlic,
 or, for more garlic flavor, chop it

½ pound spaghetti or macaroni
1 large egg
⅓ cup grated Parmesan cheese (or
 Romano or a combination)
Freshly ground black pepper

1. In a small skillet, combine the bacon and butter or oil. Cook over low heat until some of the bacon fat is rendered. Add garlic and increase heat little by little so bacon renders most of its fat and eventually becomes crisp. This will take about 20 minutes.

2. Cook the spaghetti in at least 3 quarts of boiling well-salted water until done to taste.

3. Meanwhile, in the serving bowl in which you are going to toss the pasta, beat the egg well with a fork.

4. Drain spaghetti, then stir a large forkful into the egg to warm it. Add the remaining spaghetti and the bacon fat. Toss to begin blending. Add the cheese and toss again. Put the bacon bits on top. Grind on plenty of black pepper.

5. Serve immediately, tossing at the table to blend in bacon and pepper.

Spaghetti all'-Amatriciana

Somehow I don't find the intrusion of hickory flavor in this very popular Italian dish as distracting as in carbonara. In fact, I rather like it. Like carbonara, this is a standard dish in Roman trattorias. On American menus it is often wrongly called spaghetti alla Matriciana, which doesn't mean anything. Its name comes from the fact that it originated in Amatrice, a town east of Rome, near the border between Abruzzi and Umbria. Different regions therefore take credit for its invention, which only proves how beloved it is. Hot pepper is an essential here, but I've left out an amount. Only you know how hot your pepper is and how hot you can take it. (A point on authenticity: Fifty years ago—and maybe still in some Italian homes and trattorias—this dish would have been made with lard, as well as bacon, but now olive oil is the usual fat.)

Serves 3 or 4

4 slices bacon or pancetta (about 4 ounces), cut into ¼-inch strips
1 tablespoon olive oil
1 medium onion, finely chopped
Hot pepper flakes
One 28-ounce can Italian plum tomatoes, very well drained (see Note)
Salt
1 pound spaghetti, linguine, bucatini, or tubular macaroni such as ziti
⅓ cup grated Parmesan or pecorino cheese, plus extra cheese

1. Put on a pot of salted water to boil, then start the sauce.

2. In a medium skillet, over medium heat, combine the bacon or pancetta with the oil. After the bacon starts sizzling, sauté for about 3 minutes.

3. Add the onion and hot pepper flakes to the bacon and continue to cook 5 more minutes.

4. Add the pasta to the boiling water.

5. Add the tomatoes to the skillet and break up with the side of a wooden spoon. Let simmer about 8 minutes, until reduced to a thick, chunky sauce. Remove when done.

6. Drain the pasta and, in a large serving bowl, toss with the hot sauce, then toss again with ⅓ cup cheese.

7. Serve immediately with extra cheese on the side.

Note: To drain the tomatoes as they must be for this dish, split each tomato and let the interior juices drip out. Then put the tomatoes in a dish for the few minutes it takes to cook the bacon and onion. Drain again.

Bananas

As my grandmother would not travel more than ten blocks from home without a few bananas in a little cloth sack or brown paper bag, I have always considered bananas the fruit of survival. Home always seems more homey with a bunch of bananas ripening on the kitchen counter or on top of the refrigerator. Or should I say overripening? To me they are best when the skin is covered with brown speckles and the pulp tastes almost alcoholic. But even for me there is a point when there is no point. That's when I peel them, cut them into hunks, and freeze them for the banana shake that follows. They keep for about 3 months, then begin to get bitter.

Incidentally, bananas are the second leading fruit crop in the world—after grapes, most of which go to make wine—and the most popular fruit in America.

Banana Shake

This filling thick shake—a breakfast drink, snack, restorative, post-workout pick-me-up, whatever—is almost as good as ice cream. (So I exaggerate.)

Serves 1

1 frozen banana
½ to 1 cup milk
2 ice cubes

Or

1 unfrozen banana
½ to 1 cup milk
4 ice cubes

1. Combine the banana, ½ cup milk, and the ice cubes in a blender. Process on high speed until smooth.

2. Check for thickness and add a little more milk if a thinner drink is desired. Process again.

3. Drink immediately, before it melts and deflates.

Banana-Walnut Bread

My dear friend Alan Damon makes this tea cake all the time, with the planned overripe bananas he always has in his house; then he freezes the cake for emergencies.

Makes one 9-inch loaf

3 ripe bananas
2 eggs
¾ cup sugar
5 tablespoons butter
1½ cups flour
1 teaspoon baking soda
1 teaspoon cream of tartar
½ teaspoon salt
⅔ cup shelled walnuts

1. Preheat the oven to 350 degrees. Grease a 9-by-5-by-3-inch loaf pan.

2. Put the bananas and eggs into a food processor and blend until smooth. (Or mash the bananas and eggs together by hand or with an electric mixer.)

3. Add the sugar and butter to the processor and, with a few on-off pulses, blend well. (Or, if making by hand or with an electric mixer, add sugar and butter gradually, beating well between additions.)

4. Add remaining ingredients and, again pulsing the machine, blend well. (Or beat the dry ingredients in by hand or with an electric mixer, in which case the walnuts must be previously chopped, fine or coarse depending on the texture you want.)

5. Pour into the prepared loaf pan and bake for 50 minutes. When done, a tester inserted in the center will come out clean. Let cool 10 minutes before turning it out. Let cool completely before wrapping for room-temperature storage or freezing.

Bananas Foster

Though this is one of several flamboyant dishes that Brennan's in New Orleans made famous, the combination of bananas, rum, and caramel is as obvious as Desi Arnaz and a conga drum, and appears in all kinds of cookbooks, guises, and settings under any number of names—these days, something often as prosaic as "Sautéed Bananas in Caramel Rum Sauce" on vanilla ice cream. But Bananas Foster is what I like to call it. It has more glamour. I clearly remember my first Bananas Foster. It was at my first breakfast at Brennan's, August 18, 1969—the morning after Hurricane Camille, then the worst tropical storm of the century; Charlton Heston was at the next table, and here I was having flambéed bananas for breakfast. It was one of my most decadent moments. (For the record, the Brennan's recipe contains banana liqueur as well as rum and there's no option on the cinnamon.)

Serves 2

1 tablespoon butter
2 tablespoons brown sugar
  (preferably dark)
2 tablespoons rum (preferably dark)
1 medium to large banana, cut in
  half lengthwise, then cut in half
  crosswise
Vanilla ice cream

1. In a small skillet, combine the butter, brown sugar, and rum. Blend with a wooden spoon.

2. When the mixture begins to sizzle, add the 4 banana pieces. Keep turning the banana pieces until glazed and the sauce itself has become syrupy, about 1 minute or so.

3. In a bowl or on a plate, place the bananas alongside each ice cream serving and pour the syrup over all.

4. Eat immediately.

Variation: Add ¼ teaspoon cinnamon if you like the flavor. Flambé the mixture by adding another 2 tablespoons rum to the skillet as soon as the syrup has thickened. Ignite and spoon the flaming syrup over the bananas in a dramatic fashion until the flames die out.

Other recipes featuring bananas

Mixed Fruit Salad (see page 197)

Barley

Barley, one of the oldest cultivated grains, is currently the fourth-ranking cereal in the world, after wheat, corn, and rice. Much of that production goes into the making of beer and whisky, and less than half of the American crop is used for human food, including alcoholic beverages. But bags of processed barley—called either pearl barley or Scotch (or pot) barley—are inexpensive and available in almost every supermarket, usually in the dried bean department, not on the cereal shelves.

Barley easily keeps a year in its unopened bag or box or in a covered container at room temperature. It is handy for adding body to soups, and though it is bland, it makes a satisfying pilaf that takes to almost any kind of seasoning. In wild rice country, primarily northern Minnesota, barley is the standard extender of the local delicacy, very often with mushrooms as a flavoring. The affinity of barley and mushrooms is also evident in the mushroom and barley casseroles and soups of Eastern Europe (see pages 170–71).

Barley gives off a lot of starch as it cooks, so it thickens liquids as well as bulking them up. If you look in the back of old cookbooks, in the typical final chapter on food for the sick and invalids, there is usually a recipe for barley broth or lemon-flavored barley water because barley cooking liquid can stop diarrhea and relieve indigestion.

Barley, Lentil, and Pea Salad

Serves 4 to 6

1 cup barley
½ teaspoon salt
1 cup lentils
One 10-ounce package frozen green
    peas (2 cups)

For dressing

6 tablespoons red or white wine or
    sherry vinegar
1 teaspoon Dijon mustard
3 tablespoons olive oil
2 medium carrots, finely diced (about
    ⅔ cup)
1 small onion, finely diced (about
    ½ cup), or ⅓ cup finely chopped
    shallots
Salt and freshly ground pepper

1. In a medium saucepan, cook the barley in 6 cups of rapidly boiling salted water for 45 minutes, until tender. Drain. You should have 4 cups of cooked barley.

2. In another saucepan, cook the lentils in 2½ cups of rapidly boiling unsalted water for about 20 minutes, until tender. Drain if necessary. You should have 2½ cups cooked lentils.

3. In a small saucepan, or in the microwave, cook the peas for 2 minutes in boiling water or 1 minute in a microwave.

4. In a large serving bowl, make the dressing: Using a fork, beat the vinegar and mustard together to blend. Beat in the olive oil.

5. Add the warm barley and lentils, the peas, carrots, and onion. Toss well. Season with salt and pepper and toss again.

6. Let cool in the refrigerator for 30 minutes or longer, if possible, and toss occasionally. The salad is even better if you let it stand at room temperature to cool, tossing a few times, then refrigerate it for several hours. However, do not serve the salad deeply chilled.

Vegetable and Barley Broth

This is a homey, sustaining vegetable soup.

Serves 4

3 tablespoons butter or vegetable oil
1 medium onion, chopped (about 1
  cup)
2 medium carrots, chopped (about ⅔
  cup)
2 ribs celery, chopped (about 1 cup)
½ cup barley
Two 13¾-ounce cans beef or chicken
  broth, or 3½ cups bouillon
1 large parsnip, chopped (about 1
  cup)
1 cup water (optional)
Freshly ground black pepper

1. In a medium saucepan, heat the butter or vegetable oil over medium heat and sauté the onion for 3 minutes.

2. Add the carrots and celery and cook 5 minutes.

3. Add the barley, broth, and water and bring to a full boil.

4. Boil, partially covered, for 30 minutes.

5. Add the chopped parsnip and continue cooking another 15 to 20 minutes, until barley is very tender. If necessary, add a little more broth or water.

6. Can be served immediately, but for improved texture let stand 30 minutes or longer, then reheat to serving temperature. Add freshly ground pepper and serve.

Variations: Toward the end of cooking, season the soup with dried dill or tarragon. Or, if using beef broth, add a spoon of dry sherry to each serving.

Substitutions: Instead of an onion, use chopped shallots or leeks. Instead of a parsnip, use a chopped turnip or two (though the parsnip is a sweeter alternative).

A Fresh Touch: Add almost any fresh vegetable, chopped (such as zucchini or yellow squash, fennel bulb, green beans, green cabbage. Among fresh herbs, parsley, dill, and tarragon are the most appropriate.

Other recipes featuring barley
Mushroom Barley Soups I and II
(see page 171)

Beans and Other Legumes *(Dried and Canned)*

Beans, beans, they have everything going for them. As any child or angina patient knows, they're "good for the heart"—because they are a high-fiber, high-protein food with virtually no fat. They're also easily grown, cheap, simple to cook, and, in their dry state, they last (theoretically) indefinitely on a dry, dark kitchen shelf without losing any of their nutrition. Lately beans are even chic, turning up in the most elegant restaurants as precious purees, "salsas," and salads, and coupled with shrimp, lobster, caviar, smoked salmon, and truffles.

To me, the humble bean is still best as the humble bean, however. As one of the oldest foods known to humanity and still a main source of protein and carbohydrates for a vast number of the world's people, many cultures have established bean cuisines that provide us with a huge repertoire of delicious and nutritious dishes. Actually, beans are just one of the many members of the legume family—seeds that grow in a pod—all of which have a similar nutritional and gastronomic profile. Chickpeas, lentils, peas, and split peas, as well as peanuts, soy beans, and clover are legumes.

Most beans come dried in 1-pound plastic sacks or cardboard boxes. The plastic bags are good storage containers, but to reduce further dehydration boxed beans should be transferred to a glass jar for long storage. Older beans may require longer soaking and cooking time, but eventually some beans get so dry that they can not practically be cooked soft. This has happened to me with chick-peas and black beans.

Lentils and split peas don't require soaking and are tender in 20 to 25 minutes, and it is possible to cook beans without soaking them first, but the results aren't as good. Unsoaked beans tend to burst their skins because they reconstitute less evenly. Overnight soaking is not necessary, however. Instead, combine them with cold water to cover by a couple of inches, bring the water to a boil, boil 1 minute, then let the beans stand 1 hour. Though I know I am flushing nutrition down the drain, I always throw off that first water and cook the beans with fresh. It may not be scientifically proven, but my observation is that some of the gas problem associated with eating beans goes down the pipes, too.

Chick-peas and several kinds of beans—mainly kidney beans, black beans (also called turtle beans), pink or pinto beans, and cannellini beans (sometimes called white kidney beans)—also come in cans. Fully cooked canned beans are a big convenience—especially for recipes in which the beans are pureed, when their softer texture is not important—but they don't keep as long as dried beans. Processors say they keep well for a year. You can count on a few months longer than that.

Black Beans

A popular legume in Latin American cooking, black beans are best known as the main ingredient of a black bean soup. Cans of Cuban-style black bean soup are, in fact, available in many, if not most, supermarkets. Heated (on top of the stove or in a microwave oven) and poured over a mound of boiled rice, then garnished with chopped raw onion, several dashes of bottled hot sauce, and perhaps some grated cheddar or Jack, they make a great meal. To prepare an equally good black bean soup from scratch, however, calls for some ingredients you are not likely to have on hand—at the very least some bell peppers, though a ham hock or piece of sausage is what makes black bean soup sing.

José's Black Bean Spread

(Refried Black Beans)

My Guatemalan barber, José de Leon, dictated this to me as he clipped my hair. Figuring he was talking to a fancy "gourmet," he gave me very detailed and particular instructions about soaking and cooking the dried beans. I asked him if he ever used canned beans. "Of course," he laughed, "all the time. This is America, isn't it?" José uses half of a large, sweet Spanish (or Bermuda) onion, and he likes it sliced so, as he describes it with relish, "there are little strings of onion in the beans." I prefer the onion chopped. Spread it on bread or crackers, as José does, or use it to fill quesadillas (see page 252), as a dip for corn chips, or simply as a side dish to broiled fish, meat, or poultry.

Makes 1¼ cups

2 tablespoons olive oil
1 small onion, very thinly sliced or finely chopped
1 small clove garlic, finely chopped or crushed
One 16-ounce can black beans, drained, pureed in the blender

¹/₄ teaspoon oregano
Few dashes cayenne or Tabasco

1. In a skillet, over medium-high heat, sauté the onion in the olive oil until it is just beginning to brown, about 4 minutes.

2. Lower the heat to medium, add the garlic, and sauté another minute or so.

3. Add the pureed black beans and oregano. Stir well.

4. Stir constantly over medium heat until the puree becomes a moundable paste, about 5 minutes. The bottom of the pan will become visible as you stir, and the mixture will not run back.

5. Season with cayenne or Tabasco sauce and stir another 30 seconds.

6. Serve hot or cooled to room temperature. To store in the refrigerator a few days, pack into a crock or bowl and cover with plastic.

Variation: Use pinto or kidney beans instead of black beans.

A Fresh Touch: Use fresh, finely chopped cilantro—1 teaspoon—instead of oregano.

Cannellini

These large white kidney beans are easy to find in cans, difficult to find dried. The dried beans, most of which are imported, come to market in mid- to late fall and are often sold out by New Year's. However, it's worth searching in Italian markets and specialty food stores for dried cannellini, and worth buying a large supply when you find them. They'll keep at least a full year in a tightly closed jar and are one dried bean that is dramatically superior to the canned variety. They are firmer, fuller tasting, and, because you reconstitute them yourself, you can suffuse them with other flavors in the process.

Roman Bean Soup

The Roman emperors wore crowns of bay laurel leaves, hence the accolade laureate (as in poet laureate). So I suppose it is natural that this simplest of Roman bean soups would be flavored with bay, too, even though it is unusual in Italian cooking to see bay leaves flavoring tomatoes. Because the aromatic oils in bay leaves need time to be released, their flavor is stronger in the longer cooked version made with dried beans. By adding cooked macaroni, you can turn this into "pasta fazool," too.

Serves 4 to 6

To prepare with dried beans:

Cannellini beans as prepared in Steps 1 and 2 of Tuscan-Style Beans and Macaroni (see page 36), made with 2 bay leaves instead of sage
Sugo Finto (tomato sauce) (see page 249)
About ⅓ cup grated Parmesan cheese (optional)

1. Stir the cooked beans and the tomato sauce together and, if desired or necessary, adjust consistency to taste with additional water, tomato juice, or broth.

2. Remove the bay leaves and serve very hot, with or without grated cheese. (Can be made ahead and reheated.)

Serves 3 or 4

To prepare with canned beans:

Sugo Finto (see page 249)
2 large bay leaves
Two 16- or 19-ounce cans cannellini beans, drained
Freshly ground black pepper

1. In a medium saucepan, prepare the tomato sauce, adding the bay leaves and 1 cup of water. Simmer 15 minutes, instead of 10 minutes.

2. Add the drained beans, season with pepper, stir, and simmer another 10 minutes.

3. Remove the bay leaves and serve very hot, with or without grated cheese.

Tuscan-Style Beans and Macaroni

(Pasta e Fagioli)

The Tuscans are notorious all over Italy as "the bean eaters." With bean dishes as simple and fulfilling as this, who's to blame them? This is my standard and very basic pasta and bean recipe—pronounced "pasta fazool" by most Italian-Americans. For all the delight I can take in a soup with tomatoes, diced vegetables, a variety of herbs, plus bacon, ham, or sausage, I still find this extremely primitive, creamy white version the most seductive and satisfying.

Serves 4 as a main course

To prepare from dried beans:

2 cups dried cannellini beans
2 or 3 large whole cloves garlic,
peeled
2 teaspoons dried leaf sage, or 5 or 6
leaves fresh
1 teaspoon salt
½ teaspoon freshly ground black
pepper
3 tablespoons extra-virgin olive oil
½ pound tubular macaroni, such as
penne or ziti, cooked al dente
4 tablespoons extra-virgin olive oil, to
drizzle on top (optional)

1. Soak the beans overnight in about 2 quarts of cold water. Drain and rinse before using, picking over the beans and discarding any that are shriveled or discolored. Or, combine beans and water in a saucepan and bring to a boil over high heat. Boil 1 minute. Let stand 1 hour. Drain and rinse, picking over the beans.

2. In a medium saucepan, combine drained beans with enough water to cover by about 2 inches, garlic cloves, sage, salt, pepper, and olive oil. Bring to a boil, then adjust heat so beans simmer gently for 30 to 40 minutes, or until tender. If necessary, add more water to keep the liquid at least 1 inch above the beans. Discard the sage leaves if using fresh. I don't bother removing the garlic. (The beans can be prepared ahead to this point, but will require more water when they are reheated.)

3. If desired, thicken the soup by pureeing some of the beans, then stirring the puree back into the pot.

4. Just before serving, stir the cooked macaroni into the beans and bring to a simmer, adding a little more water if necessary. There should be just enough liquid to cover everything.

5. Serve immediately, with or without additional olive oil to drizzle on top of each portion.

To prepare from canned beans:

3 tablespoons extra-virgin olive oil
2 cloves garlic, finely chopped
½ teaspoon dried leaf sage
Two 19-ounce cans cannellini beans
2 cups water
½ pound tubular macaroni, such as
penne or ziti, cooked al dente
4 tablespoons extra-virgin olive oil, to
drizzle on top (optional)

1. In a medium saucepan, over low heat, combine the oil and garlic. Let cook about 5 minutes. Do not let the garlic brown.

2. Add the sage to the oil and cook 30 seconds.

3. Add the beans with their liquid, and the 2 cups of water. Increase heat to medium and bring to a simmer. Cook gently for 10 minutes.

4. Just before serving, stir the cooked macaroni into the beans and return to a simmer.

5. Serve immediately, with or without additional olive oil to drizzle on top of each portion.

Bean Cream

Similar to hummus, but smoother, this bean dip is receptive to all kinds of creative fiddling.

Serves 4 as an appetizer

One 19-ounce can cannellini beans, drained
1 or 2 cloves garlic, cut in small chunks
2 tablespoons olive oil (optional)

Suggested seasonings: An herb (mint, rosemary, or oregano) or combination of herbs (thyme and fresh parsley); cumin, with or without cayenne or hot paprika; curry powder; chili powder; pureed reconstituted dried ancho chili

1. Combine the beans, garlic, and olive oil in a food processor and puree until creamy.

2. Add desired seasoning and process to blend well.

3. Serve at room temperature, with raw vegetables, crackers, pita, or pita crisps.

Other recipes featuring cannellini
Tuna and Beans (see page 258)

Kidney Beans, Pink Beans, and Pinto Beans

The International Chili Society's rules define chili as an all-meat dish. No beans are allowed at cook-offs. Nevertheless, it's in a bowl of chili that most of us ran into our first red kidney beans, pink beans, or pinto beans. Or was it, for you, in a sweet-and-sour three-bean salad encountered at a picnic or salad bar? These are the most common beans in America, used most conspicuously and extensively in Southwestern, Mexican, and Latin American cooking. I find good brands of canned kidney beans almost as firm as home-cooked dried beans, but, if the intent is to keep them whole, not puree them, you must be careful not to boil them. You'll end up with hollow bean skins.

Chili Beans

This comes out a gorgeous mahogany color and, depending on the chili powder or dried chili pepper, can be hot enough to make your mouth merely glow or powerful enough to meet the highest heat standards. If you like a burn, include some of the seeds of a dried chili, supplement chili powder with hot red pepper flakes or cayenne, or serve the beans with hot sauce on the side. To contrast the hot peppers, serve the beans on plain boiled rice, on cornmeal mush, over hominy, or on a baked potato, with or without chopped onions and/or shredded cheddar or jack cheese on top. I can also easily make a meal of this as is, with corn chips or corn tortillas on the side. To be more elaborate, roll the beans in softened corn or flour tortillas with shredded cheese and, if available, shredded iceberg lettuce.

Serves 2 to 4, depending on how you eat them

2 tablespoons vegetable oil
2 large cloves garlic, smashed or pressed
1 tablespoon chili powder, or 1 dried pasilla chili or ancho chili, seeds and stem discarded
One 14-ounce can Italian plum tomatoes, with their juice (1¾ cups), chopped
Two 16-ounce cans red kidney beans or pinto beans, drained

1. In a medium saucepan, over medium-low heat, combine the oil and garlic.

2. While the garlic is cooking slowly, add the chili powder, or, if using a dried chili, use scissors to cut the chili into very fine strips directly into the pan. Stir every once in a while. Cook about 2 minutes.

3. Add the tomatoes, stir well, and increase heat slightly. Let the sauce simmer 15 minutes, until thickened.

4. Add the beans and stir well again. Bring to a simmer and let simmer very gently another 10 minutes. (Can be prepared ahead, but may need a little additional water when reheated.)

5. Serve very hot.

Variations: Chili powder contains oregano and cumin. If using a dried chili, add ½ teaspoon dried oregano and ¼ teaspoon cumin, if desired. (You might want to add these even if using chili powder.)

A Fresh Touch: Chopped fresh cilantro (coriander) and/or a few drops of lime juice are to the taste of some people.

Kidney Bean Salad

The viscous juice in a can of beans has just the right consistency to make a fat-free salad dressing in which you won't miss the oil. (Well, not too much.)

Serves 2 or 3

One 19-ounce can red kidney beans, undrained
1½ cups finely chopped celery (preferably inner ribs with their leaves)
1 medium onion, finely chopped (about 1 cup)
1 small clove garlic, minced (optional)
2 tablespoons wine, cider, or malt vinegar

1. Mix all ingredients together and chill lightly.

2. Eat as is, as a salad, or toss with greens as a salad dressing.

Chick-peas

Of all the legumes that commonly come in a can, chick-peas are probably the best—they stay firm—and possibly the most neglected, in this country anyway. Unlike kidney beans and pinto beans, they haven't mainstreamed into nachos, tacos, burritos, and chili. Unlike the navy bean, the U.S. Senate doesn't make them into soup. They're the wrong size for Boston, which likes pea beans, and the wrong color for black beans and rice or red beans and rice. Mediterranean cooks use them. Arab and Indian cooks live by them and on them. I haven't been without a can of chick-peas on the shelf in 20 years.

Chick-pea Soup

This recipe is from Marcella Hazan's first cookbook, *The Classic Italian Cookbook* (Harper's Magazine Press, 1973), and it can't be topped for simplicity or flavor. It is one of my personal favorite quickie meals.

As Marcella Hazan points out, cooked dried chick-peas have slightly better texture than canned—use ¾ cup dried chick-peas—but for this soup the difference is practically undetectable, especially if you puree it. Instead of rosemary, use ¾ teaspoon dried oregano if you prefer.

Serves 4

4 large cloves garlic, peeled
⅓ cup olive oil
1½ teaspoons finely crushed
*   rosemary leaves (see Note)*
⅔ cup canned Italian tomatoes,
*   roughly chopped with their juices*
Two 16-ounce cans chick-peas,
*   drained*
1 cup beef broth, or 1 beef bouillon
*   cube dissolved in 1 cup water*
Salt, if necessary, and freshly ground
*   pepper*
Grated Parmesan cheese (optional)

1. In a medium saucepan, over medium-high heat, sauté the whole garlic cloves in the olive oil until they are a nutty brown. Remove the garlic.

2. Add the crushed rosemary and stir, then immediately add the chopped tomatoes with their juices. Cook over medium heat for 20 minutes.

3. Add the drained chick-peas and stir into the tomato sauce.

4. Add the broth, stir, and bring to a simmer. Simmer 15 minutes.

5. Taste and add salt if necessary, pepper to taste.

6. Serve immediately, as is, or puree all or part of the soup in a blender, food processor, or with a food mill, then reheat to serving temperature. (Can be made ahead and reheated.) Either way, serve with grated cheese if you have some on hand.

Note: To crumble rosemary leaves, which are like little twigs, put them in the palm of one hand and rub with the heel of the other, until herb is a fine powder. I do this with all herbs to some degree. The finer herb, heated slightly by your hands rubbing, releases more flavor and aroma.

Variations: To make Chick-pea and Rice Soup: Add 3 cups of broth or bouillon to the pureed soup, bring to a boil, then stir in ½ to 1 cup white rice. Cover and simmer, stirring several times, until rice is tender, about 15 minutes.

To make Chick-pea and Pasta Soup: Puree about half the soup and combine in a saucepan with the unpureed portion and 2½ cups of broth or bouillon. Bring to a boil and stir in ½ pound small macaroni. Boil until macaroni is tender, 8 to 10 minutes.

Chick-pea Chili Soup

(Mock Menudo)

Menudo is a legendary tripe soup/stew of Mexico and the Southwest United States, where the joints that serve it often don't open until midnight. *Menudo* can, its devotees say, prevent a hangover. Tripe soup eaters all over the world claim this, so it must work. Experts on such nutritional/medical matters explain that it's the protein from the tripe and the liquid of the soup medium that stave off the side effects of overindulgence. Theoretically, high-protein chick-peas in soup should have a similar effect. It's a moot point. I eat this strictly for pleasure.

Serves 2

1 medium onion, chopped (about 1 cup)
2 tablespoons olive oil
3 large cloves garlic, minced (about 1 tablespoon)
1 tablespoon chili powder
1 teaspoon dried oregano (preferably Mexican)
2 cups water
1 beef bouillon cube
One 19-ounce can chick-peas, drained
3 tablespoons tomato paste
One 16-ounce can hominy, or ⅔ cup raw white rice

Possible garnishes

Bottled hot sauce
Sour cream
Chopped raw onion
Corn chips
Chopped pimento-stuffed olives

1. In a 2½- to 3-quart saucepan, over medium heat, sauté the onion in the olive oil for about 3 minutes.

2. Stir in the garlic and continue to sauté 2 more minutes. Do not brown the garlic.

3. Stir in chili powder and oregano. Sauté another minute.

4. Add water, bouillon cube, chick-peas, and tomato paste. Stir well to dissolve bouillon and tomato paste. Bring to a simmer and simmer steadily for 15 minutes, stirring occasionally. (Can be prepared ahead and reheated.)

5. Meanwhile, cook rice separately. Or, if using hominy, heat through in a separate saucepan.

6. To serve, put a portion of rice or hominy in a soup bowl, then ladle in hot soup. Serve with hot sauce and all or some of the garnishes set out in small bowls.

A Fresh Touch: Add diced avocado to the garnishes.

Other recipes featuring chick-peas

Hummus with Tahini (see page 243)

Felafel, Fried or Not

F elafel—which are fritters also made with legumes other than chick-peas—are a basic, everyday food in the Middle East, a lunch food, a snack food, an appetizer, dinner. In New York, with our large population of Israelis, Egyptians, Lebanese, Syrians, and other Middle Easterners, felafel has achieved similar status. They're served up from street carts, pizzerias, full-service restaurants, and stands that specialize in nothing but felafel and the foods that go around it; tahini cream, hot red pepper sauce, pickled peppers, olives, salad. They're served in so many places that they're rarely prepared at home. But here's a chance to be creative. I have never tasted two felafel that were alike. They are like Middle Eastern opinions. I've found the seasoning formula below harmonious. You can add or subtract to please yourself. Here's a revolutionary idea, however: Don't even fry the mixture. Eliminate the flour and egg and just spread the paste inside a pita pocket. (The beans are already fully cooked.) Top with shredded lettuce for plenty of crunch, then dress the sandwich with Tahini Cream (see page 243), sprinkle on some hot pepper flakes. As a spread for bread, this mixture is also great on dense, nutty, whole grain breads. A few slices slathered like that and you can take a high-carbo holiday.

Serves 3 or 4

2 small cloves garlic
One 19-ounce can chick-peas
6 tablespoons bread crumbs
2 tablespoons flour
1 egg
½ teaspoon ground cumin
1 rounded teaspoon dried mint
½ teaspoon dried oregano
¼ teaspoon ground allspice
¼ teaspoon cayenne
Vegetable oil

1. Cut the garlic into several pieces and put in a food processor. Process as small as possible, which is usually not very small.

2. Drain chick-peas, reserving liquid, and put them in processor.

3. To the chick-peas, add the bread crumbs, flour, egg, and as much seasoning as you want. Process with several on-off pulses. Check for seasoning and texture. Remember the seasoning will become muted in cooking. The texture should be manageable in your palms, not loose or sticky nor too dry. Generally, you will need to add up to ¼ cup reserved chick-pea liquid.

4. In a heavy medium saucepan, heat ½ inch vegetable oil until a pinch of bread crumbs sizzles as soon as it hits the fat. Make balls or patties using a well-rounded tablespoon of felafel mixture for each. Fry about 3 minutes a side, until crisp and lightly browned.

5. Drain on paper towels.

6. Serve while still hot with tahini cream for dipping and olives and/or pickled peppers as a condiment. Or serve inside a pita pocket with lettuce or other salad (i.e., diced tomatoes, cucumbers, and onions).

Lentils

Hardly anyone longs for lentils anymore, but mankind was devoted to them at one time. They were one of our earliest crops, cultivated as early as 3,000 B.C. and gathered for food in their wild state long before that. In the world's first city, Jericho, archaeologists found proof that people stored lentils for future consumption even before pottery was invented. And before Jericho, there is the account in the Bible: Coming home from the hunt, Esau, grandson of Abraham, son of Isaac, and twin brother of Jacob, longed for lentils so much that, Genesis says, he sold his birthright for a mess of lentil pottage. To this day, Middle Easterners dote on a dish of lentils and rice that, they like to think at least, is the very same pottage Esau was so mad to eat.

Lentils last indefinitely, losing no nutrition if kept in a dry environment. If exposed to light, they may darken but their eating quality will not diminish.

Most lentils available in American stores are brown lentils grown almost exclusively in Idaho and Washington State. Some red lentils are also produced in the Northwest. They are sold split, like peas; they lose their color when cooked, cook more quickly than brown lentils, and do not keep their shape. Use them only for soup or Indian lentil purees (dal). Specialty food stores also carry French *lentiles vertes du Puys,* a dark green-blue lentil that is smaller than our browns. They keep their shape beautifully and are therefore the best lentil for salad.

Lentil Chili

Think of this as the basic black dress of vegetarian chilies. Just dress it up—accessorize it—to suit the situation. You can add blanched fresh vegetables, such as green beans, broccoli, or zucchini. You can add cooked dried or canned kidney, pinto, or black beans. You can sauté some green and/or red sweet peppers along with the onion. As garnishes, you can add chopped raw onion and peppers, cubed avocado, shredded cheese, shredded lettuce . . . you get the picture.

Serves 4 to 6

2 medium onions, coarsely chopped
(about 2 cups)
2 tablespoons vegetable oil
3 to 4 large cloves garlic, smashed
and coarsely chopped
4 tablespoons chili powder
1½ teaspoons dried oregano
1 teaspoon ground cumin
One 28-ounce can plum tomatoes in
puree (3½ cups) chopped
1 cup lentils
½ cup bulgur

1. In a medium saucepan or casserole, over medium heat, sauté onions in oil for 10 minutes, until beginning to brown. Stir in garlic and sauté another minute. Stir in chili powder, oregano, and cumin. Sauté another minute.

2. Add tomatoes and simmer 20 minutes.

3. Meanwhile, in salted water to cover by 2 inches boil lentils about 20 minutes, or until tender.

4. Add cooked lentils and bulgur to tomato base. Simmer together 10 minutes, until bulgur is soft. (Can be made ahead to this point, but will require more water when it is reheated.)

5. Serve very hot.

Lentils and Rice

(Mujaddarah)

It is said that this, a standard Middle Eastern home dish, is the "mess of pottage" for which Esau sold his birthright. It is almost understandable. The earthy taste of lentils is tempered by the rice and set off with well-caramelized, really almost burned, onions. Cumin is my preferred seasoning; it is, for me, what makes the dish irresistibly seductive and not just terrific, but many Middle Easterners prefer the flavor of allspice or a combination of both.

Serves 4

3 tablespoons olive oil or vegetable oil
3 medium onions, thinly sliced
3½ cups water
1 cup brown lentils
1 cup white rice
1 teaspoon salt
1 teaspoon ground cumin, or
    ¼ teaspoon ground allspice

1. In a medium skillet, over high heat, heat olive oil and sauté onions, stirring regularly, until wilted. Reduce heat to medium and continue to cook until onions are lightly browned. Remove one-third of them and set aside. Continue to cook the rest until they are very well browned, even black here and there.

2. Meanwhile, in a medium saucepan, bring water to a boil over high heat. Add lentils, reduce heat to low, cover, and simmer for 15 minutes.

3. Add the reserved onions, the rice, salt, and cumin or allspice. Stir well, cover, and continue to cook for 15 minutes, until rice is tender.

4. Remove from heat, then either stir in or top with the well-browned onions. Cover and let stand about 10 minutes.

5. Serve as is, hot or at room temperature. Or mound the mixture in a serving bowl or on a platter, make a well in the center, and fill with yogurt.

Variation. Depending on the way you want to present the dish, either stir in or top with cooked frozen leaf or chopped spinach. You might also want to serve the dish with lemon wedges for additional seasoning at the table.

A Fresh Touch: A salad of diced cucumber, tomato, and scallions, dressed only with a little lemon juice or a combination of lemon juice and olive oil, is a standard accompaniment; serve the salad on the side, put it on top of the lentils and rice, or border a platter with the salad, then heap the lentils and rice in the center.

Lentil Salad

Lentil salad is one of those many earthy European foods, essentially working-man's foods, that have taken turns at being chic in the last decade. Though it now sells for zillions of dollars a pint at your local fancy takeout, it could not be easier or cheaper to make from scratch. The following recipe uses only ingredients you might have on hand, but lentils are receptive to fresh diced tomatoes, diced cucumber, fresh herbs, any number of fillips and fancies.

Makes 5 cups without additions, serving 6 to 10

1 pound lentils
¼ cup red wine or sherry vinegar
½ teaspoon salt
3 or 4 tablespoons Dijon-style or
    grainy mustard
2 tablespoons olive oil

Optional additions

Freshly ground black pepper
2 or 3 shallots, finely chopped
1 or 2 ribs celery, finely chopped
2 or 3 medium carrots, boiled until
    crisp-tender, then finely chopped

1. In a medium saucepan, boil the lentils in 6 cups of boiling water 20 to 25 minutes, depending on lentils. Be careful not to overcook; the lentils should not fall apart.

2. Meanwhile, in a large bowl, beat the vinegar, salt, and mustard together, then beat in the olive oil.

3. Drain the lentils and pour into the bowl. Immediately toss with the dressing.

4. Add any or all optional ingredients and toss again.

5. Let stand as long as possible (at least 30 minutes but even overnight), tossing occasionally.

6. Serve at room temperature.

Lentil Soup with Carrots and Rosemary

For a crisp, sharp contrast to this thick, soothing soup, serve it topped with thin garlic toasts (see page 54) drizzled with extra-virgin olive oil and sprinkled with rosemary (in which case leave out the final fillip of rosemary in the recipe).

Serves 4 to 6

3 tablespoons olive oil
1 large onion, chopped (1¼ to
    1½ cups)
2 medium cloves garlic, chopped
4 medium carrots, sliced or chopped
    (about 1¼ cups)
1 teaspoon dried rosemary, crumbled
    fine (see Note, page 41)
2 cups lentils
Two 13¾-ounce cans chicken or beef
    broth, plus 1 quart water or
    2 bouillon cubes dissolved in
    3½ cups water
½ teaspoon freshly ground black
    pepper
Salt

1. In a medium saucepan, heat the oil and sauté the onion over medium heat until golden, about 8 minutes.

2. Add the garlic, mix well, and sauté another 30 seconds.

3. Add the carrots, mix well, and continue to cook, tossing frequently, another 5 minutes, adding ¾ teaspoon rosemary for the last minute.

4. Add the lentils, broth, 1 quart water, and pepper. Stir well, increase heat, and stir frequently from the bottom until liquid begins to boil.

5. Adjust heat so soup simmers gently for about 45 minutes, or until lentils are very tender. Stir occasionally, and after 30 minutes mash some of the lentils everytime you stir.

6. Taste for salt and pepper. (The salt in the broth or bouillon is often quite enough.) For an extra rosemary oomph, add an additional ¼ teaspoon rosemary just before serving.

Lima Beans

D ried limas are beige, fresh limas are green, and their flavor and texture is so different that dried limas and fresh limas might as well be different legumes. One isn't better than the other, just different. Fortunately, frozen limas are as good as almost any fresh ones you can buy and are available in any supermarket. They keep, in their unopened box, for about six months, after which they become noticeably dehydrated. If you are using part of a box, rewrap the remainder tightly in a plastic bag and return it to the freezer immediately.

Dried Lima Beans, Greek Style

G reeks make their beloved, fat *gigantes* beans this way. If by chance you happen on some at an ethnic or fancy food market (though they are by no means "fancy"), buy a good stock. They're one of the most comforting beans and will keep in a jar for better than a year.

Serves 4 or 5

1½ cups dried lima beans, soaked in
   cold water for at least 8 hours, or
   covered with water, brought to a
   boil, and left to stand 1 hour
1 small to medium onion, finely
   chopped (about ⅔ cup)
1 heaping tablespoon coarsely
   chopped garlic (about 3 medium
   cloves)
3 tablespoons olive oil
2 tablespoons tomato paste
1 medium carrot, diced
½ teaspoon dried oregano
Freshly ground pepper

1. Drain the beans, rinse in a colander or strainer, and set aside.

2. In a small saucepan, combine the onion, garlic, and oil. Set over medium heat and cook about 8 minutes, until onion is golden.

3. Add the tomato paste and carrot. Stir well.

4. Add the beans and enough water to cover them completely. Season with oregano and several turns of the peppermill.

5. Simmer until beans are very tender, about 1½ hours.

Lima Beans with Garlic and Mint

This is the frozen (fresh) lima version, a quickly cooked version of the preceding traditional Greek recipe.

Serves 2 or 3

1 tablespoon extra-virgin olive oil
1 large clove garlic, finely chopped
One 10-ounce package frozen baby
   lima beans (2 cups)
1 cup drained canned plum tomatoes
Freshly ground pepper
1 tablespoon finely chopped fresh
   mint, or 1 scant teaspoon dried
Salt, if necessary

1. In a small saucepan, over medium-low heat, combine the oil and garlic and cook together until the garlic begins to sizzle.

2. Add the frozen lima beans and canned tomatoes. With the side of a wooden spoon, break up the tomatoes.

3. Add a few turns of the peppermill. Cover, lower heat, and cook gently for about 10 minutes.

4. Taste a bean. If tender, add mint, salt, if desired, and cook, uncovered, over medium-high heat to evaporate any excess liquid. If beans are still slightly hard, cover and continue to cook until tender.

5. Serve hot, warm, or at room temperature.

Split Peas

Peas are ancient. This we know. According to Waverly Root in *Food,* one archaeological pea find, in a cave on the border between Burma and Thailand, was carbon-dated at 9750 B.C. The first mention of eating dried peas, however, is from ancient Rome. Peas are a legume, and like their kin—lentils and beans —they maintain all their nutrients (which are substantial) and flavor when dried, even when stored for a couple of years at warm room temperatures.

Most dried peas, both yellow and green, are sold split, are very inexpensive, and, I think, as decorative as they are delicious. Keep them in a canning jar that has a rubber gasket, in a screw-top jar, or in a jar with a ground glass stopper and display them on a counter or shelf. Besides being attractive, this will also make you think of them some late fall or winter day when you want to eat something substantial but don't know what.

Split Pea Soup

This is a very thick soup, but in no way a stodgy soup. Plenty of onion, carrot, and celery see to that. A food processor comes in handy here, not only to puree the soup at the end, but also to chop the carrots, onions, and celery very fine so they release their flavor in a relatively short cooking time. If you don't own a food processor, shred the vegetables on a medium grater and puree the soup in a blender or with a food mill. From start to table, the soup can take as little as just over an hour.

Serves 6 to 8

1 pound green or yellow split peas
  (2 cups)
1 cup very finely chopped carrot
  (about 2 medium or 3 small)
1 cup very finely chopped onion
  (1 large or 2 or 3 small)
1 cup very finely chopped celery
  (2 or 3 ribs)
7 cups water

1 large bay leaf
1 teaspoon salt
Freshly ground pepper
Croutons (optional) (see page 54)

1. In a large pot, combine all the ingredients except salt, pepper, and croutons. Bring to a boil, lower heat, cover, and simmer about 50 minutes, until peas are soft.

2. In two or three batches, puree the peas and vegetables in a food processor or blender or through a food mill.

3. Season with salt and pepper.

4. Return to a simmer and cook briefly to make very hot for serving—with or without croutons. (The soup will keep for several days in the refrigerator, but you will need to add more water when it is reheated.)

Variations: If desired, add a ham bone, smoked ham hock, or diced bacon to all the other ingredients. (The ham hock will flavor the soup, but it won't really cook through in an hour.) If not using a meat flavoring, serve with a dollop of sour cream.

Substitutions: This is a vegetarian soup and it has a clear, sweet pea flavor. I prefer it to a meat-muddied soup, but chicken broth does add a depth that can be desirable. Use canned broth for some of the water, or, if after pureeing and seasoning the soup you think it needs some extra oomph, add 1 or several vegetable or chicken bouillon cubes.

Dal

The Indian word *dal* really refers to any legume, though, to Americans, it has come to mean a puree of lentils or peas. This is not an authentic Indian recipe, but it is very delicious and both a good soup or side dish.

Serves 4

1 cup green or yellow split peas
(½ pound)
3 cups water
1 teaspoon salt
4 tablespoons butter
1 tablespoon vegetable oil
1 medium onion, finely chopped
1 clove garlic, finely chopped
1 teaspoon curry powder
¼ teaspoon cayenne
¼ teaspoon ground cinnamon
¼ teaspoon ground ginger

1. In a medium saucepan, combine the split peas and water. Bring to a simmer and cook gently until peas are tender enough to beat with a wooden spoon into a rough, thick puree, about an hour, depending on how old the peas are. Add more water if necessary to keep the peas covered, or to thin out the puree after they are cooked.

2. After they are cooked, season the split peas with salt.

3. Meanwhile, in a small skillet, heat the butter with the oil and sauté the onion until golden, about 8 minutes, adding the garlic for the last 2 minutes.

4. Stir the spices into the onion and garlic, then cook another minute, until the aroma of the spices rises.

5. Serve each portion of peas topped with a spoonful of flavored onion-garlic butter-oil.

Variation: Add water, broth, or bouillon to bring dal to soup consistency. Serve as above.

Bread

"A loaf of bread," the Walrus said,
  "Is what we chiefly need."
        —Lewis Carroll, *Through the Looking-Glass*

My sentiments exactly. Of course, bread can be frozen for the times you can't buy it fresh or bake it, but it suffers in the process. Nevertheless, since it is what I chiefly need, I always do keep a few favorite loaves of solid, crusty bread on ice. I wouldn't dream of taking up freezer space with supermarket sliced bread. Aside from quality considerations, it's available at any all-night convenience store.

To refresh my cherished locally baked handmade loaves, I heat the mostly thawed bread directly on the middle shelf of a 350-degree oven; the exact length of time depends on the size and density of the loaf. You'll have to experiment with the different breads you buy to figure how long that is, but it is rarely more than 10 or 12 minutes.

Wrapping bread—frozen or not—in foil before putting it in the oven is generally not a good idea—the bread becomes soggy, sometimes rubbery. And don't buy partially baked bread that, its baker will tell you, is produced half-baked to make it more freezer worthy. This sort of thing is done in many suburban and rural areas, but I find the bread never gains the crumb or crust of a properly baked loaf. It's better to have the crust crack and be a little over-browned and brittle—a common result of re-heating frozen bread—than to have a still raw-tasting product with a beautiful but merely thick exterior.

Any bread—fresh, day-old, slightly stale, or previously frozen—can also be revived (or salvaged) by toasting it. Dense loaves make particularly good garlic bread.

English Muffins

English muffins, unlike crusted oven breads, are supposed to be half baked. That's why you have to toast them before you eat them and why they last so long in the refrigerator. They are the closest thing to freshly baked bread that you can keep on hand. From my experience, the muffins can be kept, closely wrapped and under refrigeration, for about a month. I've left them even longer, though after 2 weeks they're never as moist as they should be. Keep them in the freezer for a long storage. Though they are slightly sweet for the job, I've even made garlic toast with English muffins.

Garlic Toast

(Bruschetta, Fatunta, Croutons)

Toast ½- to 1-inch-thick slices of bread on both sides, either on a baking sheet under a broiler, or in a toaster or toaster oven. Rub one side of the bread with a cut clove of garlic, drizzle with olive oil, season with salt and pepper. Eat.

A Fresh Touch: Top with diced tomatoes and chopped garlic and olive oil.

Pita

If kept in the refrigerator, super-market-bought pita, the daily bread of the Arab world, has significantly longer lasting power than any European-style bread. All it takes is a few minutes in the oven or in a toaster and days-old pita is revived, though this is a short-lived miracle. If you let the pita cool, it becomes harder and staler tasting than it did before its revival.

Pita "crisps" are another solution for long-kept pita. Cut the pocket breads into two separate rounds, cut each round into triangles, spread them with butter or brush with oil, season to taste with garlic, curry, sweet paprika, cumin, an herb mix, or whatever you like that goes with the dish (if any) with which the pita will be served. Place on a baking sheet and bake in a preheated 350-degree oven until crisp and lightly browned, about 10 minutes.

Sliced White Bread

Though there certainly are many oversweetened, all too fluffy su-permarket brands to ridicule, white bread has its place. It has been well over 100 years since we realized that dark bread or whole-grain bread is better nutritionally, but sliced white bread continues to comfort us, to make fine sandwiches, toast, and French toast, among other uses. Here are some.

Sautéed Bread Crumbs for Pasta

In poor times and war times, when cheese for grating was scarce or unavailable, toasted bread crumbs were used in Italy to top many pasta dishes. In Sicily, it is still the favored topping for pasta con le sarde, the dish of macaroni with fresh sardines, fennel, raisins, and pine nuts. It's great on any fish pasta, especially Spaghetti with Anchovies (see page 16), but also Tuna-Noodle Casserole (see page 256). In a pinch, use it on tomato-sauced pastas.

Makes ½ cup

2 slices white bread, preferably somewhat dried out, crusts removed
2 tablespoons olive oil

1. Using your fingertips, crumble and pull the white bread into small crumbs no bigger than a pea, but even smaller if you have the patience. Alternately, you can use a blender or food processor, but don't make super-fine crumbs.

2. Heat the oil in a small skillet over medium-high heat. When very hot, add the crumbs and stir and toss immediately. Lower heat. (Some crumbs will absorb a lot of oil, some won't. It doesn't matter.)

3. Sauté, stirring, tossing, and turning frequently if not constantly, until crumbs are golden brown and crunchy, about 4 minutes.

4. Sprinkle over pasta while the crumbs are still hot.

Substitution: Because commercial soft white bread is made with sugar, use a sturdier, sugar-free Italian loaf if available.

Chocolate Raspberry Strata

Why does the *strata,* which is clearly American, have an Italian name? (It means layer.) I can't find the answer. A savory bread pudding assembled in layers, sort of a sandwich baked in custard, a strata in old cookbooks was always filled with cheese. Then there was a vogue in the 1950s and 1960s for cheese-and-other-ingredient stratas, the other ingredient being a salad of tuna, crab, shrimp, or ham, elevating this simple family dish to buffet and brunch fare. I've extended the notion to make dessert stratas, which are essentially bread puddings. Use the smaller amount of milk for a pudding texture, the larger amount for a more souffléed effect.

Serves 1 or 2

1 teaspoon butter or margarine
2 slices sandwich bread or an
    equivalent amount of sliced
    French or Italian bread, crusts
    removed if brittle
Kirsch or another white spirit or
    liqueur
1 rounded tablespoon raspberry jam
1 ounce chocolate (any kind of
    chocolate—bittersweet, sweet,
    unsweetened, bits, bars, or blocks),
    chopped or grated, if necessary to
    make small pieces
1 egg
½ to 1 cup milk
1 tablespoon sugar

1. Preheat the oven to 350 degrees.

2. Butter a small ovenproof dish just large enough to hold a slice of sandwich bread (or use a loaf pan for double the recipe).

3. Put a slice of bread on the bottom (or 2 or 3 slices from a long loaf) and sprinkle lightly with your spirit of choice.

4. Spread on or dot with the jam.

5. Cover with bits of chocolate.

6. Top with remaining bread.

7. Sprinkle top slice lightly with spirit.

8. Beat together the egg, milk, and sugar until sugar is dissolved, then pour over the sandwich in the dish. Let stand at room temperature for at least 30 minutes, though 1 hour is better.

9. Bake for 35 minutes, until top has browned lightly.

10. Serve immediately, warm or at room temperature.

Variations: For a peanut butter and chocolate strata, use 1 tablespoon smooth or chunky peanut butter instead of the jam, and sprinkle on from 1 teaspoon to 1 tablespoon sugar if the chocolate is unsweetened. To make the pudding particularly nutty, sprinkle with chopped peanuts before baking.

Other flavor combinations can be apricot preserves and chocolate, or apricot preserves and cream cheese. Toasted slivered, sliced, or chopped almonds make the pudding look and taste extra special. Even untoasted almonds are a good fillip. Either way, sprinkle them on before the pudding is baked.

Cheese Strata

This is the more classic strata combination, one of those dishes that taste wonderful for breakfast, lunch, or dinner. Any good melting cheese will do, even American slices.

Serves 1 or 2

1 teaspoon butter or margarine
2 slices sandwich bread
1 ounce cheese (Swiss Emmenthaler
 or Gruyère is perfect)
1 teaspoon prepared mustard
1 egg
½ to 1 cup milk

1. Butter a small ovenproof dish just large enough to hold a slice of bread (or a loaf pan for double the recipe).

2. Put a slice of bread on the bottom. Arrange cheese over the bread, as if you were making a sandwich.

3. Spread mustard on the other slice of bread and place mustard-side down on cheese.

4. In a small bowl or cup, beat the egg and milk together well, then pour over the sandwich in the dish. Let stand at room temperature for about 1 hour.

5. Preheat the oven to 350 degrees. Bake for 35 minutes, until top has browned lightly.

6. Serve immediately, warm or at room temperature.

Variations: Almost anything you would eat between slices of bread can be glorified into a strata.

Bread and Allium Soup

Allium is the botanical family name for shallots, garlic, onions, and leeks. Any one of them will work in this peasanty bread-thickened cream soup. What allium you use, as well as which dairy enrichment, depends entirely on what you have on hand. The bread thickening is called a *panade* in French and many recipes of this sort call the whole soup *panade*.

Serves 4

6 slices firm or even stale white bread
 (preferably made without sugar),
 crusts removed and broken into
 pieces, or 2 cups cubed dry French
 or Italian bread, crusts removed
2 cups milk
2 tablespoons butter
1 cup coarsely chopped shallots, or
 10 large cloves garlic, coarsely
 chopped; or 1½ cups coarsely
 chopped leeks or onions, or a
 combination of these
2 cups chicken broth or bouillon
Freshly ground pepper
Freshly grated nutmeg
1 cup milk, yogurt, sour cream, heavy
 cream, or a combination (optional)

1. Combine the bread and milk. Set aside to soak.

2. In a 2- to 3-quart saucepan, melt butter over medium heat. Add your allium of choice, and sauté about 3 minutes, until wilted.

3. Add the chicken broth and bring to a simmer over medium heat. Simmer, covered, for 10 minutes.

4. Meanwhile, with a wooden spoon, mash the bread into even smaller pieces.

5. Add the bread and milk to the saucepan and stir frequently with a wire whisk or wooden spoon while bringing the mixture to a simmer. Simmer, covered, another 10 to 15 minutes, or until the bread has dissolved and the soup has thickened. The soup may not look perfectly smooth, but you should not feel any lumps in your mouth.

6. Season with a few grinds of pepper and nutmeg to taste. (Salt is generally not necessary because broth contains enough.) For a thinner or richer soup, blend in one of the dairy additions.

7. Serve very hot, with a peppermill to add more pepper to taste.

Variations: Beat up to ½ cup Parmesan cheese into the soup just before serving. Or, pour the soup into individual crocks, top with Gruyère, and place bowls in a preheated 375-degree oven, until cheese melts and gets a brown glaze.

A Fresh Touch: Add an allium and garnish with chopped chives or garlic chives. Or garnish with any chopped fresh herb.

Broth *(Canned)*

A freezer full of homemade chicken broth and beef stock hardened into ice cubes and packed in plastic zipper bags is the serious cook's idea of emergency meal heaven. After all, homemade broth is a noble and nourishing meal unto itself. And, as any cooking classicist will tell you, the difference between a good dish and a great dish is often the stock that's used to make it.

I accept it: Canned broth is definitely a compromise. And it's expensive. But it is a more genuine product than bouillon cubes and, as salty as it is, it is less salty than they are. It can be reduced slightly without becoming absolutely vicious with salt and it has enough flavor to be diluted when necessary.

Canned broth is, obviously, a ready base for soups and sauces, but also think of it as a cooking medium that enhances the flavor of other foods. Both macaroni and rice become more of an eating event when boiled in broth instead of water. Vegetables take on an additional flavor.

I prefer ready-to-use broth over condensed, not only for flavor reasons, but also because the 13¾-ounce or 14-ounce can is a handy amount. Under the assumption that I can never have too much broth in the cupboard, I buy a few cans on every major supermarket outing. Low-salt broths are now available also. But be warned, some are low-flavor, too.

Macaroni in Brodo

There is no easier meal, which is one reason this is so satisfying when you're hungry and tired. Don't worry about the broth being too diluted. A lot of it evaporates and, with the starch from the macaroni, it regains enough strength and texture to make a full-bodied soup.

Serves 1

One 13¾-ounce can chicken broth
1 canful of water
1 cup macaroni (any kind)

1. In a small saucepan, bring the broth and water to a rolling boil.

2. Add the macaroni and boil, uncovered, stirring occasionally, for 8 to 10 minutes, until the macaroni is done to your taste.

Variations: I can eat this soup as is and enjoy it, but if you need embellishments to make you happy, sprinkle the soup with grated cheese. Or with a season-all product such as Spike or (for low-salt diets) Mrs. Dash. A few drops of Tabasco are a revelation: All the smoky-sweet subtlety of the hot sauce is exposed in the broth—just as the flavors in a fine whisky are brought out by a little water.

A Fresh Touch: The options are obviously endless, and you can easily make this into a catch-all soup for leftovers—vegetables, chicken, meat. More simply, add chopped herbs, scallions, a grating of fresh ginger.

Oriental Noodle Soups

The international popularity of packaged Oriental noodles-in-broth products is proof of their primal appeal. You know how they work: Add the contents of a flavoring packet to boiling water then simmer or steep the noodles.

Here's how to one-up them: Start with canned chicken, beef, or clam broth diluted with an equal amount of water. Add a sliced carrot, perhaps some slices of onion and/or celery, a few slivers of gingerroot, and a few drops of soy sauce, bottled hot sauce, or sesame oil. Boil until the vegetables are crisp-tender, about 3 minutes, depending on the size of the vegetable pieces. Add ramen (Japanese egg noodles), mein (Chinese egg noodles), cellophane (transparent) noodles, or soba (Japanese buckwheat noodles), even spaghetti or linguine, then steep or cook until noodles are tender.

A Fresh Touch: Beat 1 to 2 teaspoons finely chopped fresh parsley or basil into the egg and cheese.

Stracciatella

This homey Roman soup is satisfying as a restorative supper for one, though I have never understood why it is on the menus of fancy Italian restaurants.

Serves 1

One 13¾-ounce can chicken or beef broth
1 egg
2 tablespoons (or more) grated Parmesan cheese

1. In a small saucepan, bring the broth to a boil.

2. Meanwhile, in a small bowl or cup, with a fork, beat the egg with the cheese.

3. With the broth at a rolling boil, use the fork to stir in the egg-cheese mixture.

4. Eat immediately, with or without extra grated cheese.

Bulgur

Bulgur, sometimes spelled bulghur, is whole grains of wheat that have been precooked (steamed), then dried, then cracked. It is sold in fine, medium, or coarse grains. Though used mainly in Middle Eastern cooking, it is now often sold in supermarkets and health-food stores. Buy carefully, however, because some packaged bulgur products are preseasoned with dried herbs and vegetables and are not nearly as versatile as pure bulgur.

As a whole grain with its germ and natural oils, bulgur eventually turns rancid, so for storage of up to a year, keep it in a plastic container in the freezer, or at least in the refrigerator. It will keep only 4 to 6 months in a jar on a shelf at room temperature.

Because bulgur is precooked, it does not require further cooking. It need only be soaked to reconstitute it into a fluffy, nutty-tasting grain. Cover 1 cup bulgur with either 3 cups boiling water or very hot tap water and let it soak from 40 minutes to 1 hour. Or, use cold water and let it soak for several hours. Either way, when the bulgur has expanded and is tender, expunge the excess water by squeezing the grain in fistfuls. One cup of bulgur will yield about 3 cups when soaked. Reconstituted bulgur can be kept in a tightly covered container in the refrigerator for about a week.

Bulgur mixed with at least an equal amount of chopped fresh parsley and/or mint—and often as much as double the amount of herbs—a little olive oil, lemon juice, and perhaps finely chopped scallions and diced tomato is called *tabbouleh,* a salad that is ubiquitous throughout the Middle East and the most familiar bulgur dish in this country, too. Bulgur also makes a delicious hot pilaf. Depending on the embellishments, it can be a meal unto itself, or a side dish to any broiled or braised meat, fish, or poultry.

Bulgur Pilaf

Many bulgur pilaf recipes have us cooking the wheat for as long as 30 minutes. This results in a creamy mass that may be delicious (see Tomato Bulgur, which follows) but isn't pilaf to me. I like a separate grain, which you can get only by soaking the wheat, then briefly heating it through. The ingredients you toss with the bulgur are up to you and your cupboard supplies. I find the following mix delicious all by itself—a cereal supper—and it is a wonderful side dish to any broiled meat or poultry. (For a quick, full feast I buy an already roasted chicken from the supermarket deli department, pull off the skin and cut it into strips, then pull off the meat and cut it into strips. I add the skin strips with the carrot, proceeding as below, then top the pilaf with the chicken meat.)

Serves 2 or 3

2 tablespoons butter, vegetable oil, or olive oil
1 small to medium onion, finely chopped
1 small to medium carrot, grated
2 tablespoons sliced, slivered, or chopped almonds, or chopped walnuts
2 tablespoons raisins, plumped in hot water, or chopped dried apricots
1/2 cup chicken broth, orange juice, or water
1/2 teaspoon ground cumin or dried mint
2 cups reconstituted bulgur (2/3 cup dry)
Salt and freshly ground pepper

1. In a medium skillet, heat the butter over medium heat and sauté the onion until tender, about 5 minutes.

2. Add the carrot and continue to cook 3 or 4 minutes.

3. Add the almonds or walnuts; raisins or apricots; broth, juice, or water; and cumin or mint. Simmer 1 to 2 minutes.

4. Add the bulgur and toss over heat until bulgur is heated through, 3 or 4 minutes. Season with salt and pepper to taste.

5. Serve immediately. (May be reheated.)

Bulgur and Tuna Salad

Toss together a can of drained tuna and ½ to 1 cup of reconstituted bulgur. Season to taste with lemon juice; balsamic wine, or sherry vinegar, chopped olives, capers, chopped celery, shallots, or chopped onion, chopped parsley, dill, or basil.

Tomato Bulgur

This is freely adapted from a recipe of the late Bert Greene that appears in his book *The Grains Cookbook* (Workman, 1988). It is a creamy-textured grain dish with a distinctly Middle Eastern flavor and, as Bert notes, it goes supremely well with scrambled eggs, which Bert puts over the bulgur and I would put next to it on the same plate.

Serves 3 or 4

2 tablespoons olive oil
1 medium to large onion, finely
   chopped (about 1¼ cups)
2 large cloves garlic, finely chopped
   (1 scant tablespoon)
One 14-ounce can Italian plum
   tomatoes, with their juices
   (1½ cups), chopped
Big pinch of sugar
½ teaspoon dried oregano
2 anchovy fillets
Scant ½ teaspoon ground allspice
One 13¾-ounce can beef broth, or
   1¾ cups beef bouillon from cubes
1 cup bulgur

1. In a medium saucepan, heat the olive oil over medium-high heat and sauté the onion for 3 minutes.

2. Add the chopped garlic and sauté 2 more minutes.

3. Add the chopped tomatoes and their juices, the sugar, oregano, anchovies, and allspice. Reduce heat and simmer gently, stirring occasionally, for 15 minutes, until the sauce is thick.

4. Add the beef broth, increase heat, and bring to a boil.

5. Add the bulgur and reduce heat again, cover, and cook over lowest possible heat for 20 minutes.

6. Remove from heat and let stand, covered, for another 10 minutes.

7. Serve hot.

Cabbage

Produce charts and guides give green head cabbage a refrigerator life of no more than 2 weeks; some say 1 week. This is not my experience. I have had whole, unwashed heads of green cabbage live safely in the vegetable crisper, in a plastic bag, for as long as a month. Even after that length of time, only the outside layers of leaves are badly wilted, yellowed, or spotted; the interior is still firm and pale green, ready for cooking or to eat raw in a slaw.

Be careful when purchasing cabbage to keep on hand, however. The hard head cabbage we buy in the supermarket has often spent time in storage already. You can be certain it is not at its peak of freshness if the outer dark green leaves have already been stripped off, which is why those leaves, still dark and crisp, are what to look for when making a selection. Also choose cabbages that feel tight and heavy for their size.

Cabbage has an unfortunate reputation as an unpleasantly smelly vegetable and a mainstay of the poor, but it was not always so. It is one of the oldest cultivated vegetables and was considered a hangover remedy by ancient Egyptians, a source of good nourishment in ancient Greece, and a noble food fit for the Caesars in ancient Rome. In fourteenth-century France, there is said to have been a variety that, when cut, gave off an aroma more intoxicating than musk. This may be hard to imagine, given today's cabbages, which contain sulphur compounds that react with an enzyme when the leaves are cut and produce a compound with what we consider a "rotting" smell.

The trick to keeping cabbage sweet and delicate, both in taste and aroma, is not to cook it at all, or not to cook it too long.

Smothered Cabbage

This is the best way to cook cabbage when you want to serve it for its own sake. Butter and onion enhance the cabbage's sweetness.

Serves 2 or 3

2 tablespoons butter
1 medium onion, thinly sliced
   (1 rounded cup)
1 pound shredded cabbage (generally
   less than a small head, about
   2½ cups)

1. In a medium saucepan, over medium heat, melt butter and sauté onion until golden, about 8 minutes.

2. Add the shredded cabbage and toss to mix it with the onion and coat it lightly with butter.

3. Cover the pot, reduce heat to low, and let steam 8 to 10 minutes, until just tender.

Microwave Method: Combine butter and onion. Microwave on HIGH for 2 minutes. Add cabbage, toss well, then cover and microwave on HIGH another 4 to 6 minutes, tossing once or twice. Let cabbage rest 2 minutes before serving.

Smothered Cabbage and Noodles

My paternal grandmother, Rose (Cohen) Schwartz, who was born in Brooklyn and was of Hungarian and Polish heritage, made what she called "cabbage varnishkes," smothered cabbage tossed with egg noodles. In the old country, she told me, they probably used chicken fat or goose fat for such a dish, and so one holiday season when I had roasted goose, I made cabbage varnishkes with the rendered goose fat. I guess Rosie knew: It's better with butter.

Serves 2 or 3

1 recipe Smothered Cabbage (see opposite page)
4 ounces wide egg noodles, cooked and drained

1. When the cabbage is tender, toss, in the pot, with the drained noodles. (Add another tablespoon of butter if you dare.)

2. Serve immediately.

Cabbage and Noodle Kugel

This takes my grandmother's "cabbage varnishkes" one step further and makes it stretch further, though I now make the whole kugel from scratch for its own sake.

Serves 4

½ cup yogurt or sour cream
2 eggs
1 recipe Smothered Cabbage and Noodles (see opposite page)

1. Preheat the oven to 350 degrees.

2. In a mixing bowl, beat the yogurt or sour cream together with the eggs until well blended.

3. Stir in the cabbage and noodle mixture, making sure it is evenly coated with the egg mixture.

4. Spread mixture in a buttered 8- or 9-inch-square baking pan and bake for 30 minutes.

5. Serve hot, warm, or at room temperature. (I prefer it warm or at room temperature.)

Cabbage and Noodle Soup

Here's another way to stretch a pound of smothered cabbage.

Serves 3 or 4

Two 13¾-ounce cans chicken broth
1 recipe Smothered Cabbage (see opposite page)

*4 ounces fine or wide egg noodles,
cooked and drained*

1. Add the chicken broth to the smothered cabbage with 1 broth can full of water. Bring to a simmer and let simmer 5 minutes.

2. Add the drained noodles.

3. Serve immediately.

Oriental Slaw

U se this as a salad, or turn it into a wok and make a stir-fried side dish. As a slaw, it will keep in the refrigerator for several days, while it continues to marinate and become limper.

Serves 4 to 6

*3 tablespoons (or more to taste) rice
   wine vinegar or unflavored white
   wine vinegar*
1 tablespoon sugar
1 tablespoon soy sauce
*¼ teaspoon ground ginger, or
   ½ teaspoon (or more to taste) finely
   minced gingerroot*
Big pinch (or more to taste) cayenne
*3 tablespoons sesame oil or vegetable
   oil, or a combination of both*
*One 2-pound head cabbage, cored,
   quartered, and shredded as fine as
   possible (about 5 cups)*

1. In a small bowl, blend together the vinegar, sugar, soy sauce, ginger (or gingerroot), cayenne, and oil. (Or place all ingredients in a jar and shake well.)

2. In a serving bowl, toss the shredded cabbage with the dressing.

3. If served immediately, the slaw will be a crisp salad. For more wilted cabbage, let it stand at least 30 minutes before serving, tossing occasionally and tasting to adjust seasoning.

Variation: Turn the slaw into a hot dish by stir-frying the cabbage in the oil, then adding the sauce and allowing the cabbage to steam a few minutes. Cold or hot, you can always add chopped garlic.

All-American Cole Slaw

T he law on cole slaw is cabbage and vinegar. All the rest is interpretation. I happen to like mine with mayonnaise—sometimes half mayo and half sour cream, never too much—and with grated onion, some carrots, and no sugar. I can appreciate oil-and-vinegar-dressed slaws, and "creamy" slaws with more mayonnaise, and slightly sweetened slaws, with sugar but no raisins, but I never make one of those. Adjust the following recipe to taste: Add more mayonnaise, substitute sour cream or yogurt for some (but not all) of the mayonnaise, or add a supplement of one or the other. Add diced green and/or red pepper if you have one, celery or caraway seeds if you like that kind of thing, or shredded celery for an extra fresh taste.

Serves 4 to 6

One 1½-pound head (or a little more) green cabbage, cored, quartered, and shredded as fine as possible
3 tablespoons cider, malt, or distilled white vinegar
¼ teaspoon salt
1 small onion, grated (optional)
2 medium carrots, grated
⅔ cup mayonnaise

1. In a large mixing bowl, toss the cabbage with the vinegar and salt.

2. Grate the onion directly into the bowl.

3. Grate in the carrots.

4. Toss well.

5. The slaw can be served immediately, but it is much better—more melded and tender—if allowed to stand and tossed occasionally for 30 minutes to 1 hour. For a very limp slaw, refrigerate several hours or overnight.

Capers

"T he piquant, elegant, tasty little beads known as capers are the pickled unopened flower buds of a trailing shrub which since antiquity has been giving a lift to foods otherwise insipid." So wrote the great gastronome and journalist Waverley Root in *Food* (Simon & Schuster, 1980).

For the purposes of this book, his definition couldn't be more apt.

Sprinkle a few capers over a baked potato and it becomes something exotic. For a lift, add them to tomato sauce (see page 247), or to tuna salad (see page 255), sprinkle them on a bowl of spaghetti with garlic and oil (see page 184) or Spaghetti with Anchovies (see page 16). Add a few to a Tuna-Noodle Casserole (see page 256).

There are two basic kinds of capers available: Capers preserved in brine with vinegar and capers preserved dry in salt. Tiny capers, whether in brine or salt, are called nonpareil, "without peer," though I personally prefer the fuller flavor of fatter, larger capers. Capers in brine should be drained and rinsed under cold tap water before you use them. Salted capers must be rinsed, then soaked in cold water for at least 15 minutes, or, if very salty and slightly dehydrated from long storage, soaked in several changes of cold water for up to 1 hour. Brined capers can be held, covered in brine, indefinitely in the refrigerator. Salted capers will hold several years if kept in a tightly covered jar at room temperature.

Capers, Browned Butter, and Lemon

This classic trio of flavors is used to season fish and vegetables and sautéed sweetbreads. Use it on a baked potato, boiled potatoes, pasta, or rice.

Enough for 2 baked potatoes or ½ lb. pasta

3 tablespoons butter
1 tablespoon small capers or chopped large capers
2 tablespoons lemon juice

1. In a small skillet, heat the butter until it starts sizzling.

2. Add the capers and stir until butter begins to brown.

3. Add lemon juice and sizzle another 10 seconds.

4. Use immediately.

Macaroni with Capers and Hot Pepper

Excellent olive oil is essential here, not to mention a taste for capers.

Serves 2 as a main course, more as a side dish

½ pound macaroni or spaghetti, cooked
2 to 3 packed tablespoons finely chopped capers (drained if in brine, soaked if in salt)
2 tablespoons extra-virgin olive oil
At least 1 big pinch hot red pepper flakes, or more to taste

1. Toss cooked macaroni or spaghetti with the capers, oil and hot pepper flakes. Because capers are salty, no salt is usually necessary.

2. Serve hot or cooled, but not cold—and without grated cheese.

Variation: To make this feel more like a full-meal dish, flake in a can of tuna fish, or serve with sardines or hard-boiled eggs.

Carrots

Carrots are both the workhorses and the hussies of the emergency larder. Their garish color, crispness, and indefatigable sweetness can freshen up and bring to life almost anything and any meal. They are loaded with vitamin A, and the amount actually increases during their first five months in storage. Carrots, as much as onions, are an almost essential ingredient in soups and sauces, just to name the dishes encountered in this book.

Bagged carrots, as we buy them in the supermarket, may have already been stored several weeks. Still, I've kept carrots as long as 3 months, wrapped in a plastic bag in the vegetable crisper of the refrigerator. Carrots sold with their green tops may be more recently harvested than bagged carrots, but the greens quickly sap the carrots' nutrition and flavor and these may, in fact, have a shorter shelf life than the carrots that come bagged.

Look for bags with bright-colored carrots of similar size —not too large—and without splits. Don't be fooled by the orange printing on the bags; you have to read between the lines.

Carrots with Cumin

This is a standard Middle Eastern treatment, and these carrots are often served as part of an appetizer assortment. They are better than raw carrots to nibble with a drink (provide toothpicks), and I think they are more delicious at room temperature than hot. Even so, they make a great hot vegetable to go with roasted or broiled lamb or poultry.

Serves 2 or 3

4 carrots, peeled and cut into ¼-inch-
    thick slices on the bias (about
    2 cups)
1½ teaspoons ground cumin
½ teaspoon salt
Dash cayenne
1 clove garlic, smashed
1 or 2 tablespoons olive oil
1 teaspoon wine vinegar or lemon
    juice

1. In a small saucepan, combine the carrots, water to cover them, 1 teaspoon cumin, salt, cayenne, and garlic. Bring to a boil, simmer about 8 minutes, until carrots are tender but firm. Drain well. Discard garlic if desired.

2. In a small bowl, toss the carrots with olive oil, then with the wine vinegar or lemon juice. Sprinkle on ½ teaspoon cumin and toss again. Serve hot or at room temperature.

Carrot and Orange Soup

This is extremely refreshing as a cold summer soup, but can also be served hot.

Serves 4

2 tablespoons butter
1 medium onion, sliced
1 teaspoon chopped fresh gingerroot
1 pound carrots, peeled and sliced
    (about 3 cups)
Two 13¾-ounce cans chicken broth
1 cup orange juice
2 tablespoons white rice
Sour cream (optional)

1. In a medium saucepan, over medium heat, melt the butter and sauté the onion until golden, about 8 minutes.

2. Add ginger and carrots and toss with the onion and butter. Sauté another 2 minutes.

3. Add the chicken broth, orange juice, and rice. Cover and bring to a simmer. Reduce heat and simmer for 25 minutes.

4. Remove from heat and allow to cool.

5. In a food processor or blender, puree in several batches.

6. Reheat puree to serve hot, or chill well before serving. Either way, you can float a dollop of sour cream on the top.

Carrot Ribbons with Orange Glaze

A swivel-bladed vegetable peeler can cut carrots into noodle-thin and wide pieces, which, when braised like this, become a carrot dish liked even by carrot haters.

Serves 4

1 pound carrots
4 tablespoons butter
½ teaspoon salt

Freshly ground pepper to taste
½ cup orange juice

1. Scrape the carrots with a swivel-bladed vegetable peeler. Then, using medium pressure with the peeler, make the carrot ribbons by cutting the carrots into lengthwise strips, rotating the carrot as you go. Eventually, the carrot will be all core. Discard the core.

2. In a medium to large skillet, melt the butter over medium-high heat and sauté the carrot ribbons for about 2 minutes. Season with salt and pepper.

3. Add the orange juice, stir well, then reduce heat to medium.

4. Cover the skillet and let the carrots steam in the juice for about 3 minutes.

5. Uncover the skillet and continue cooking over medium-high heat, tossing the carrots constantly, for about 2 more minutes, until the liquid has mostly evaporated and the carrots are glazed.

6. Serve immediately.

Egg Noodles with Carrots

You can use carrots to dress macaroni, too, but I think they blend better with rich egg noodles. If using macaroni, you may want to top the dish with Sautéed Bread Crumbs for Pasta (see page 55) instead of grated Parmesan.

Serves 2

½ pound wide egg noodles
3 tablespoons butter
4 medium carrots, coarsely grated
Salt
⅛ teaspoon cayenne
2 tablespoons water
Grated Parmesan cheese

1. Cook the noodles in boiling salted water until *al dente*. While the water is coming to a boil and the noodles cook, prepare the carrots.

2. In a medium skillet, heat the butter over medium heat and sauté the grated carrots, tossing frequently, for about 8 minutes. Add the salt, cayenne, and water.

3. Drain the noodles and toss them with the carrots.

4. Serve immediately, with grated cheese on the side.

Carrot Slaw

Grated carrots make a fine salad that can be dressed any number of ways. Mayonnaise, or a mixture of mayonnaise and sour cream or yogurt, is a standard start. Sometime in fairly recent American food history, raisins and nuts began to be added. White distilled or cider vinegar, vegetable oil and a little sugar is another all-American style dressing. Rice wine vinegar, vegetable oil, a few drops of sesame oil and, if desired and available, some grated fresh gingerroot give the carrots a brisk Chinese flavor. Olive oil, lemon, garlic and cumin is an Arab-Mediterranean interpretation, while olive oil, red wine vinegar, garlic and mint is very Italian. Carrot slaws can be eaten as soon as they are prepared, when they are crisp, or they can be allowed to marinate and become limp for several hours or a day.

Celery

Celery is the most perishable of the three workhorse vegetables—onions, carrots, and celery—that every kitchen should have stocked. Buying the freshest celery available and storing it properly are the keys to keeping it for several weeks, if not longer.

Leaves that are only slightly wilted are one indication that celery is fresh, which is one reason you should look for celery with leaves, not leafless stalks. The stalks themselves should be firm and crisp, glossy and green—not yellowish—and without rust spots or big blemishes. If it appears that outer ribs have been removed from the stalk, the celery is probably not fresh. They have been removed because they were wilted or yellow.

For maximum storage time, wrap celery in plastic and keep it in the vegetable crisper of the refrigerator. Wilted celery can often be recrisped for eating raw by soaking it in very cold water. For cooking, wilted celery, if still green, can be used just as you would fresh celery.

Withered Celery Soup

Who hasn't bought a whole bunch of celery just to have a rib or two for a recipe? The rest of the celery sits in the refrigerator until it withers, then dies. This takes about a month in the vegetable crisper, though I've retrieved celery, in its last gasps of life, well into its sixth week of storage.

Serves 4

2 tablespoons butter or olive oil
3 cups diced celery (1 bunch, minus a
*   couple of outer ribs)*
1 cup finely chopped onion
*   (1 medium)*
½ teaspoon salt
3½ cups water
⅓ cup white rice (any kind)
¼ cup grated Parmesan cheese

1. In a saucepan, melt the butter or oil over medium-high heat. Add celery and onion; toss in butter. Lower heat to medium-low, cover, and let vegetables steam (they are sometimes said to sweat or stew) for 10 minutes, stirring once or twice.

2. Add water, increase heat, and bring to a boil, covered. Simmer 15 minutes. (May be prepared ahead to this point. Bring back to a simmer before continuing.)

3. Add rice and simmer another 12 to 15 minutes, until rice is tender.

4. Stir in the grated Parmesan cheese and serve immediately.

Variation: A teaspoon or so of dried dill or mint is a nice addition for the last few minutes of cooking.

Substitution: Made with chicken stock instead of water, the soup is richer but loses some of its refreshing celery delicacy.

Ants on a Log

This used to be a favorite children's snack before processed snack foods became a major industry.

Celery
Cream cheese
Raisins

1. Trim off the leaves and broad white end of crisp celery.

2. Fill the celery with cream cheese.

3. Stud with raisins.

Caraway Celery Sticks

Even when a long-stored bunch of celery looks like a total loss, it may be good for this pickling treatment, which in turn will let you keep the celery another 2 weeks or so if you continue to refrigerate it.

Makes about 1 quart

1 incomplete bunch celery
1 cup thinly sliced onion (1 medium)
⅓ cup vegetable oil
¼ cup white distilled vinegar
1 tablespoon caraway seed
1½ teaspoons salt
1 teaspoon sugar
¼ teaspoon freshly ground pepper

1. Trim the celery of any badly dehydrated portions and wash well.

2. Cut the ribs into 3-inch-long pieces then cut each length into quarters. Soak the sticks in very cold water to cover for about 1 hour, if the celery is in very bad shape. Drain, if necessary.

3. In a bowl, combine the celery and onion slices with the remaining ingredients. Cover and refrigerate for several hours or overnight, or up to 2 weeks.

A Fresh Touch: Chopped fresh parsley is an excellent addition.

Cheese

Making cheese was, at the beginning of civilization, a way of preserving excess milk and, at the same time, enhancing the economic value of the milk: it could be stored, then transported to be sold or traded for other goods. That turning milk into cheese also transformed it into one of the most seductive foods man makes was merely a by-product of necessity. Over the centuries cheese makers learned that even the smallest variables of climate and ecology, production and handling could create a different cheese. And the process goes on.

There are thousands of aged cheeses in the world today and they are generally classified into categories according to texture—soft, hard, firm, and semifirm—with blue-veined cheeses in a category by themselves. Fresh cheese, another category by itself, includes such unaged cheeses as cottage cheese, pot cheese, farmer cheese, and mascarpone (an Italian cream cheese that has recently become popular in the United States). They are beyond the scope of this book because they have such short shelf lives. A container of cottage cheese, for example, will keep in the refrigerator for 1 to 2 weeks without actually becoming moldy or spoiling dangerously, but it almost immediately develops an acid edge that most of us find very unappealing.

American-style cream cheese is, technically, a fresh

cheese, too. But only in a cheese store, health-food store, or advanced supermarket cheese department will you find true, fresh cream cheese without preservatives (and gum for firm texture). The more typical preservative-loaded cream cheese sold in supermarket dairy cases, albeit delicious, will keep in the refrigerator an almost frighteningly long time. Ditto processed cheeses—American cheese slices being the chief kind in that category.

High-quality, pure, natural cheeses can have a very long storage life as well. The rule of thumb is: The harder the cheese, the longer the life.

All cheeses must be kept refrigerated. Heat is destructive to cheese and many changes in temperature will shorten its life. Be careful to return cheese to the refrigerator as soon as you have cut off the amount you need. If mold develops on the surface, which it sometimes does, cut it off with an additional ½ inch of cheese. The cheese under that portion will be unaffected.

Following are the five kinds of cheese that are the most readily available, storable, versatile, and cookable, though let's not forget that cheese, as is, can be almost a meal unto itself. A chunk of cheddar or Parmesan, an apple or pear, some crackers or fulfilling bread, a glass of wine (red or white, sweet or dry, whatever you like). That's my idea of a sublime meal.

Cheddar

Cheddar is America's favorite cheese and consequently half the cheese made in America is cheddar, or at least an aged cow's milk cheese something like cheddar.

The best cheddar I can get is white and from Vermont. There are some superior cheddar producers in New York, Wisconsin, Canada, and, I hear, Kentucky, but I find that of the cheeses that are regularly available through mainstream, not specialized, sources, Vermont white cheddar has the most consistently high quality. It is sold in hunks and wedges from large wheels, and it is also available in small wheels of 2, 3, or 5 pounds each. (These can also be obtained by mail order.) The national brand bricks of cheddar sold in the supermarket can be satisfactory but they are not significantly lower in price than the best cheese.

Once you've found superior cheddar you can buy a lot of it. Kept wrapped in plastic film or in a resealable bag in the top third of the refrigerator, cheddar should keep for about 2 months. An unopened whole wheel can be kept 2 years or more at the bottom of the refrigerator; it will in fact continue to age and improve quite dramatically; just turn it over every month or so.

Melted Cheese

Many's the long night I've dreamed of cheese, toasted, mostly," said Ben Gunn, the old man in Robert Louis Stevenson's *Treasure Island*. For me, it is more specifically a toasted English muffin bubbling with Vermont white cheddar, though I don't put my nose in the air to orange cheese from Canada or New York, or to a firm slice of wholegrain bread instead of a muffin. I can eat melted cheddar for breakfast (with coffee), for lunch (with beer), and for dinner (with wine) and be very happy.

Serves 1

1 English muffin
2 ounces cheddar cheese

1. Split and toast the muffin on both sides in either a pop-up toaster or toaster oven.

2. Put about 1 ounce of cheese on top of each muffin half; that's about ¼ inch of cheese. Don't let any cheese overhang the muffin.

3. Melt the cheese under a broiler (on a baking sheet if necessary) or under the top element of a toaster oven. I pull the muffin out when the cheese bubbles nicely. Some people like the cheese tinged with brown.

Variations: Put a slice of apple or pear—or tomato or onion—under the cheese. Top with a slice of bacon or a dab of mango chutney.

Substitutions: Swiss, Gruyère, and blue cheese work just as well as cheddar. Mustard is good on the muffin under Swiss or Gruyère; the apple or pear is excellent with blue cheese.

Welsh Rabbit

There is an eternal debate about the derivation of the name of this classic British dish. Is it rabbit or rarebit and why? What does it all mean? I think it means it's a funny name either way and sounds delicious whatever it's called, so people keep talking about it, if not actually eating it. As some recipes direct, it's possible to make rabbit, or rarebit, without an egg yolk. But it won't get light and puffy and hold on to the bread as this one does. It'll be more like fondue, and better mopped up with bread than broiled on it, though there's nothing wrong with that. Either way, rabbit is a snack or light meal that goes particularly well with beer, red wine, or port.

Serves 2

4 ounces cheddar cheese, shredded or grated, or 1⅓ to 1½ cups shredded or grated combination of firm cheeses
2 splashes Worcestershire sauce
1 egg yolk
½ teaspoon dry mustard
1 to 2 tablespoons milk or beer
4 slices white bread

1. In a mixing bowl, combine all the ingredients—except the white bread —and, with a fork, mix together well.

2. Toast the bread on both sides (either in the oven or in a toaster).

3. Spread one side of the toast with the cheese mixture, then place under the broiler until bubbly.

4. Serve immediately.

Cheddar Soup

This is an extremely rich soup even when made with skim or low-fat milk. It's best to serve it in relatively dainty 1-cup servings as a first course, though a 2-cup portion poured over a couple of slices of dried or toasted bread, or topped with croutons or crumbled crackers, is a substantial lunch or supper. The soup also goes well with corn bread (see page 111) or Drop Biscuits (see page

142)—especially if you have a few slices of ham to put in the biscuits.

Makes 1 quart, to serve 2 to 4

2 tablespoons butter
3 tablespoons flour
One 13¾-ounce can chicken broth
1 small onion, very finely grated
1½ cups milk
¼ teaspoon ground cayenne
6 ounces cheddar cheese, grated (1½ cups loosely packed)

1. In a small or medium saucepan, over medium-low heat, melt butter, then blend in flour. Let bubble for 3 minutes, then remove from heat.

2. When bubbling has stopped completely, stir in the chicken broth and grated onion.

3. Place saucepan over medium-high heat and, stirring constantly, bring to a simmer. Simmer 1 minute. (Can be made ahead to this point. Return to a simmer before continuing.)

4. Add the milk and cayenne and bring almost to the simmering point. As soon as soup begins to bubble, reduce heat.

5. Stir grated cheese into the very hot, but not simmering, soup until cheese is completely melted, less than 1 minute.

6. Serve immediately, sprinkled with a little extra cayenne, if desired.

Variations: Before adding the milk, stir in 1 cup of frozen peas. They'll be cooked perfectly by the time the milk verges on a simmer. Crumbled bacon is a welcome garnish with or without the peas.

Ronald Reagan's Favorite Macaroni and Cheese

This is a rich man's dish, and for one who is not afraid of really rich food. The recipe, as it was handed out by the White House in 1986, calls for a full 3 cups of grated cheddar. That's an entire 8- or 10-ounce supermarket stick of cheese, about 880 to 1,100 calories worth; it serves 2 though. You can make a decent dish of its kind with significantly less cheese (page 92), but why would you want to if you didn't have to?

Serves 2 to 4

½ pound elbow macaroni or other
  small macaroni, preferably
  tubular
1 teaspoon butter
3 cups grated sharp cheddar (about
  10 ounces)
1 cup milk
1 egg
1 teaspoon dry mustard dissolved in
  1 tablespoon hot tap water
  (optional)
½ teaspoon salt
Freshly ground pepper (optional)

1. Preheat the oven to 350 degrees. Butter a shallow 8- or 9-inch-square casserole.

2. Cook macaroni in boiling salted water until still slightly firm. Drain well, then turn into a mixing bowl. Toss with butter, then with cheese, reserving about ½ cup of the cheese.

3. Using a rubber spatula, transfer the macaroni to the casserole.

4. In a small bowl or cup, beat together the milk, egg, dissolved mustard, and salt. (Add freshly ground pepper, if desired. It is not in the original recipe.)

5. Pour the liquid mixture over the macaroni and sprinkle with reserved cheese.

6. Bake for 45 minutes, until top is crusty and flecked with brown.

7. Serve very hot.

Cream Cheese

Have you ever looked at the last date of sale on a package of cream cheese? You can buy it on Halloween, and if it's left unopened in the refrigerator, it'll still be fine as a chip dip for Super Bowl. And even if you use only half the package then, what's left may still be good to smear on green bagels for St. Patrick's Day.

The largest selling national brand of cream cheese, Kraft's Philadelphia, has preservatives that keep it going and going. But even pure, "all natural," unprotected cream cheese keeps for a month or so. When a trace of mold develops, cut it off with an extra ½ inch of the cheese. Opened packages will, of course, deteriorate quicker than unopened ones. Keep opened cream cheese wrapped in plastic. Dump it when it dries out or becomes too moldy to save.

Cream Cheese and Tuna Spread

Many people offered me this recipe for this book and said it tastes like a fine fish pâté. It doesn't fool me, but I like it anyway.

Makes about 1½ cups

One 8-ounce package cream cheese
One 6½-ounce can tuna fish, well drained
2 tablespoons lemon juice, or 1 tablespoon lemon juice and 1 tablespoon Pernod

1. In a mixing bowl, combine the three ingredients. With a fork, blend them together until smooth. Or, for the fine fish pâté simulation, place ingredients in the bowl of a food processor and, with the metal blade, process until smooth.

2. Pack into a crock or mound on a serving plate.

3. Can be served immediately. If kept refrigerated, remove 30 minutes or so before serving time. It spreads better if not deeply chilled.

Variations: Add from 1 teaspoon to 1 tablespoon dried dill weed. Or add about 2 teaspoons finely chopped capers, up to 2 tablespoons of finely chopped green olives, finely chopped sweet or sour gherkins, or sweet pickle relish.

A Fresh Touch: Chopped fresh dill, parsley, or chives, lemon balm, lovage, or celery leaves are extremely good. However, if you have as much as a rounded ¼ cup of finely chopped fresh herbs, you can forget the tuna altogether. With some mashed garlic, you will then have what some cookbooks call "mock Boursin," referring to the flavored French cream cheese. Though by calling the fresh version a copy of the commercial, it's like saying Lipton's is the model for French onion soup.

Cream Cheese and Sardine Spread

This is along the lines of the above but, to me, an even better combination.

Makes about 1½ cups

1 or 2 shallots, peeled
One 3¾-ounce can sardines, drained
One 8-ounce package cream cheese
1 tablespoon lemon juice, or to taste
  (optional)

1. In a food processor, using the metal blade, chop shallot until fine.

2. Add the drained sardines, cream cheese, and lemon juice. With a few on-off pulses, process until smooth.

Cheesecake Custard

A great cheesecake is something of a production. This stove-top custard isn't, but it tastes like it is.

Serves 4 to 5

One 8-ounce package cream cheese
½ cup sugar
2 eggs
1 cup milk
1 teaspoon vanilla extract

1. In a blender or food processor, combine the cream cheese, sugar, and eggs. Process until smooth.

2. Add the milk and process again until well blended.

3. Pour into a medium saucepan and stir constantly with a wooden spoon over medium heat for about 10 minutes, until mixture has thickened. Just before mixture has fully thickened, surface will become steamy. When done, mixture will coat the back of a wooden spoon.

4. Ladle into 4 or 5 custard or pudding cups and chill for at least 2 hours before serving. Stir in the vanilla extract.

Feta

Feta is best known as a Greek cheese—the cheese that is crumbled over a Greek salad—but it and cheeses like it are produced in Romania, Bulgaria, Albania, and throughout the Caucasus. Traditionally it is a sheep's milk cheese, but today it is often made entirely of cow's milk or partly with sheep's milk. It is sharp, crumbly, and salty and keeps extremely well because it is preserved in brine—in this country a mixture of salt, water, and milk.

Feta has become a supermarket item in recent years and can be purchased either cut into pieces and packed in a screw-top jar or as a block in a vacuum plastic wrap that holds a small amount of brine. Both jars and plastic packages of feta can carry a last date of sale that is 9 months ahead of the purchase date.

However, once opened, the jarred cheese is easier to store because pieces of the feta can be picked out without disturbing the brine that keeps the remaining cheese fresh. Once a plastic package is opened there is not enough brine to cover the unused portion of cheese. Keep it wrapped in plastic or in a covered bowl or crock, submerged in a solution of 1 teaspoon salt to 1 cup water. It should last either way for several weeks.

Greek Salad

What we call a Greek salad, the Greeks call "country salad," *horiatiki*. It usually includes cucumber and tomato, often sweet green or red pepper, too, none of which are likely to be available in a pinch. But a salad of only iceberg lettuce attractively topped with crumbled feta, Kalamata olives (or other good olives), some anchovies, red onion, perhaps marinated artichoke hearts and capers, plus an olive oil and vinegar dressing with garlic and oregano is Greek enough for me.

Iceberg lettuce, chopped coarsely
Feta cheese
Kalamata or other dark olives
Anchovy fillets
Onion, sliced or chopped (preferably red or sweet Bermuda)
Small pickled green peppers, sometimes called Tuscan, sometimes Greek (optional)
Marinated artichoke hearts (optional)
Capers

For about ½ cup dressing:

½ teaspoon salt
3 tablespoons red wine vinegar
1 small clove garlic, crushed or mashed
1 rounded teaspoon dried oregano
½ teaspoon freshly ground black pepper
6 to 8 tablespoons olive oil

1. In a salad bowl, or on individual plates or shallow bowls, make a bed of the lettuce.

2. On top of the lettuce, crumble the feta cheese, then arrange all the remaining ingredients.

3. To make the dressing, in a small bowl, dissolve the salt in the vinegar, then add all remaining ingredients, except the oil. Stir to mix, then beat in the oil with a fork or whisk.

4. If tossing the salad in a big bowl, serve within 30 minutes of adding the dressing. If salad is arranged on plates, serve the dressing on the side.

A Fresh Touch: It would certainly be nice to have cucumbers and tomatoes. Chopped fresh parsley is a good addition to—not substitute for—the oregano.

Macaroni and Cheese Like a Greek Salad

I f you take the same ingredients and put them on pasta instead of lettuce, you'll also have an excellent salad.

Serves 1 or 2

¼ pound macaroni
1½ tablespoons fruity olive oil
1 tablespoon wine vinegar
2 ounces feta (one-fourth most
*   supermarket packages)*
4 or 5 Kalamata or other Greek
*   olives, pitted and quartered*
¾ teaspoon dried Mediterranean
*   oregano*
Freshly ground pepper

1. Cook the macaroni until tender. Drain well.

2. Pour into a mixing bowl and toss immediately with the oil.

3. Add vinegar and toss again.

4. Add the feta, olives, oregano, and several grinds of the pepper mill. (Because the cheese is salty, additional salt is probably unnecessary.) Toss again. Serve hot or at room temperature.

Saganaki

I n fancy Greek restaurants—or for festive occasions at home—*saganaki,* or fried cheese, is often brought to the table flamed in brandy. This is probably not something you would do for yourself eating a plate of fried cheese and a hunk of bread for supper in front of the TV. But, then again, why not?

Serves 1

2 tablespoons butter
¼ pound feta, sliced
Juice of ½ lemon
1 tablespoon brandy (optional)

1. In a small skillet, heat the butter over medium heat until it sizzles.

2. Add the feta and fry 2 minutes on each side, until melted and lightly browned.

3. Squeeze on the lemon juice and eat immediately. Or pour on the brandy, ignite, and when the flames go out, sprinkle on the lemon juice and eat.

Variation: Butter unquestionably adds to the appeal of the cheese, but feta is also good melted under a broiler or in a toaster oven, on bread or not, with lemon juice or not.

Parmesan

According to *The Cheese Book* (1964; revised edition Fireside paperback, 1985), a standard reference by Vivienne Marquis and Patricia Haskell, " 'No Italian export, with the possible exception of our Sophia Loren, has brought so much pleasure to the world,' as one Milanese put it."

But I must stress, as Marquis and Haskell do several times, any grating cheese called Parmesan and not the genuine article—what is called Parmigiano Reggiano by Italian law and stamped with that name all over the rind—could very well bring disgrace to Italy. You do not want anything that comes already grated and in a box, or that is domestically made, or made in a country other than Italy, and/or sold in the supermarket dairy case in a plastic-wrapped, evenly cut wedge. Parmigiano Reggiano is produced in a limited area (it's part of a particular agricultural ecosystem) by strict production standards and there is simply nothing like it.

Even in New York City you have to go to a special store to buy authentic Parmigiano Reggiano. Fortunately, in a large hunk, ungrated and wrapped tightly in plastic or in a zipper bag, it can keep for many months in the refrigerator, preferably in the upper third. I know expert Italian cooks who freeze their Parmesan—even grated—and are happy with it. I've never felt the need. If anything, I use up the cheese too fast.

Parmesan is an essential flavor of the Italian kitchen. Be careful cooking with it, however. It does not melt well, and when it is browned under the broiler it gets sharp and salty, though that is a flavor many people like. In this book it is used on and in soups, pasta, and risotto. It is also an excellent eating cheese, and a hunk of Parmesan with a glass of red wine is about as perfect a snack or dessert as I can imagine.

Baked Thin Spaghetti or Little Macaroni

This is an Italian-style dish, not American macaroni and cheese. The top is intentionally left dry to give it a chewy texture with the occasional hit of a crunchy bit of browned pasta.

Serves 2

*½ pound thin spaghetti, small
    elbows, or soup-size bow ties
3 tablespoons butter, cut into bits or
    melted
2 ounces Parmesan cheese, about
    2-by-3-inch chunk (1 loosely
    packed cup of grated cheese)
Freshly ground pepper
2 eggs
½ cup milk*

1. Preheat the oven to 425 degrees.

2. Cook the spaghetti or macaroni in boiling salted water until still slightly firm. Drain well.

3. Immediately toss the pasta with the butter.

4. Toss again with the cheese, until the pasta is evenly coated.

5. Pour the dressed pasta into a baking dish—an 8-inch-square pan, 10-inch oval gratin dish, or equivalent rectangular or similarly sized oven-to-table ware. Spread the pasta evenly. Season the top lightly with pepper. (Can be set aside until ready to be baked. If refrigerated, bring back to room temperature, if possible.)

6. In a small bowl or cup, beat the eggs and milk together.

7. Pour the egg mixture over the pasta and bake about 20 minutes in the preheated oven, or until lightly browned.

8. Serve immediately or at room temperature.

Substitutions: Instead of butter, use olive oil. Instead of Parmesan, use a combination of cheeses, or all Swiss or all cheddar. Use 1 egg instead of 2.

A Fresh Touch: Diced boiled ham (up to about ½ cup) is a fine addition, so are peas. So are both together.

Parmesan Wafers

Serve these rich, fragile crackers with drinks, salad, or soup, or with apples for dessert.

Makes about 2 dozen

8 tablespoons (1 stick) butter, at room temperature
½ cup grated Parmesan cheese
1 cup flour

1. Preheat the oven to 400 degrees.

2. With a fork, cream together the butter and cheese.

3. With a wooden spoon, blend in the flour.

4. Chill until mixture is firm enough to roll out.

5. On a lightly floured board, roll the dough to a ¼-inch thickness.

6. With a cookie cutter or glass tumbler, cut the dough into rounds.

7. Place on an unbuttered baking sheet and bake in the preheated oven for 8 to 10 minutes, until lightly browned.

8. Cool thoroughly before serving. (May be stored in a tin for several weeks.)

Swiss and Gruyère

What we call Swiss cheese, the smooth, mellow, sweet, and distinctly nutty-tasting cheese with the big holes, is actually called Emmenthaler and it is Switzerland's largest food export. It is so popular here and in other countries—as a table cheese, sandwich cheese, and cooking cheese—that it is imitated by many of them, including the United States. Much of what is sold in our supermarkets is domestic Swiss, which can be good but never the same as true Swiss, which is identified by the word Switzerland printed in red all over the rind. Jarlsberg, which is a Norwegian version of Swiss, is a pleasant cheese, too, but it lacks the real sweetness and nuttiness of true Switzerland Swiss.

Gruyère, also a Swiss cheese, is very much like Emmenthaler, but more so. It is also smooth and mellow tasting, but even nuttier. It is the preferred cheese for fondue and other cooking purposes, such as to flavor a soufflé or gratin, though, in a pinch, Emmenthaler can be used whenever Gruyère is called for in a recipe.

Both cheeses keep very well in the refrigerator, up to a couple of months if they are in a large piece. I keep my cheese in plastic wrap and after several weeks it may develop some mold that needs to be cut off before the cheese is used. Some cheese connoisseurs prefer wrapping their cheese in wax paper. This allows the cheese to breathe, inhibiting mold, but it also speeds dehydration. In that case, it's the dry end that has to be cut off.

Gougère

This Burgundian snack is nothing more than cream puff pastry (Pâte à Choux; see page 140) with cheese added for flavor and an extra-rich texture. Use it as a bread to go with soups or salads, as a snack with wine, or a complement to apples or pears for dessert.

Serves 4 to 6 as an appetizer

8 tablespoons (1 stick) butter, cut into
    large pieces
1 cup water
½ teaspoon salt
1 cup flour
4 eggs
2 ounces Swiss or Gruyère, grated
    (about ¾ cup)

1. Follow instructions on page 141 for Pâte à Choux, adding the eggs 1 at a time.

2. Stir in all but about a couple of tablespoons of the cheese.

3. With a tablespoon, scoop out heaping spoons of dough and drop on a greased baking sheet. Drop the dough balls next to each other to form a ring about 8 inches in diameter.

4. Sprinkle the top of the ring with the remaining grated cheese.

5. Bake in the oven for about 50 minutes, until the ring is well puffed and browned.

6. Serve hot.

Variations: Instead of using all the cheese in the dough, reserve about half, then make a double ring of dough, one on top of the other, with the cheese in the middle. Instead of making one large ring, make individual puffs by dropping the spoonfuls of dough about 2 inches apart on the baking sheet and baking for only 20 to 25 minutes.

Cheese Soufflé

Nothing impresses people like a soufflé. Nothing impresses me like a soufflé. It is a constant source of human fascination the way beaten egg whites can balloon in heat and form architecture as inspiring as any ancient wonder of the world.

Serves 2

4 tablespoons butter
4 tablespoons flour
1 cup milk
4 eggs, separated
1 cup grated cheese (Swiss, Gruyère, cheddar, or one of those in combination with up to ½ cup Parmesan)
½ teaspoon salt
⅛ teaspoon cayenne
Freshly grated nutmeg

1. Preheat the oven to 350 degrees. Butter a 1-quart soufflé dish then dust it with flour. Set aside.

2. In a small saucepan, melt the butter over medium-low heat, then blend in flour. Let bubble over medium low heat for 3 minutes, stirring frequently.

3. Remove from the heat and when the bubbling stops, beat in the milk.

4. Place the saucepan over medium heat and, stirring constantly, bring to a simmer. The sauce should be thick and smooth.

5. Remove from the heat again and stir in the egg yolks, then the grated cheese, salt, cayenne, and nutmeg. Scrape into a large mixing bowl.

6. In another mixing bowl, beat the whites until they hold stiff peaks.

7. Place the egg whites on top of the cheese mixture and fold together.

8. Pour into prepared dish and bake for 35 minutes.

9. Serve immediately.

Chocolate

There is life without chocolate, but who would want to live it? In the form of unsweetened cocoa, semisweet bits, and unsweetened and semisweet squares, my cupboard is never without it. Cocoa, which is the powdery, flavor essence of the cocoa bean after most of the cocoa fat has been removed, keeps the longest—1½ to 2 years would not be stretching it if it is kept on a dry shelf tightly covered in a jar or tin. The cocoa butter is the part of chocolate that spoils, though even full-fat chocolate bits and squares keep for at least a year, tightly wrapped in their original packaging or a plastic bag. If solid chocolate develops a white or gray surface—called "bloom"—don't throw it out. It may look unappetizing, but it doesn't indicate spoilage. It's fat separation caused by temperature changes, or in the case of solid milk chocolate, it can mean sugar separation.

The recipes in this book were all tested with old-fashioned, unsweetened Hershey's cocoa, a nonalkylized cocoa that, I feel, has more flavor than more expensive imported Dutch cocoas, which have been treated with alkylides to make them less acidic. (Hershey also makes Dutch-style cocoa now.) The different cocoas are interchangeable in most but not all recipes. Here, you can use either if necessary.

Cocoa can substitute for unsweetened chocolate in some recipes. Use 3 tablespoons of cocoa plus 1 tablespoon of butter to replace 1 ounce of chocolate.

Chocolate Brownies

I was just about to embark on what I thought would be a never-ending search for the origin of brownies when *Maida Heatter's Book of Great American Desserts* was published (Knopf, 1983). There it was, America's favorite baking book writer had unearthed the whole story, at least as much as I needed to know:

"Brownies are totally American. I don't know of any other country where they are made. Their history and origin are unknown and guessed at. One theory is that someone forgot to use the leavening and the chocolate cake did not rise. There is a rumor that this historical event occurred in Bangor, Maine, in the early 1900s.

"At the Maine Historical Society in Bangor, Mrs. 'Brownie' Schrumpf, a local food authority and an octogenarian, remembers a cookbook published by the local YMCA in 1914. It had a recipe for brownies. That might have been the first brownie recipe in print."

Coincidentally, the recipe I had been using for a number of years uses exactly the same proportions as "Brownie" Schrumpf's—as given by Maida Heatter. The procedure here is considerably different, however. It's a recipe that has been stripped down to its bare essentials—everything is mixed in a single saucepan with a wooden spoon. Not even a mixing bowl gets dirtied.

Makes a 13-by-9-inch panful; cut them as you want

8 tablespoons (1 stick) butter
1 cup cocoa, or 4 ounces unsweetened chocolate
2 cups sugar
4 eggs
1 cup flour
2 teaspoons vanilla extract
½ teaspoon salt
¾ cup coarsely chopped walnuts or pecans (more or less)

1. Preheat the oven to 350 degrees. Grease a 13-by-9-inch baking pan.

2. In a 1-quart or larger saucepan, over medium-low heat, melt the butter. If using chocolate, melt the chocolate with the butter. If using cocoa, stir the cocoa into the melted butter using a wooden spoon.

3. Stir in the sugar.

4. Still using a wooden spoon, beat the eggs into the chocolate mixture one at a time, incorporating each before adding the next.

5. Stir in the flour, vanilla, and salt to make a smooth, dark batter.

6. Blend in the nuts, unless you only have a few, in which case, reserve them to sprinkle over the top.

7. Scrape batter into the prepared pan and bake for 30 to 35 minutes, until a toothpick inserted in the center comes out clean.

8. Cool thoroughly before cutting into squares.

Variation: The same ingredients in the same proportions can also be made into a perfect chocolate pound cake. Instead of melting the butter, cream it with the sugar, using an electric mixer. Then beat in the eggs one at a time, beating very thoroughly between additions. Beat in the cocoa thoroughly, then beat in the flour, salt, and vanilla. When all the ingredients have been added and thoroughly blended, beat an additional 90 seconds or so. You will see the batter turn a lighter color. Pour into a greased 9-inch-square cake pan and bake as above. The only trouble with this cake is that it is significantly better the day after it is baked and it doesn't always last that long.

Mocha Mock Mousse

A classic French mousse has whipped cream folded into it. This one gets its volume and requisite sponginess from beaten egg whites only.

Serves 6

6 ounces semisweet chocolate (any kind)
5 tablespoons double-strength coffee or espresso
5 eggs, separated
1 teaspoon vanilla, or 2 tablespoons rum, brandy, or Scotch
Pinch of salt

1. In a heavy saucepan, combine the chocolate and coffee. Place over very low heat and melt the chocolate, stirring occasionally to blend it with the coffee until mixture is absolutely smooth.

2. While the mixture is still warm, stir in the egg yolks, then stir in the vanilla or rum, brandy, or Scotch. Scrape into a mixing bowl and set aside.

3. In another mixing bowl, beat the egg whites with a pinch of salt until the whites form stiff peaks.

4. Carefully pour the chocolate mixture down the side of the bowl with the egg whites, then fold together until there are no more puffs of egg white.

5. Spoon into 6 serving cups or stemmed glasses. Refrigerate at least 2 hours before serving.

Variation: Substitute 2 tablespoons of brandy, bourbon, or Scotch for 2 tablespoons of coffee. For an interesting contrast in flavors and textures, either fold in ½ cup chopped salted peanuts with the egg whites, or top with a few whole salted peanuts.

James O'Shea's Mocha Ice

James O'Shea, proprietor of the West Street Grill in Litchfield, Connecticut, whips this mixture in the food processor to give it a finer texture. I find it is more refreshing if left in larger crystals.

Serves 6 to 8

⅓ to ½ cup sugar
1 tablespoon cocoa (optional)
4 cups strong coffee
6 ounces semisweet chocolate
Orange liqueur, such as Grand
    Marnier, Cointreau, Curaçao, or
    Triple Sec

1. In a saucepan, over medium heat, stir the sugar and cocoa into the coffee until both sugar and cocoa are dissolved. Let cool 5 minutes.

2. Add the chocolate, return the saucepan to low heat, and stir occasionally until chocolate has melted and mixture is perfectly smooth.

3. Pour into freezer trays, preferably metal ones. Freeze several hours, stirring the frozen edges into the center every 20 minutes or so. The ice will never become smooth. It is supposed to have relatively large crystals.

4. Serve with or without a drizzle of orange liqueur poured on top of each serving.

Variation: Top with whipped cream.

Miraculous Microwave Chocolate Cake

This moist cake layer is rich and satisfying, it's ready to eat in as few as 20 minutes from the moment you start mixing the batter, and it requires only 1 egg. Could you ask for more? (If you do: The cake is made with vegetable oil, not butter, and it is therefore low in cholesterol, too.) The only problem you may have in making it is finding the right pan. The perfect one—a 1½-inch deep, 8-inch round plastic or glass pan—comes in the box with Pillsbury's microwave cake mixes: Buy one, get one free.

Makes one 8-inch-diameter cake, to serve about 6

¼ cup cocoa
⅔ cup water
¾ cup plus 2 tablespoons all-purpose flour
1 cup sugar
½ teaspoon baking soda
¼ teaspoon baking powder
¼ teaspoon salt
¼ cup plus 2 tablespoons vegetable oil
1 egg
2 teaspoons vanilla extract

1. Cut out a circle of wax paper to fit the bottom of the cake pan. Fold another long piece of wax paper in quarters the long way—to make a collar to line the sides of the cake pan and come up about 1 inch higher than the pan.

2. In a small bowl or cup, combine the cocoa and ⅓ cup water. Don't bother to stir; the cocoa won't dissolve. Microwave on HIGH for 40 seconds. Stir until smooth; mixture will be thick. Set aside.

3. In a mixing bowl, combine the flour, sugar, baking soda, baking powder, and salt. Mix thoroughly.

4. Make a well in the center of the dry ingredients and add the cocoa mixture, the remaining ⅓ cup water, vegetable oil, egg, and vanilla.

5. With a spoon, mix the wet ingredients thoroughly, then blend in the dry ingredients until the batter is smooth.

6. Pour the batter into the prepared pan and microwave on HIGH for 5 to 6 minutes, until the cake begins to pull away from the sides of the pan. Check the cake after 5 minutes, and if it isn't pulling from the sides, return it to the microwave for another minute.

7. Let stand 10 minutes. Carefully pull out wax paper collar. Turn it out onto a serving plate.

8. The cake can be served as soon as it cools, but its texture improves after a rest of 1 hour. If desired, sift confectioners' sugar over top, or glaze with melted chocolate.

Another recipe featuring chocolate

Sour Cream Coffee Cake (see page 235)

Canned Clams and Clam Juice

I have to be honest. Canned clams are a compromise. They're on my pantry shelf because they keep their quality for at least a year and I think they can be turned into a pretty good spaghetti sauce—especially if there is parsley to freshen up their flavor—and pretty good chowder, but I stop there. You will find no clam dips here or baked clams or casseroles. Canned clams can only be a flavor fillip, never a main event.

Brands vary, but I haven't found any objectionable national domestic brands of chopped or minced clams. However, I have tasted some distressingly salty, flabby, or metallic whole tiny clams imported from Southeast Asia. Shop around and see what's available. Whatever you do, do not cook canned clams; it only toughens them further. They are already cooked and need only be heated through.

Bottled clam juice is another handy product to keep on the shelf, and a better product than the clams themselves. It is a satisfactory substitute for fish broth and, with a little freshening up by simmering it with a sliced carrot, a rib of celery, and a thick slice of onion, it's a pleasant soup to sip for its own sake.

Spaghetti with White Clam Sauce

T he olive oil and garlic are as vital to this sauce as the clams. Unless the oil is first rate and fruity and you use plenty of garlic, the dish will be flat.

Serves 2

¼ cup extra-virgin olive oil
2 or 3 large cloves garlic, finely chopped
½ pound spaghetti or linguine
One 6½-ounce can clams (¾ cup)
Freshly ground black pepper or hot red pepper flakes

1. In a small saucepan, combine the olive oil and garlic over medium heat. Let sizzle gently while cooking the spaghetti in boiling salted water.

2. When the spaghetti is a few minutes from being done, and the garlic is a light, nutty brown, drain the clam juice into the saucepan. Season with pepper and bring to a simmer.

3. Add the clams and let heat through while draining the spaghetti.

4. In a warm serving bowl, toss spaghetti with sauce and serve immediately. (Do not add grated cheese.)

A Fresh Touch: There is nothing like finely chopped parsley to freshen up the taste of canned clams: use 2 or 3 tablespoons.

Manhattan Clam Chowder

I read somewhere that Manhattan clam chowder is also called Coney Island clam chowder. I grew up near Coney Island and it's true that you used to be able to buy a pretty good cup of chowder at a few places along the boardwalk. But as I remember, it was called Manhattan clam chowder even there. In the same vein, no one in Coney Island would ever refer to a hot dog as a Coney, but in many parts of America that's exactly what they are called. Tomatoes and thyme are the ingredients everyone associates with Manhattan chowder, but carrot and celery are equally important for the real thing.

Serves 3 or 4

2 strips bacon
1 cup diced carrots
1 cup diced celery
1 cup diced onion
2 cups diced potatoes
One 28-ounce can Italian plum
  tomatoes, with their juices
  (3½ cups), chopped
1 cup water or bottled clam juice
½ teaspoon dried thyme
Freshly ground black pepper
Two 6½-ounce cans minced clams
  (about 1¼ cups)

1. In a medium saucepan, over low heat, cook bacon until crisp. Remove, crumble, and set aside.

2. Add the diced carrots, celery, and onion to the bacon fat in the saucepan. Increase heat to medium and sauté until tender, about 10 minutes.

3. Add the potatoes, mix well, and sauté another 2 minutes.

4. Add the chopped tomatoes and all their juices, the water or clam juice, the thyme, a few grinds of black pepper, and the clam juice from the canned clams. Simmer together for 15 minutes.

5. Add the clams and heat through.

6. Serve very hot with oyster crackers or pilot crackers or hot biscuits.

Substitution: Instead of clams, use two 6½-ounce cans tuna fish, preferably chunk light, drained.

New England Clam Chowder

Salt pork, not sugar-cured and smoked bacon, gives the authentic Cape Cod flavor. But what's authentic, after all? I knew an old-time Falmouth cook, now long deceased, who used only canned evaporated milk in her chowder. If you happen to have salt pork, you can use it. If you happen to have evaporated milk, use it. I find the following quite comforting, which, to me, is what New England chowder is supposed to be.

Serves 2

2 slices bacon
1 medium onion, chopped
1 large potato, diced (about 1½ cups)
1 cup bottled clam juice
One 6½-ounce can minced clams
1 cup milk

1. In a medium saucepan, over low heat, cook bacon until crisp. Remove, crumble, and set aside.

2. Add onion, increase heat to medium, and sauté until golden, about 8 minutes.

3. Add the diced potato. Toss and coat with fat and sauté about 2 minutes.

4. Add the clam juice, the clam juice drained from the clams, and the milk. Bring to a gentle simmer, and cook 10 minutes, until potatoes are tender.

5. Add the chopped clams and heat through.

6. May be served immediately, but the texture of the chowder will improve with standing. Let stand at room temperature for at least 1 hour, then reheat gently. Or, refrigerate overnight.

Corn *(Frozen)*

Corn begins to lose sweetness as soon as it is picked. Hence the old cooking advice about putting the water up to boil then going out to pick the corn. And that's why, except during your local corn season, frozen corn—like frozen peas—is more reliably sweet than fresh.

As one of the most popular vegetables in the frozen food case, corn is sold in several forms, in several differently sized packages, and in combination with various seasonings, sauces, and other vegetables. I don't bother with frozen corn on the cob because its texture is wrong for eating that way, and I don't buy any of the seasoned, sauced, or combo corn products. Large bags of corn kernels I find very useful, but once opened, the corn must be used within a month or so.

Succotash

There was a time I would have made gross faces at the thought of succotash. It is one of those all-American foods for which my relatively ethnic upbringing had not prepared me, just as a boy from Maine might not be ready for chopped liver. Until fairly recently, I thought succotash was always a sludgy mess, as it was in my Southern college's cafeteria, where I had my first taste of it. With a new love for lima beans, I began to find the idea of succotash appealing, though, and looking through old cookbooks, I found it isn't always so heavy. It is, in fact, any combination of lima beans and corn kernels, which isn't a bad combination in itself. The two vegetables taste sweet and light simply tossed together with a little butter. Or try this creamed version. Even with frozen vegetables it's surprisingly fresh tasting.

Serves 3 or 4

One 10-ounce box frozen baby lima
    beans (2 cups)
1 cup frozen corn kernels
1 small onion, halved and very thinly
    sliced (about ⅓ cup)
1 cup milk
1 tablespoon butter
1 teaspoon sugar
Salt

1. In a small saucepan, combine the limas, corn, onion, milk, butter, and sugar. Bring to a boil, reduce heat, and let simmer about 20 minutes, until limas are very tender and milk has reduced to a few tablespoons.

2. Increase heat and, stirring constantly, cook the milk down so that it is just a creamy glaze over the vegetables. Season with salt.

3. Serve hot.

Corn Chowder

Soups called corn chowder have been on trendy American restaurant menus of late. Young chefs gussy it up with purees of red pepper, bits of esoteric ham, or other fillips that remove it from its humble origin as everyman home food. The new chowders have their appeal as fancy restaurant food, I suppose, but the following recipe, as simple as can be, is a bowlful of sweet comfort.

Makes 1 quart to serve 2 as a whole meal, 3 or 4 as a first course

2 tablespoons butter
1 medium onion, chopped
2 medium potatoes, cut in ⅓-inch
    dice (about 2 cups)
2 cups milk
½ teaspoon salt
Freshly ground pepper
1 to 2 cups frozen corn kernels

1. In a medium saucepan, heat butter over medium heat and sauté onion until golden, about 8 minutes.

2. Add the potatoes and toss them around with the onions for a minute.

3. Add the milk, salt, and a few grinds of the peppermill. Simmer gently until potatoes are tender, 10 to 15 minutes.

4. Add the corn and return to a simmer.

5. Can be served immediately or reheated, at which time more milk or some chicken broth will have to be added.

Variations: With the onion, sauté a rib of celery, finely chopped. If desired, simmer a bay leaf in the soup. Also, if desired, instead of butter, use the fat from a rendered strip of bacon (I prefer butter).

A Fresh Touch: About ½ cup finely diced sweet red pepper, or minced hot red or green pepper to taste, or a combination of both, makes a fine addition. In either case, you may want to garnish each serving with finely chopped fresh coriander.

Corn Pancakes

A little cornmeal in the batter makes these more interesting than simply dropping corn kernels into regular pancake batter. However, if that's what you want to do, go right ahead (see page 136).

Makes 6 to 8, to serve 2

½ cup flour
¼ cup cornmeal
2 teaspoons baking powder
1½ tablespoons sugar
½ teaspoon salt
½ cup milk
1 egg
2 tablespoons melted butter, corn oil, or vegetable oil
½ cup frozen corn kernels, defrosted

1. In a large bowl, combine the flour, cornmeal, baking powder, sugar, and salt. Stir to mix well.

2. Use a 2-cup measure to measure out the milk. Break in the egg and beat with a fork to mix well.

3. Stir the melted butter and corn into the egg and milk.

4. With the fork, stir the liquid ingredients into the dry ingredients until just blended.

5. Drop the batter by ¼ cupfuls onto a heated, lightly greased griddle. When bubbles begin to break on the surface, turn the pancakes. Cook another minute.

6. Serve immediately.

Cornmeal

Because of its low cost, cornmeal is recognized as one of the most economical sources of food energy in the form of low-fat, complex carbohydrates." That's the way the Quaker Oats Company, the nation's largest cornmeal processor, explains cornmeal's place in our diet. Translation: It's cheap and filling.

A lot of us think it is delicious and a comfort, too—simply for its own sake, hot from the pot with a lump of butter—and are amused to see that, like so many other peasant and poor people's foods, cornmeal has become chic. Cornmeal pancakes are now used as a base for smoked salmon and caviar. Fancy Italian restaurants serve wild mushroom or cheese or sauce-topped wedges of toasted polenta as if they were jewels. Cornbread, corn muffins, and corn sticks appear on swank Sunday brunch buffets. Spoonbread, puffed with egg whites, is held up as an example of American culinary elegance.

There are basically two kinds of cornmeal, with the germ and without the germ. Stone-ground cornmeal contains the germ of the kernel with all its vitamins, proteins, and fat. Because of their minimal processing and higher oil content, these products can be fairly coarse, are fuller flavored than common cornmeal, and spoil much more quickly. Stone-ground cornmeal should be kept in the refrigerator or freezer in a tightly closed container, usually for not more than a couple of months in the refrigerator, for up to 6 months in the freezer. Be sure to smell for rancidity before you use stone-ground cornmeal.

The more common cornmeal has been "degerminated" and is labeled as such. Some of the germ's nutrition is restored, however, and the product is also called "enriched." Degerminated cornmeal will keep on a dry shelf for at least a year. It comes in white and yellow, and though some cornmeal aficionados swear that one is sweeter than the other, for all practical purposes they are the same and interchangeable. The only difference nutritionally is that the yellow cornmeal contains carotene, a natural coloring that contains vitamin A, while white cornmeal does not. All of the recipes here have been formulated using the degerminated cornmeal available in supermarkets.

Polenta

Call it *polenta* (in Italian), *mammaliga* (in Romanian), or plain, humble cornmeal mush. It's all about the same, and a lot easier and quicker to make than most recipes let on. I've seen recipes that give such a scare about lumps and coarseness ("Sift the cornmeal in very gradually, otherwise . . . ," "Make sure to stir only clockwise, or else . . .") that you'd never dare to make it. I've even seen Italian recipes that insist you stir constantly with a wooden stick in a round-bottomed, unlined copper pot for nearly an hour—otherwise it is simply not polenta worth eating. What is really not worth eating are the imported "instant" polenta meals and precooked, vacuum-packaged polenta I see in Italian groceries and fancy food stores. Yet the only trick to smooth, carefree polenta is simple: Start the cornmeal in cold water. Why haven't Italian cooks learned this in the more than 400 years they've been cooking it?

Serves 2

1 cup cornmeal
4 cups cold water
1 teaspoon salt

1. Combine the cornmeal and cold water in a medium saucepan. Stir

constantly over high heat until mixture begins to simmer.

2. Reduce heat to medium and simmer, stirring frequently, but not necessarily constantly, for 15 minutes. At this point the cornmeal is ready to eat immediately with any number of toppings (suggestions follow).

3. Or, to make a very thick polenta that can be sliced once it has cooled, continue stirring another 5 minutes, until the mixture is so thick it pulls from the sides of the pan as you stir.

Note: American cornmeal, though of different granulation than cornmeal for polenta imported from Italy, makes a gruel that is every bit as smooth and delicious. I prefer American cornmeal, in fact, because it has a slightly cornier flavor, maybe because it comes to us fresher.

Microwave Method: Combine the cornmeal and water in a 3-quart casserole. Microwave on HIGH for 5 minutes. Stir well to smooth out the mixture. Return to microwave on HIGH for 10 more minutes, stirring two more times.

Variations: Beat butter and grated Parmesan cheese into hot polenta, or simply top with butter and cheese. For Romanian *mammaliga,* top with a pat of butter, crumbled feta cheese, and, if possible, a dollop of sour cream or yogurt. Polenta is also excellent topped with cottage cheese, any grated firm cheese, such as ched-dar or Swiss, or with tomato sauce (see pages 247–249).

A Purist's Southern Corn Bread

My friend and former *Daily News* colleague, Suzanne Hamlin, the Brenda Starr of food, grew up in Kentucky where corn bread is important food. For more than the decade that we've broken bread together, whenever it is corn bread she complains, "Too much sugar." When pressed on the matter, however, even she admits that a little sugar takes the bitter bite out of a sturdy, nearly all-cornmeal corn bread. It also makes the crumb a little finer. The following contains just enough sugar to do those two things, but it is essentially no-compromise corn bread. (For fully compromised but nonetheless delicious corn bread, see the back of any cornmeal package.) It is best eaten hot from the oven, and because it has no evident sweetness, it is also suitable for savory treatments: Try it topped with melted cheese, shredded iceberg lettuce, and salsa, or topped with Sautéed Spinach with Garlic (see page 239) and jalapeños. Plain and hot out of the oven, it is an excellent breakfast or brunch bread. To me, it doesn't even need a slathering of butter. Jalapeño jelly makes it perfect. This is also a good corn bread to use as a base for corn bread stuffing—inside a bird or out or next to a plate of scrambled eggs.

Serves 6 to 8

1 teaspoon butter
2 cups white or yellow cornmeal
1 tablespoon baking powder
1 tablespoon flour
1½ teaspoons salt
2 tablespoons sugar
3 eggs
2 cups buttermilk, or 1¾ cups milk
  blended with ¼ cup white vinegar
4 tablespoons (½ stick) butter, melted

1. Preheat the oven to 450 degrees. Butter a 13-by-9-inch baking pan with 1 teaspoon butter. Set aside.

2. In a mixing bowl, combine the cornmeal, baking powder, flour, salt, and sugar. Blend well with a wooden spoon, crushing any tiny clumps of baking powder with the back of the spoon. Set aside.

3. In another mixing bowl, beat the eggs with the wooden spoon until well blended.

4. Using the spoon, beat in the buttermilk or soured milk, then the melted butter.

5. Pour the dry ingredients into the wet ingredients and stir until just blended.

6. Pour into the prepared pan and bake for 18 to 20 minutes. When done, the bread will be slightly pulling away from the pan, brown on the sides, and firm in the center. Be careful not to overbake.

7. Serve hot or warm. To reheat, wrap in foil and place in a preheated 350-degree oven for 10 minutes.

Variation: Stir in chopped canned green chilies to taste along with the liquid ingredients.

Spoonbread

Spoonbread is a soufflé of corn bread, but don't let the word *soufflé* scare you off this recipe. It's much lighter and more dramatic than corn bread but it is not that much more difficult to prepare. Traditionally served as a side dish in the South—particularly with country ham or roasted pork or poultry—it makes an impressive main event for breakfast with a couple of strips of crisp bacon, or for brunch or a light supper, when you might want to add vinaigrette-dressed vegetables or a salad. It is also a great way to dress up a supper of French Onion Soup (see page 191), Chick-pea Chili Soup (see page 42), or any chowder (see pages 103, 104, and 107).

Serves 2 to 4

2 cups milk
½ cup cornmeal
½ teaspoon salt
2 tablespoons butter
2 teaspoons baking powder
3 eggs, separated

1. Preheat the oven to 350 degrees. Butter a 1-quart souffle dish.

2. In a medium saucepan, over medium-high heat, combine the milk, cornmeal, and salt. Stirring constantly, bring to a simmer.

3. Lower heat and cook for 2 or 3 minutes, until mixture has fully thickened and you can see the bottom of the pot as you stir.

4. Remove from heat and stir in the butter and baking powder.

5. In a small bowl or cup, beat the egg yolks to blend, then blend thoroughly into the cornmeal mixture.

6. In another mixing bowl, beat the egg whites until they hold stiff peaks. Fold into the cornmeal mixture, right in the saucepan.

7. Pour into the soufflé dish and bake for 30 to 40 minutes until top is lightly browned.

8. Serve immediately.

Cornmeal Crisps

These are fragile crackers with a wavy edge. They're a good snack with melted cheese, Chili Beans (see page 39), or beaten cream cheese. Or serve them with soup.

Makes about 4 dozen

½ cup cornmeal
½ cup flour
¼ teaspoon salt
¾ cup milk
3 tablespoons butter or margarine,
  melted
Vegetable oil

1. Preheat the oven to 400 degrees. Line a cookie sheet with aluminum foil and grease lightly with vegetable oil.

2. In a mixing bowl, combine the cornmeal, flour, and salt. Add milk and butter or margarine and mix until smooth.

3. Drop by teaspoonsful 2 inches apart on prepared pan and bake for 11 to 13 minutes, until the edges are golden brown.

4. Cool on a wire rack. May be stored in a tin.

Cornstarch

I t's worth keeping a box of cornstarch in the house if only to soothe rashes, stop itching, and make chocolate pudding. That seems to be the national consensus: Eighty-six percent of American households have that familiar yellow cardboard box on a shelf somewhere, according to Best Foods, makers of both Argo and Kingsford-brand cornstarch.

Of course, cornstarch has other uses: It thickens gravies and soups and the juices in fruit pies. It's the most common thickener of Chinese sauces. And again, especially in the Chinese kitchen, it's used for batters and dry coatings for fried foods.

Considering its prominence in the Chinese kitchen, it's surprising that the modern method of extracting this silky starch from corn was not invented until 1842, by Thomas Kingsford, whose company soon had a competitor called Argo. By the turn of the century, the two brands, among the first packaged grocery items, had virtually monopolized the market. Argo is now the largest selling brand in the country, though Best Foods continues the Kingsford name in some regions. The products are identical.

Theoretically, cornstarch can be used to replace flour as a thickener (1 tablespoon of cornstarch equals 2 tablespoons of flour), but the results are very different. Cornstarch gives liquids a slicker texture and glossier surface; sometimes a virtue, but often not. If used in excess, in the wrong place, cornstarch mixtures can taste gluey. In addition, cornstarch-thickened sauces and soups need to be carefully reheated because overheating breaks them down. Cornstarch is at its full thickening capacity when the liquid comes to a full, rolling boil. Many recipes call for 1 minute of boiling to ensure that the cornstarch has swelled fully. If the mixture is boiled too long, however, or stirred too briskly, the mixture may begin to thin. When adding ingredients to an already thickened liquid, stir them in off the heat and gently. To add cornstarch to a cooking liquid, first dissolve it in a small amount of cold water. The cornstarch will separate from the water as it stands, so give it a quick stir again before adding the mixture to a liquid.

Chocolate Pudding

Making pudding from scratch is so simple it makes the idea of cooking pudding from a box embarrassing. Unfortunately, either way, and as quick as it is, pudding has to be chilled for at least 2 hours for the full effect. Hot pudding is a child's indulgence. These days I can manage to wait at least 1 hour before diving in with a spoon.

Makes 3 cups

¾ cup sugar
¼ cup cornstarch
6 tablespoons cocoa
2½ cups milk
1 teaspoon vanilla extract

1. In a medium saucepan, combine everything but the vanilla extract.

2. With a wooden spoon, stir slowly over medium-high heat, continually scraping the sides and bottom of the pan and breaking up any lumps with the back of the spoon.

3. When mixture is smooth and beginning to thicken, reduce heat slightly and, still stirring, bring to a boil. Boil 1 minute, stirring slowly but constantly.

4. Remove from heat and stir in vanilla extract.

5. Pour into cups and refrigerate until chilled. In ½-cup servings, the pudding is cool enough to enjoy in about 1 hour.

Chocolate Pudding in a Mug

In the early days of microwave ovens, a recipe like this was always part of the demonstrations given by manufacturers' home economists. It proved how fast and how much fun the microwave could be. It still does.

Serves 1

1 tablespoon cornstarch
2 tablespoons cocoa powder
2 tablespoons sugar
¾ cup milk
¼ teaspoon vanilla extract

1. In a large mug (at least 12 ounces), dissolve the cornstarch, cocoa, and sugar in the milk.

2. Microwave on HIGH for 90 seconds, or until mixture boils.

3. Stir in the vanilla extract.

4. Chill in refrigerator at least 1 hour.

Substitutions: Instead of cocoa, use 3 tablespoons of chocolate bits. Stir them into the hot pudding with the vanilla. Instead of vanilla, use orange zest, grated or very finely julienned.

Corn Syrup

'd keep a bottle of corn syrup on hand even if all I ever used it for was to make dessert sauces and pancake syrups, where it is better than sugar because it does not crystallize as readily.

As sweeteners go, however, corn syrup has a relatively short shelf life. An unopened bottle will hold up for a mere 6 to 8 months at room temperature and refrigerating the syrup will not extend its life. Once opened, the bottle will keep at least 6 months—unless, of course, it was opened near its last date of sale. Again, refrigeration doesn't improve the situation. In any case, it is easy to tell when corn syrup is going bad. It either ferments, which causes bubbles to gather on the surface, or it becomes moldy, also on the surface. Remember to wipe the threaded top of the bottle each time you use it; syrup under the cap will prevent the cap from sealing properly and may also attract insects.

Microwave Brittle Candy

Peanut brittle is one of those things that microwave oven demonstrators like to show off, and, for me, this recipe is reason enough to keep a bottle of corn syrup in the cupboard—for late-night munchie emergencies or plain old fun on a lazy afternoon. Candy making is like magic to most people, and this candy bubbles and sputters and foams, then becomes as hard as . . . brittle. You don't really need nuts to make brittle, though they do make it much, much better. They add textural contrast, not only flavor. On the other hand, if your sweet tooth aches for candy and you have no nuts, I am here to testify that plain brittle can be very satisfying.

Makes 1 approximately 12-by-8-inch sheet

1 tablespoon vegetable oil
1 cup sugar
½ cup light corn syrup
Dash salt
1 to 1½ cups nuts (peanuts, walnuts, pecans, or almonds) (optional)
1 tablespoon butter
1½ teaspoons baking soda
1 teaspoon vanilla extract

1. Pour the vegetable oil on a baking sheet and spread it around with a paper towel to completely grease sheet. It must be ready for the hot brittle to be poured on it.

2. In a 3-quart microwave-safe bowl or casserole, combine the sugar, corn syrup, salt, and nuts. There is no need to stir now.

3. Microwave on HIGH for 3 minutes. Remove and stir. Microwave on HIGH for 5 or 6 more minutes, until the foam turns light brown. (If the edge begins browning before the middle, stir an extra time.)

4. Working quickly, immediately add the remaining ingredients, sprinkling the baking soda over the surface. Stir well. The mixture will foam up and turn creamy looking.

5. Immediately pour mixture onto the prepared baking sheet. With the back of a spoon, spread it out as thin as possible, but don't worry if you can't get it terribly thin.

6. Let the brittle cool thoroughly, then lift it off the pan in large pieces with a spatula. Put it on paper towels to blot off the oil from the baking sheet.

7. Break the brittle into pieces to serve. Store in a wax-paper-lined tin.

Variations: To make a plain brittle, because of the reduced volume, the cooking time needs to be reduced by almost half. In Haiti, and perhaps some other Caribbean islands, brittle is made with molasses and nutmeg. Try it with cashews, too, replacing half the corn syrup with molasses or dark corn syrup and adding about a rounded ¼ teaspoon freshly grated nutmeg at the beginning.

Hot Fudge Sauce

It's the corn syrup in this recipe that gives the sauce its essential gloppiness. And note: This is the rare hot fudge sauce that does not require cream or evaporated milk.

Makes 1½ cups

3 ounces unsweetened chocolate
3 tablespoons butter
½ cup water
¾ cup sugar
3 tablespoons light corn syrup
Big pinch salt
2 teaspoons vanilla extract

1. In a small saucepan, over low heat, combine the chocolate, butter, and water. Stir until smooth.

2. Add the sugar, corn syrup, and salt. Increase heat to medium and bring to a boil, stirring constantly until the sugar is dissolved.

3. Let simmer gently for about 8 minutes.

4. Remove from heat and stir in vanilla.

5. Serve hot or warm.

Microwave Method: In a 1-quart measuring cup or bowl, combine the chocolate and butter. Microwave on MEDIUM-HIGH for 1½ minutes. Stir until chocolate and butter are melted and smooth. Add the remaining ingredients, except vanilla, and microwave on HIGH for 1½ to 2 minutes, until boiling. Stir well, then microwave on MEDIUM-HIGH for 7 minutes, until thickened. Add vanilla extract.

Butterscotch Sauce

Makes about ¾ cup

½ cup corn syrup
½ cup dark brown sugar
2 tablespoons butter
1 teaspoon vanilla extract

1. In a small saucepan, combine the corn syrup and brown sugar. Stir over medium heat until sugar has dissolved and mixture is translucent, about 5 minutes.

2. Stir in the butter until melted.

3. Stir in vanilla extract until well mixed.

Variations: If you have no vanilla extract, add 1 tablespoon rum or whisky to make a flavored caramel sauce, though even then the vanilla is desirable. To make a buttered raisin-rum sauce, add 2 tablespoons plumped raisins, using brandy or rum to plump them, if desired. For a caramel-nut sauce, add 3 or 4 tablespoons coarsely chopped toasted walnuts or pecans, or chopped unsalted roasted or dry-roasted peanuts.

Microwave Method: In a 2-cup measuring cup or bowl, combine the corn syrup and brown sugar. Microwave on HIGH for 45 seconds. Stir well, then microwave on HIGH for 1½ minutes. Add butter and vanilla extract. Stir until smooth.

Caramel Popcorn

This is adapted from *The Microwave Cook's Complete Companion* by Rosemary Dunn Stancil and Lorela Nichols Wilkins (Fawcett Columbine), which is filled with marvelous, magical candy recipes.

Makes 3 Quarts

3 quarts popped popcorn
8 tablespoons (1 stick) butter
1 cup light or dark brown sugar
¼ cup light corn syrup
¼ teaspoon salt
¾ teaspoon vanilla extract
¼ teaspoon baking soda
½ cup roasted peanuts (optional)
½ cup raisins (optional)

1. Place popcorn in a large paper bag and set aside.

2. In a 2-quart microwavable casserole, combine the butter, sugar, corn syrup and salt. Microwave on HIGH for 6 minutes, or until boiling.

3. Stir and continue to microwave on 70% power for 6 more minutes. Quickly stir in the vanilla extract and baking soda.

4. Immediately pour the hot syrup over the popcorn and toss to coat. Roll up the top of the bag and place the bag in the microwave. Cook on HIGH 1 minute.

5. Shake the bag well, return it to the microwave and cook on HIGH 1 to 1½ minutes longer. Stir in peanuts and raisins, if desired.

6. Pour caramel corn into a large bowl and let cool until crunchy, stirring several times. To speed the cooling, place the bowl in the freezer.

Dried Fruit

Apricots may be the "apples" of the Garden of Eden, dates were part of the promise of the Promised Land, and as early as 1551 B.C., figs were known to be a healthful food. An Egyptian inscription notes that figs, which appear to be the first fruit humankind dried, are a tonic for the entire body. Modern science did not catch up with ancient science nor even the folklore on dried fruits until the last half of this century. Now that we understand the impact of dietary fiber on heart disease, gastrointestinal ailments, and cancer, dried fruits are now officially—not just because grandma told us—one of the best things we can eat to satisfy a sweet tooth.

Let's not forget their other virtues, however. Dried fruits are as fine tasting a sweet out-of-hand snack food as there is; they can dress up salads, slaws, grain pilafs, muffins, biscuits, quick breads, and cakes. And they are designed for long storage.

The best place to keep all dried fruit is in a tightly closed jar or plastic bag, in a relatively cool place. The warmest spot in the refrigerator—generally a middle shelf—is what is often advised as an optimum storage environment for keeping dried fruits up to a year. I've found that they can be kept almost as long in an airtight container at room temperature. If you notice white crystals developing on the surface of a fruit, this sugaring is generally due to dramatic changes in temperature or an inappropriate storage temperature or humidity. The fruit will taste gritty when eaten out of hand, but, to a point, you can salvage it by plumping it or cooking it in a liquid.

Dried fruits as they are, especially dates and figs, are a good simple dessert, but they do take on some glamour when simmered or steeped in a liquid. Water will do if there is nothing else, in which case it adds interest to put in a slice of citrus peel, some cinnamon or cloves or allspice or black peppercorns, or some combination of them. Strong tea of any kind is an excellent liquid to use, particularly with prunes and figs. And I've played with herb and spice teas, such as ginger tea with figs and prunes, orange-spice or chamomile tea with apricots. Orange juice has the right flavor for reconstituting dried fruits, and a steeping in wine or spirits transforms dried fruits into fancy fare. Among the spirits that can be dashed into a dried fruit compote, consider Kirsch, brandy or Cognac, bourbon, and Scotch. Vodka won't add flavor, though it does add punch.

There are several ways to go about steeping dried fruits. If you can wait overnight, simply bring the liquid to a boil, then pour it over the fruit and let it stand at room temperature until morning. If you're in a hurry, combine the fruit and liquid in a saucepan, bring to a boil, boil a minute or so, then let the fruit steep. Dried fruit compotes are even good warm.

Apricot Puree or Sauce

Without any thickening this can be served in cups as a pudding, or poured on ice cream, pancakes, or crêpes. Add the cornstarch only if you want a very thick pudding, called *kissel* in German.

Serves 3 or 4

1 well-packed cup dried apricots
1½ cups water
1 to 2 tablespoons sugar
Drop almond extract (optional)
1 tablespoon cornstarch dissolved in
  ¼ cup water (optional)

1. In a small saucepan, combine the apricots and water and place over medium heat. Simmer until the apricots are very tender, about 15 minutes.

2. Puree the apricots and water together in a blender.

3. Sweeten to taste and add almond extract, if desired.

4. For a thicker pudding, return the puree to the saucepan and stir in the dissolved cornstarch. Bring the mixture to a boil.

5. Serve at room temperature.

Variations: Add a shot of orange liqueur, brandy, or bourbon.

Prunes in Red Wine

I keep a jar of this going from October through spring, adding leftover dribs and drabs of red wine and enough prunes to keep up with the wine. Be careful: Prunes not covered with wine will spoil—you'll discover hideous green mold.

Prunes, pitted or with pits
Red wine (any kind)

Combine prunes with enough red wine to cover them by about ½ inch. Let stand at least 1 day before eating with prune-flavored wine syrup.

Other recipes featuring dried fruits

Curried Rice Salad or Pilaf (see page 220)
Oatmeal Peanut Butter Bars (see page 178)
Ants on a Log (see page 79)

Eggs

Eggs are the magical ingredient. They leaven, bind, thicken, emulsify, and enrich other ingredients, and, all on their own, they taste good boiled, fried, scrambled, poached, and baked. What's more, they keep for several months in the refrigerator if stored in those clever cardboard boxes in which they're sold. A stored egg may not be a fresh egg but it is better than no egg at all.

Eggs used to be considered the perfect food, a convenient and reliable food, even a diet food—one large egg has only 75 calories and half of an adult's recommended daily supply of protein (with all twelve essential amino acids). But eggs have gotten a lot of bad press in the last decade. Raw or undercooked eggs may carry salmonella, and all eggs have nearly a day's quota of cholesterol—275 milligrams (out of a recommended 300), according to the latest scientific tests. They've become forbidden, and as anything forbidden does, all the more delicious for it.

Scrambled Eggs

Practically everyone says they can make scrambled eggs, but I have this arrogance: I always think mine are better. In any case, these are the scrambled eggs that go so well with the several dishes I say go so well with scrambled eggs elsewhere in this book—most notably Zarela's Home-Style Hominy (see page 150), Curried Potatoes and Peas (see page 213), and Tomato Bulgur (see page 65). The following technique turns out fluffy, large-curd eggs; whether you make them dry or creamy depends on your taste. See, I'm flexible.

Serves 1 to 3

2 to 6 eggs (if you need to make more, make 2 batches)
1 to 3 tablespoons butter
Salt

1. Use a 6- or 7-inch skillet for 2 or 3 eggs, an 8- to 10-inch skillet for 4 to 6 eggs. (Never try to scramble more than 6 eggs at a time; 6 is pushing it.)

2. Break the eggs into a mixing bowl and, with a fork, beat very, very well, until eggs are foamy on the surface.

3. Melt the butter over high heat and when it is sizzling (but before it browns), pour the eggs into skillet. (Give the eggs a final beating with the fork just before and as you pour them in.)

4. Immediately reduce heat to medium-low. When you see that the edge of egg around the pan has set, with the fork, draw the cooked part to the center and the center to the sides. Allow the liquid eggs to set again and continue drawing the eggs into large masses as they cook. If you want drier eggs, turn the masses over and let them cook on the other side.

5. Serve very hot, which is to say immediately.

Hard-boiled Eggs

It's not just me. Everyone is finicky about their eggs, though I must say I am particularly particular about hard-boiled eggs. The yolks must be soft and creamy, the white firm but not rubbery. There must be no line of green between the two and not a whiff of sulfur. How to achieve these eggs? Bring a pot of water to the boil. Make a hole in the small end of each egg. Place the egg(s) in boiling water and let boil 2 minutes from the time the water returns to the boil. Remove from the heat, cover the pot, and let the eggs stand in the water for 15 minutes. (Alternately, simmer the eggs for 12 minutes.) Drain the eggs and run them under cold water as you shell them. That's it.

Dress the eggs with mayonnaise— or, for egg salad, mash them with a fork with mayonnaise. Serve them with crusty bread and Sardine Tapenade (see page 229), or just a plain olive dip (see page 188), or crossed with anchovies, to name just a few possibilities.

Eggs and Onions Salad

This was one of my father's favorite summer suppers, one of the many cold dishes we ate when my mother considered it too hot to cook, which was most nights from Memorial Day through Labor Day. As a course before this we had cold borscht served in a bowl with a boiled potato and a dollop of sour cream, or in a glass with the sour cream stirred into it. Along with the salad came a platter of tomatoes, cucumber, and whole scallions, and some dense sour rye bread, which is called "corn bread" in New York, though it really should be "corned" bread; it's a sourdough rye. If my mother had some chicken fat in the refrigerator, she'd sauté the onions in it. Otherwise, oil would do, as it still does.

Serves 2

1 medium onion, chopped
2 tablespoons vegetable oil (or half
  butter, half oil)
4 hard-boiled eggs

1. In a small skillet, over medium heat, sauté the onion in the oil until golden, about 8 minutes.

2. Meanwhile, roughly cut up the eggs into a small mixing bowl.

3. When the onion is done, scrape it and any fat in the pan into the eggs.

4. Blend and mash until you have mixture that holds together.

5. Serve warm or cold.

Spanish Omelet

If this isn't one of the great dishes of the world, period, then it is at least one of the great egg dishes of the world. Cut into small squares it is perfect finger food (serve with napkins), which is what it usually is in Spain, where it is one of many tapas —small plates the Spanish make into meals. I find that to make a superb, not just good, omelet, you must use two pans, a large one to cook the potatoes and onions, and a smaller one for the omelet itself. If you are willing to compromise a little quality for the sake of having only one pan to wash, opt for the smaller pan.

Serves 6 as an appetizer, 2 or 3 as a main course

4 tablespoons olive oil
1 pound potatoes (3 medium), peeled and cut into ½-inch cubes
1½ cups finely chopped onions (2 or 3 small)
1 teaspoon salt
6 eggs

1. In an 8- or 10-inch skillet, heat the oil over medium heat, stir in the potatoes and onions. Sprinkle with ½ teaspoon salt, then immediately reduce the heat to low.

2. Cook, stirring frequently and shaking the pan occasionally, until the potatoes are tender and the onions are very soft, about 20 minutes. (Neither vegetable should brown.)

3. Meanwhile, in a mixing bowl, beat the eggs with the remaining salt until well blended.

4. When the vegetables are done, remove them with a slotted spoon and add to the eggs.

5. With a rubber spatula, scrape any remaining oil in the large skillet (there should be about 1½ tablespoons) into a 5- to 7-inch skillet.

6. Set the small skillet over medium heat. When the oil is hot, pour in the eggs, then immediately reduce heat to low. Cook 5 to 8 minutes, until all but the very top and center of the omelet is set.

7. Place the omelet, still in the skillet, under the broiler for less than 1 minute, just to set the top.

8. Loosen the edges of the omelet with a fine knife and slide onto a serving plate.

9. Let cool at least 15 minutes before serving, but it is best at room temperature.

Gratin of Eggs

When did we stop eating things like this? To answer my own question, it was only about a dozen years ago, when the nutrition police told us not to eat anything with fat and cholesterol—on pain of death. This dish is a quadruple whammy—eggs, butter, milk, and cheese—but it has been one of my favorite comfort foods for a long time. And, as Jacques Pépin, the great French chef, cooking teacher, and writer says in his book *Everyday Cooking* (Harper & Row, 1982), from which the proportions for this recipe were borrowed, "The ingredients for it are always at hand, so it is a real savior when unexpected guests arrive for dinner." Nearly a decade after he wrote that, it is probably more appropriate as brunch fare.

Serves 4

6 or 7 hard-boiled eggs
2 tablespoons butter
1½ cups sliced onions
1 tablespoon flour
1½ cups milk
½ teaspoon salt
¼ teaspoon freshly ground black
  pepper, or hot ground pepper
½ cup grated Swiss cheese, or
  cheddar, or a combination,
  including Parmesan

1. Preheat the oven to 400 degrees.

2. Slice the eggs with an egg slicer or knife and arrange them in a buttered 4- to 6-cup baking dish.

3. In a saucepan, melt the butter over medium-high heat and sauté onions until they just begin to brown, about 10 minutes.

4. Blend in the flour and cook another 30 seconds.

5. Stir in the milk, salt, and pepper. Stirring continuously, bring to a simmer. Lower heat and simmer 1 or 2 minutes.

6. Pour the sauce over the eggs and, gently lifting the egg slices, let it run in and around the egg.

7. Sprinkle with the grated cheese and bake for 10 to 12 minutes. Place under the broiler for a few minutes, until top is nicely browned.

8. Serve immediately.

Skillet Soufflé

(Omelet Soufflé)

The following soufflé demonstrates to what heights a few eggs can take your emergency cooking. When egg yolks are beaten until very thick, their proteins are developed into what you might think of as rubber bands. When whites are beaten stiff, you are incorporating air into their structure. When the air is heated, it expands and makes rise whatever the whites are in. In this case, they are blended with the worked-up and lightly sweetened yolks, which stretch with the expansion of air in the whites, then stiffen into a somewhat solid structure.

Inspiration for this simplest of all soufflés comes from *Paris Bistro Cookery,* a book of reminiscences and recipes by Alexander Watt (Knopf, 1958). The original recipe, from a bistro called Chez Pierre, in the first *arrondissement,* says to "quickly sear the outside of the soufflé crisscross fashion with a hot poker," then sprinkle it with sugar, pour over warmed rum, and "blaze it at table." In fact, the sugar (confectioners') should be sifted over the omelet first, then the hot poker (a metal skewer heated over the gas burner will do) will make caramelized lines on the top. Disregarding the instructions for this glamorous presentation, I make it as below and think it's delicious (and quite dramatic enough) either plain for breakfast or with a spoonful of preserves or jam for dessert.

Serves 2

4 eggs
2 tablespoons sugar
2 teaspoons butter

1. Preheat the oven to 450 degrees.

2. Butter a 7- or 8-inch skillet.

3. Separate the eggs into two bowls. Using a hand-held electric mixer (or a wire whisk), beat the yolks until mixed well, then beat in the sugar and continue beating until the yolks are very light and thick enough to form a slowly dissolving ribbon when they fall off the beaters back onto the surface.

4. Rinse and dry the beaters very well, then beat the egg whites until stiff.

5. Fold the whites into the yolks thoroughly, then pour into the buttered skillet.

6. Bake for 10 minutes and serve immediately.

Other recipes featuring eggs
Hungarian Potato and Egg Casserole (sec page 215)

Flour

I f bread is the staff of life, then what is flour? Philosophy and baking aside, if you have any intentions of doing more than opening a can for dinner, it is hard to manage without white wheat flour. It is used as a thickener for liquids—to make them into soups and sauces and gravies—and to coat foods you'd like to have with a crisp surface, whether they are baked, fried, or sautéed. It's the main ingredient in pancakes, biscuits, cookies, cakes, and other desserts, not to mention bread.

During the processing of wheat into powdery white flour, many of the nutrients and virtually all the fat are removed. Some of the nutrition is restored—thus the name "enriched white flour"—but there is so little fat, the part that spoils most easily, that white flour can be stored in a closed container (canister, tin, or plastic bag) in a relatively dry and dark place for at least a year. Even at less than optimum conditions, it will hold up well for at least 6 months. After that you may not want to bake bread or cake with it, but it is fine as a thickener or as a coating. (Whole wheat flour, which does have oils that turn rancid, should be kept in the refrigerator or freezer for no more than 6 to 8 months.)

How can one tell if white flour is stale? Usually one can't. Weevils spoil flour more frequently than detectable rancidity. And though the flour's proteins do break down with time, this is noticeable only when baking yeast breads. Because the wheat's proteins provide structure for the bread, stale flour may not rise as well as fresh.

Food-Processor Focaccia and Pizza Dough

In the last decade, pizza has become a national passion, though few of us make it from scratch. Home-delivered pizza, fast-food pizza, frozen pizza, and restaurant pizza laden with ever more exotic toppings continue to be the hottest items in their various food-industry categories. It's the yeast that dissuades even accomplished home cooks from baking their own pizza. Yeast doughs take time and require kneading, or so we have it in our heads. In the same decade that we made pizza part of our lives, fast-rising yeast was introduced and food processors became an everyday home appliance. The first reduces the time required for a yeast dough to rise, the second reduces the need to knead. Even when using regular dry yeast, making pizza dough in a food processor consumes more time than energy. It takes 90 minutes from start to finish—most of it unattended —then 10 to 15 minutes for baking. With fast-rise yeast, the job is done in less than 1 hour.

Serves 4 to 6

1 package active dry yeast
1¼ cups warm water
3½ cups all-purpose flour
*   (approximately)*
3 tablespoons olive oil
½ to 1 teaspoon salt (optional)

1. Combine the yeast and ½ cup water in the bowl of the food processor fitted with the steel blade. Turn on a couple of seconds to dissolve yeast.

2. Add ½ cup flour and pulse the machine several times to blend into a smooth mixture. Let stand 10 to 15 minutes, until there are a few small bubbles on the surface.

3. Add the olive oil, salt, and remaining water. Pulse again to blend.

4. Add 2½ cups of the remaining flour. Pulse again to blend, then let the processor run a few seconds, until mixture binds together into a sticky mass. (If your machine sounds like it is struggling, turn it off. You don't want to burn out the motor, and in any case that shows the dough is stiff enough.)

5. With a rubber spatula, scrape this sticky mass of dough into a lightly oiled bowl. Cover with plastic wrap and let stand in a warm place until dough has doubled in size, about 1 hour for regular yeast, 30 minutes for fast-rising yeast. (To make a cozy environment for the dough, I preheat the oven to 200 degrees, turn it off, then place the bowl of dough in the closed oven.)

6. Flour a board with the remaining ½ cup flour and scrape the slightly sticky dough onto the board. Knead for about 3 minutes, just long enough to incorporate the flour and make a silken dough.

7. Divide dough in half. Proceed as desired according to the recipes that follow.

Schiacciata

Roman trattorias often serve this crackerlike bread, one of the innumerable forms of focaccia, and one of the many breads called *schiacciata*.

Serves 2

1 teaspoon plus 1½ tablespoons olive oil
½ recipe Food-Processor Focaccia and Pizza Dough (see opposite page)
Coarse salt
Freshly ground black pepper (optional)

1. Preheat the oven to 500 degrees. With 1 teaspoon olive oil, grease a baking sheet.

2. With your fingers, or using a rolling pin, stretch and pull or roll the dough out into an irregular flat that will fit on the baking sheet. (I like to hold the dough by the edge and, constantly turning it, let it stretch itself. I'm not as graceful about this as a professional *pizzaiolo,* but in the privacy of my kitchen, it's fun.)

3. Place the dough on the greased sheet and brush it with the remaining 1½ tablespoons of olive oil.

4. Sprinkle with salt (and freshly ground pepper, if desired, though this is not the way it is served in Italy).

5. Bake for 10 to 11 minutes, until lightly browned; it will bake unevenly, so be careful to remove it before the thinnest parts get too dark.

6. Can be served immediately or at room temperature.

Plain Focaccia

The dough, baked unadorned and thicker (in a cake pan or pie plate), is fine basic bread (or focaccia) to serve with soups and salads . . . anything with which you'd serve bread. Prepare exactly as above, using a full teaspoon of salt.

But instead of stretching the dough on a greased baking sheet, push the dough into a greased 8- or 9-inch-round or square baking pan. Let rise 15 to 30 minutes. Bake for 15 to 20 minutes.

Onion or Herb Focaccia

Focaccia, like pizza, is receptive to almost any topping. Sliced onions and/or herbs are a traditional and simple embellishment. Anchovies, sliced garlic, olives, tomato sauce, and mushrooms are other obvious possibilities.

Serves 2 to 4

1 teaspoon plus 1 tablespoon olive oil
½ recipe Food-Processor Focaccia
   and Pizza Dough (see page 132)
1 small onion, sliced as thin as
   possible, and/or 2 teaspoons dried
   rosemary, oregano, or a
   combination of rosemary,
   marjoram, and thyme, finely
   crushed (see Note)
Coarse salt

1. With the 1 teaspoon of olive oil, grease an 8- or 9-inch-square or round baking pan or pie plate.

2. Press the dough into the greased pan.

3. Gently press the slices of onion and/or herbs into the dough and sprinkle with salt.

4. Cover with plastic wrap and let rise 15 to 30 minutes, until puffy. Preheat the oven to 500 degrees.

5. Drizzle with remaining olive oil and bake for about 20 minutes, until browned at the edges.

6. Serve immediately.

Note: To crush dried herbs, put the herbs in the palm of one hand and rub them with the heel of the other.

Pissaladière

The dough for true French pissaladière, the Provençal pizzalike snack, is not as bready as pizza dough, but the Italian dough does better than fine.

Makes 2 12-inch rounds; serves 6 to 8 as a snack or appetizer

¼ cup olive oil
1 pound onions (3 medium), thinly
   sliced (about 3½ cups)

2 large cloves garlic, finely chopped
½ teaspoon salt
½ teaspoon dried thyme
2 tablespoons tomato paste
1 tablespoon water
1 recipe Food-Processor Focaccia and
    Pizza Dough (see page 132),
    divided in half
Anchovies
Purple or black olives, pitted and cut
    in half

1. In a medium skillet with a cover, heat the oil over medium heat, then add the onions and garlic. Toss and sauté for about 3 minutes, until onions are wilted.

2. Stir in the salt and thyme, cover the skillet, reduce heat to low and cook, stirring occasionally, for about 30 minutes, until the onions are soft and beginning to color.

3. Preheat the oven to 500 degrees.

4. Add the tomato paste and water and stir well. Cook another few minutes. Remove from heat.

5. Stretch or roll the pizza dough into a very thin 12-inch round and place on a pizza pan or make the shape more oval and place on a baking sheet.

6. Top with half the onions, then decorate the top with a crosshatch of anchovies dotted with pitted olive halves.

7. Bake for about 15 minutes and serve hot.

Basic Pancakes

(Griddle Cakes or Flapjacks)

Making pancakes for breakfast (or any other meal, for that matter) is certainly a gesture of love. Daddies do it on Sundays for their kids, and often that's the only things they ever cook. Lovers do it for lovees and sometimes serve them in bed. Hosts do it for guests they want to treat especially well. In any case, the pancake cook has to stand and make them while the pancake eaters get to sit and devour them. If that isn't love, what is?

There's no getting around this situation if you have any interest in serving pancakes at their best, which is the moment they are taken off the griddle. You can put them on a heat-proof platter and keep them warm in the oven until all the batter is baked, but, as Raymond Sokolov dryly put it in his primer *How to Cook,* they "don't improve with time."

As a "cake" of a kind, you might think pancake recipes would have to be as strict as those for oven cakes, when actually they are fairly flexible. The following formula cooks up to a relatively thin, moist, sweet, and surprisingly buttery pancake. To keep them tender, make sure not to beat the batter too much. To make them higher (and less moist), add another teaspoon of baking powder. To avoid the bitterness that baking powder can give, be certain the griddle or pan is very hot. If the pan is not hot enough, the baking powder will not fully react and the pancakes will not only be flatter than need be, but tainted with the taste of raw leavening.

Makes about eight to twelve 4-inch pancakes; serves 2 or 3

1 cup all-purpose flour
2 teaspoons baking powder
2 tablespoons sugar
Scant 1/2 teaspoon salt
1 cup milk
1 egg
2 tablespoons melted butter or
*   margarine, or vegetable oil*

1. Combine dry ingredients in a large mixing bowl. With a fork, stir to mix.

2. In a 1- or 2-cup measuring cup, measure out the milk. Using the fork, beat in the egg, then the melted butter.

3. Pour liquid ingredients into dry. Again with the fork, stir together, scraping sides of bowl to incorporate all the flour. It will take about 50 strokes to blend well. Don't worry about small lumps. Mixture should be the consistency of double cream—quite pourable but thick enough to coat the fork generously.

4. Heat a griddle or skillet over medium high heat until a drop of water bounces over the surface. Pour the batter onto the hot griddle in scant 1/4 cup measures. The batter should sizzle immediately, but if the griddle is too hot the pancake will have radiating dark marks. Adjust heat as necessary.

5. As soon as the tops of the pancakes are covered with bubbles and the edges look dry, turn them. The first side should be an even medium brown. Cook second side another 30 seconds or so, until it is lightly browned.

6. Serve immediately with butter and/or syrup or jam.

Variation: To make corn griddle cakes, stir in 1 to 1 1/3 cups defrosted frozen corn kernels with the wet ingredients.

Substitution: Instead of all white flour, use as much as 1/3 cup whole wheat flour.

Crêpes and Blintzes

After America saw Julia blending, swirling, stacking, and filling crêpes on TV in the 1960s, we went through a crêpe craze in the 1970s. Special pans were invented. Entire cookbooks were written. It seemed that every dinner party and buffet featured crêpes; for, depending on the filling or fillip, they could be served for any course, and best of all they could be made ahead, even "frozen for future use."

My grandmother made crêpes but called them blintzes. She didn't use milk, as in a French recipe. She used only water and wrapped these pancakes "you can see your fingers through" around fresh pot cheese or a peppery mixture of mashed potatoes and onions browned in butter.

That was not a meal in a pinch for her. It was a major project. And she made them by the hundreds when she made them at all, turning the pancakes out onto dish towels spread over the dining-room table extended with all its leaves. After all the pancakes were hand-filled and folded (the part I was eventually entrusted to do), they were doled out on platters, with shares to my uncle's fam-

ily, to a select few neighbors and friends, and to our household, which fortunately included my grandmother. It was up to each family to pan-fry the white-skinned blintzes until they were a nutty brown on both sides.

I always preferred potato, topped with lots of sour cream, and potato blintzes are still something that, on a rainy day, I have the urge to make. Flour, eggs, potatoes, butter, onions —there's no question of "what to cook."

I have tried making crêpe and blintz batter without letting it rest, but the pancakes are definitely not as tender and fine-textured as when the batter is made at least 1 or 2 hours ahead of time. I have also compared hand-beaten batter to blender-beaten batter, and the blender method produces a finer, more tender crêpe.

Makes fourteen to sixteen 7-inch crêpes

Crêpe batter

1 cup all-purpose flour
1 cup milk
½ cup cold water
¼ teaspoon salt
2 eggs
2 tablespoons melted butter

Blintz batter

If desired or necessary, use all water
instead of milk and water

1. Combine all the ingredients in a blender jar. Process for a few seconds to mix well. Stop the blender, scrape down the sides with a rubber spatula, then process again for about 30 seconds. The batter should be very smooth and the consistency of very heavy cream. You'll know if it is right when you make the first crêpes. For a thinner crêpe, add 1 to 2 tablespoons more water.

2. Use a skillet with a 6- or 7-inch bottom. Pour in a scant teaspoon of vegetable oil and, with a paper towel, spread it around. Place skillet over medium-high heat for French crêpes, medium heat for blintzes. French crêpes are browned on one side, blintzes should cook through without coloring.

3. When the pan is hot, lift it off the heat with the left hand and with the right hand pour a scant ¼ cup of batter into the center of the pan. Swirl the batter in the pan to cover the bottom and to make a fairly even edge. Tip the pan to get the top runny batter to fill any holes that may have been left. Let cook about 1 minute, then lift the edge of the pancake with a metal spatula or the tip of a table knife. Turn the pancake over and cook another 30 seconds. This sounds difficult but just takes a little practice. After making 2 or 3 crêpes, you'll be able to adjust the heat of the pan, the consistency of the batter, and the turn of your wrist. If your first few don't come out perfect, con-sider them the chef's share and enjoy.

4. As the pancakes are finished, turn them out onto a board or table. (There is no need to grease the pan after the first crêpe is made.) When cooled, the crêpes can be stacked.

5. To freeze, wrap together in plastic as many as you think you might use at once, putting wax paper between the layers. Defrost before attempting to separate them.

Filling for Potato Blintzes

Enough for 10 blintzes; serves 2 to 4

*3 tablespoons butter or vegetable oil
   (or a combination)
2 medium onions, finely chopped
   (about 2 cups)
¼ teaspoon salt
2 large potatoes (about 1 pound)
½ teaspoon salt*

¼ teaspoon freshly ground black or
  white pepper
Ten 7-inch crêpes (see page 137)

1. In a medium skillet, over medium-high heat, sauté onions in butter until well-browned, at least 20 minutes. Add salt and stir frequently in the beginning to prevent the onions from getting steamy. Then leave unattended to brown. They're even better if a few get burned.

2. Meanwhile, peel the potatoes, cut into quarters, and boil until tender to the center, about 20 minutes. Drain immediately.

3. Put the potatoes through a ricer directly into a medium mixing bowl. Add the browned onions, remaining ½ teaspoon of salt, and the pepper. Mix very well.

4. To make potato blintzes, put 2 rounded tablespoons of potato filling side by side in the center of a crêpe. With your fingers press lightly to form into a 3½-inch log. Fold a third of the crêpe up to cover the filling, fold in from the sides, tucking the ends closely. Then fold filled portion over the remaining third of crêpe to complete the package. May be made ahead to this point. Refrigerate, covered with foil (not plastic) only if not frying the same day. Will keep for 1 day.

5. To pan-fry: Over medium heat, melt a thin coating of butter in a skillet (size depends on how many you want to fry at a time). Place the blintzes flap-side down and cook until blistered and well-browned on both sides.

White Sauce

Béchamel, as the French call white sauce (*besciamella* in Italian), is considered terribly déclassé by cooks weaned on 1970s and 1980s nouvelle cuisine and the various supposedly "light" contemporary cooking styles nouvelle spawned. White sauce is milk thickened with flour that has been cooked briefly in butter or another fat, and flour-based sauces are thought to be too heavy these days. Gravy, béchamel's first cousin—velouté in French, *velouta* in Italian—in which the same fat-and-flour thickening (called a *roux*) is incorporated into meat, poultry, or fish stock or broth is just as frowned upon. But tell that to a Southerner about his "cream gravy," or to a Cajun cook who thinks that roux is one of the secrets of his kitchen.

Beyond their use as sauces, roux-thickened liquids are invaluable as binders for fritters and croquettes, as bases for soups and soufflés, beignets, and what Italians call *sformati*, baked molds or loaves of heavily thickened, well-seasoned sauce with bits of vegetable or other savory ingredients. And, despite a reputation for heaviness, white sauce can be a lower fat substitute for cream: So-called cream soups often contain no cream at all. They are based on white sauce.

The thickness of a white sauce depends on its flour content. A thin sauce is made with about 1 tablespoon of flour per cup of liquid. A thick sauce will contain about 2 tablespoons of flour per cup of liquid. The amount of butter or fat used should be about the same as the flour.

Lumping is the only technical problem beginning sauce makers have. To avoid it, before incorporating the liquid, pull the roux off the heat and let it cool until it stops bubbling. Then add the liquid, stirring constantly as you add. Return the mixture to the heat and, still stirring constantly, bring to a simmer. The sauce's maximum thickness is reached when the mixture starts bubbling, though it can be further thickened, if necessary, by letting the liquid reduce through evaporation—just keep cooking. Thinning a flour-based sauce is even easier—just add more liquid.

Makes 1 cup

1½ tablespoons butter or vegetable oil
1½ tablespoons flour
1 cup milk
Salt and pepper
Freshly grated nutmeg

1. In a small saucepan, melt the butter over medium heat.

2. With a wooden spoon or whisk, stir in the flour. Let it bubble over medium heat, stirring frequently.

3. Remove from heat and stir in the milk.

4. Return to heat and, stirring constantly, bring to a simmer. Let simmer about 2 minutes. Season with salt, pepper, and nutmeg.

Variations: Use broth of any kind instead of milk.

Pâte à Choux

(Cream Puff Pastry)

Cream puff shells, empty balls of buttery crust, look impossible to make, but think of them this way: The dough is a sort of very thick white sauce into which eggs are beaten as a leavener. Technically, there is nothing to it, though you do need a strong arm or an electric mixer to thoroughly beat the eggs into the stiff flour mass. As a finger food appetizer, and citing only the fillings within the scope of your theoretically at-hand ingredients, cream puff shells can be filled with Sardine Tapenade (see page 229) or Cream

Cheese and Tuna Spread (see page 87). Cheese can be incorporated into the dough (see Gougère, page 94). For a dessert, fill shells with pudding or with ice cream. Topped with chocolate sauce, ice cream–filled puffs are called profiteroles. (Piped into long lengths, filled with custard, and glazed with chocolate, they are éclairs.) Very small and unfilled puffs are also an elegant soup garnish that are often inelegantly called "soup nuts."

Makes about 2 dozen small puffs

½ cup water
4 tablespoons butter
¼ teaspoon salt, or ½ teaspoon sugar
   (depending on intended use)
6 tablespoons flour
2 eggs

1. Preheat the oven to 425 degrees.

2. In a small saucepan, over medium heat, combine the water, butter, and salt or sugar, and bring to a boil.

3. As soon as the water boils and the butter has completely melted, stir in the flour. Stir briskly over medium heat until the mixture forms a ball of dough and the dough begins to leave a light film on the bottom of the saucepan. Remove from heat.

4. Add an egg and stir briskly again until the egg has been completely absorbed and the dough forms a mass again.

5. Add the second egg and beat it thoroughly into the dough, as with the first.

6. Drop the dough by rounded teaspoonfuls, about 2 inches apart, onto a greased baking sheet. Using your finger, nudge each piece of dough into a reasonably round ball.

7. Bake for 18 to 20 minutes, until nicely browned.

8. As soon as the puffs are done, remove them from the oven and turn it off.

9. Pierce the side of each with the point of a sharp knife, then return them to the turned-off oven for another 15 or 20 minutes. (May be made ahead and stored in a tin for 1 or 2 days, or they may be frozen for up to about 6 weeks. To refresh from the freezer, place frozen puffs in a preheated 325-degree oven for 5 to 8 minutes.

Scones

(Margaret O'Shea's "Kill Me Quicks")

I know only one member of the O'Shea family, James, a restaurateur with a wickedly wry sense of humor. He claims it was his older siblings, however, who gave his

mother's delicate scones their fright-
ful nickname.

Makes 6 scones

2 cups all-purpose flour
1/2 teaspoon salt
1 teaspoon baking soda
2 teaspoons cream of tartar
6 tablespoons sugar
4 tablespoons butter or margarine
1 egg
2/3 cup milk, buttermilk, or yogurt
1/2 cup raisins

1. Preheat the oven to 400 degrees.
Flour a baking sheet.

2. In a sifter or strainer, combine the
flour, salt, baking soda, cream of tartar, and sugar. Sieve into a medium
mixing bowl.

3. Rub in the butter until the mixture resembles fine bread crumbs.

4. In a small cup or bowl, beat together the egg and milk.

5. Add milk mixture and raisins to
dry ingredients and stir until mixture forms a soft dough. (Save the
bowl from the milk mixture with its
last drops of liquid.)

6. On a floured surface, knead the
dough lightly, then pat it out into a
1-inch thick round.

7. Cut round into 6 wedges and place
on the baking sheet. Brush the last
drop of milk-egg mixture over the top
of each wedge.

8. Bake for 15 to 17 minutes, until
lightly browned.

9. Serve warm or at room temperature.

Drop Biscuits or Shortcake

The difference between biscuits
and shortcakes is largely the
amount of sugar and eggs. Leave
out the sugar entirely or use the full
measure. Use 1 egg or 2 eggs, or
make a really rich dough with only
egg yolks.

Makes 8

2 cups all-purpose flour
Up to 3 tablespoons sugar
1 tablespoon baking powder
1/2 teaspoon salt
6 tablespoons butter
1 or 2 whole eggs or egg yolks
1/2 cup milk

1. Preheat the oven to 425 degrees.

2. In a mixing bowl, stir together the
flour, sugar (if any), baking powder,
and salt.

3. Cut the butter into small pieces, letting them drop into the bowl with the flour mixture.

4. Using your fingertips, rub the butter and flour mixture together until the mixture resembles coarse meal.

5. Blend the eggs and milk together, then stir into the flour mixture, stirring just until mixture binds into a dough.

6. Drop by ¼ cupfuls onto a greased baking sheet. (May be prepared ahead to this point, and even refrigerated overnight—covered with plastic—for baking in the morning.)

7. Bake for about 15 minutes, until biscuits are tinged with brown.

8. Serve hot.

Pepper Crackers

This is an unbelievably quick fix for a cocktail snack or soup accompaniment.

Makes 2 approximately 12- by 8-inch sheets

1½ *cups flour*
½ *teaspoon salt*
½ *to 1½ teaspoons freshly ground pepper (not too fine), to taste*
2 *tablespoons vegetable oil*
7 *to 9 tablespoons cold tap water*

1. Preheat oven to 350 degrees.

2. In a medium mixing bowl, stir together the flour, salt and pepper.

3. Add the oil and stir until mixture resembles fine meal.

4. With a fork, stir in the cold water, using just enough to make the dough gather into a ball.

5. Divide the dough in half and, on a well-floured board, roll out each half as thinly as possible into a rough rectangle that fits on a baking sheet.

6. Place dough on baking sheet and, if you want neat-looking crackers, score it into squares or diamonds.

7. Bake for 25 to 30 minutes, turning after 15 minutes. Dough should be a pale brown and snap, not bend.

8. Break into crackers or irregular pieces. Can be stored in a tin.

Variations: Instead of black pepper, season with hot red pepper flakes or any other spice that seems appropriate to the crackers' eventual use. Or, don't season at all. Or, after the dough has been transferred to a baking sheet, sprinkle with coarse salt and press lightly into the top.

Garlic

If there is any indispensable flavoring—after salt and pepper, that is—garlic must be it. Men have given garlic medicinal, even magical, properties since Egyptian days—perhaps earlier. Could it be that our species has a need to rationalize our passion for this stinking bulb?

Garlic is available all year, but the garlic we buy in late winter and early spring is the previous year's crop. Because it is drier than new-crop garlic it's easier to peel, but it may have green sprouts inside. The sprouts have an extra-strong garlic flavor that some people find too strong or bitter. Cut the cloves in half and remove them if you like; they pull out easily. Fresh garlic, because it is moist and fills out its skin, is often difficult to peel. To ease the job, put the unpeeled clove on a flat surface, cover it with the broad side of a wide knife blade, and tap it lightly or hit it with the knife handle. The peel pops off.

I store garlic in a basket at room temperature and it lasts anywhere from a couple of weeks to a couple of months, depending on its freshness when purchased, the temperature and humidity in the kitchen, and how much air is able to circulate around it—the more the better. You can refrigerate garlic, but I've never found that this extends its life; it simply gets dusty with mold instead of dry as dust.

Garlic takes on several characters depending on how it is cut and at what temperature it is cooked. Cloves cooked whole and gently—either simmered or roasted—give the mildest flavor. Cloves that are smashed with the side of a knife or put through a garlic press or cooked at high heat have the strongest flavor. Never sauté garlic until it is dark brown because that brings out its most bitter, acrid side.

Peruvian Garlic Soup from Felipe Rojas-Lombardi

Felipe Rojas-Lombardi, the late chef-owner of The Ballroom in New York, remembered fondly how his mother would whip this up for him as a restorative/snack. Served in mugs, instead of a bowl, I find it's a great hot drink to serve someone who has just come in from the cold. Multiply the ingredients as needed.

Serves 1

2 teaspoons olive oil
1 clove garlic, finely chopped
1 cup water
1 egg
Salt and pepper

1. In a small saucepan, combine the olive oil and garlic and set over medium heat. Cook until garlic just begins to color.

2. Add the water and boil 2 or 3 minutes.

3. While the water boils, beat the egg in a mug or cup.

4. Remove garlic-water from heat and, with a fork, beat the hot liquid and garlic into the beaten egg. Season with salt and pepper.

5. Drink hot.

Spanish Garlic Soup

As one might imagine, there are a zillion ways garlic soup is made in Spain. Some recipes—if we can call them by so formal a word—have tomatoes, some don't. Some use fish stock or chicken stock or simply water. Some recipes don't contain eggs, some have them poached, some scrambled, some scrambled and baked into a crust. In some the bread is toasted and left crisp as a final garnish. In some the bread is toasted then dissolved in the liquid. The following offers some alternatives.

Serves 4

3 tablespoons olive oil
8 whole cloves garlic
½ teaspoon sweet or hot paprika
One 14-ounce can plum tomatoes, chopped (optional)
4 to 6 cups water, broth, or clam juice
Four 1-inch-thick slices bread from a long Italian or French loaf
4 eggs

1. In a small saucepan, over medium heat, heat the oil and sauté the garlic cloves until browned lightly on all sides.

2. Add the paprika, stirring for 30 seconds and smashing the softened garlic slightly.

3. Add the chopped tomatoes and the water, broth, or clam juice, or, if not using the tomatoes, add 6 cups liquid. Bring to a boil and boil about 10 minutes.

4. Meanwhile, toast the bread.

5. To serve, either break the toasted bread into the soup and simmer another 3 minutes, or divide the broth among 4 individual ovenproof dishes and float the bread on top. The eggs can either be beaten lightly, then stirred into the boiling broth (with or without the bread), where it will form strings, as in Italian *stracciatella* or Chinese egg drop soup. Or, the eggs can be poached and placed on top of each bread slice. (In Spain, where they live life more dangerously, the eggs may not be fully cooked at all: The bread is placed in a bowl, the raw egg broken onto the bread, then the hot soup poured over both.)

Roasted Garlic

Whole heads of roasted garlic have become a fashionable accompaniment to roasted or grilled meat. When cooked this way, the garlic is tamed to a sweetish pulp that can be squeezed out of the skins and smeared on bread or on a forkful of meat. I like to cook the garlic in the oven alongside baked potatoes. And with the oven already on, I might roast some onions, too. Now, with bread and wine, it's a meal.

Serves 1 to 4

1 whole head garlic, unpeeled
¼ teaspoon salt
2 tablespoons olive oil

1. Cut ¼ to ½ inch off the pointed end of the garlic head, enough to expose the garlic cloves.

2. Put the head of garlic in a custard cup or ramekin. Sprinkle with salt and pour on the olive oil.

3. Cook in a preheated 400-degree oven for about 45 minutes, the same time it takes to bake a large potato or a large onion.

4. Eat hot, warm, or at room temperature.

Other recipes featuring garlic

Aglio e Olio (Spaghetti with Oil and Garlic) (see page 184)
Bagna Cauda (olive oil, garlic, and anchovy dip) (see page 183)

Grits

The word *grits* is related to grist (as in "grist for the mill") and to groats, which is what milled, toasted buckwheat is called. Grits are, indeed, the coarsest milled product of corn. Some sources say it is incorrect to call them "hominy" grits, for they are not necessarily made from hominy, which is a treated corn product. But try to tell that to a Southerner, where "hominy grits" are ubiquitous and honored and abhorred with equal passion. Old-fashioned, long-cooking, coarse grits have significantly more flavor than more elegant fine-milled grits or lackluster "instant" grits, but all have a long shelf life. Kept on a dry shelf, a box of grits, stored in a plastic bag to keep out insects, will do you service for at least a year. For basic grits, to be eaten with butter (and/or cheese) for breakfast or as a side dish, follow package instructions. To make the grits recipe that is the pride of the South, see the following recipe.

Carolina Grits Soufflé

Ask a Southerner for his or her best grits recipe and you'll get something very close to this. This particular formula is adapted from *The Heritage of Southern Cooking* by Camille Glenn (Workman, 1986), who used to write a food column for the *Louisville Courier-Journal*.

Serves 4

2½ cups water
¾ teaspoon salt
½ cup hominy grits (not instant)
4 tablespoons butter
¼ cup shredded sharp cheddar
   cheese
Cayenne
3 eggs, separated

1. In a medium saucepan, over medium heat, bring the water to a boil. Add the salt and grits and simmer, stirring constantly, until the grits taste done and are thick and smooth, about 20 minutes.

2. Stir in the butter until melted and remove from the heat.

3. Stir in the cheese, cayenne to taste, and egg yolks, until thoroughly blended. Scrape into a large mixing bowl and set aside.

4. Preheat the oven to 375 degrees. Butter a 1-quart casserole or soufflé dish.

5. In another mixing bowl, beat the egg whites until they are stiff.

6. Fold the egg whites into the grits mixture (not vice versa), leaving some pieces of white showing.

7. Pour into the casserole or soufflé dish and bake until golden brown and firm in the middle, 35 to 40 minutes.

8. Serve immediately.

Hominy

Hominy is a kind of large-kernel white corn. Dried and treated with lime, it puffs up or "flowers" into soft white balls when boiled. Dried hominy is available in the Southwestern states, but most of us have to make do with already cooked canned hominy. Actually, in my few attempts to cook dried hominy I have found it frustratingly unpredictable—sometimes it flowers, sometimes it doesn't—and I now prefer the convenience of the canned, which keeps well on a cupboard shelf for several years.

Zarela's Home-Style Hominy

Zarela Martinez is the proprietor and culinary guiding force of Zarela restaurant in New York, where, due to her joie de vivre, it always feels like a party. This is how she handles hominy for a meal at home—"with just some scrambled eggs."

Serves 2 or 3

1½ tablespoons vegetable oil
1 medium onion, chopped
1 large clove garlic, crushed
One 28-ounce can Italian-style tomatoes
½ teaspoon salt
½ teaspoon dried oregano
1 dried ancho chili, soaked, seeded, and chopped
One 16-ounce can hominy, drained well

1. In a skillet, heat the oil over medium-high heat and sauté the onion for 5 minutes, until it begins to brown.

2. Add garlic and sauté another minute.

3. Drain the tomatoes very well, even split them and let their interior juices drain back into the can.

4. Add the tomatoes to the skillet and break them up well with the side of a wooden spoon.

5. Add the salt and oregano. Simmer over medium heat for about 8 minutes, until sauce is quite thick.

6. Add the chopped ancho. Simmer another minute.

7. Add the hominy and heat through for 3 to 5 minutes.

Substitution: Instead of a dried ancho chili, use about 1 teaspoon commercial chili powder.

Another recipe featuring hominy

Chick-pea Chili Soup (see page 42)

Kasha

Kasha is the generic word for cereal in Russian, but in the United States it refers to toasted, hulled buckwheat groats. So what's a groat? It's the seed or edible grain part of the plant. However, in the case of kasha, *groat* is a misnomer, because a buckwheat groat is botanically not a grain but a fruit.

Those of us who grew up eating kasha regularly, often as the starchy side dish to pot roast, have a special fondness for its nutty taste, but its popularity must be growing if its increased availability in supermarkets is any indication. Aside from its usefulness as a sort of pilaf, kasha is used to fill knishes, a savory, snack pastry and delicatessen specialty that was invented in New York and not Eastern Europe, as many people assume. And if you add bow tie egg noodles and sautéed onions to the pilaf, it becomes kasha varnishkes. Polish cooks also use it to make a sort of starch sausage called *kiska,* among other things.

Kasha is usually sold in boxes that always give directions for cooking it, though kasha is occasionally available in bulk in health-food stores, too. It comes in whole grains, as well as coarse, medium, and fine-milled grains. Whole grain kasha is best for pilaf. The medium and fine grains, which become mushy when cooked, are used for stuffings and as hot cereal.

Store kasha in a tightly closed jar, at room temperature if you expect to use it within a few months, in the refrigerator or freezer for extended storage. Like all whole grains, kasha contains oil and eventually becomes rancid: Smell long-stored kasha before cooking it.

Basic Kasha

Makes 2 cups

1 egg
1 cup kasha
2 cups boiling water or broth
½ teaspoon salt (if using water or
low-salt broth)
Freshly ground black pepper
Sautéed onions (optional)

1. In a small bowl or cup, beat the egg to mix well.

2. In a cold skillet with a cover, blend the egg into the kasha. Place over medium heat and, with a wooden spoon, stir constantly until the grains are separate. Be careful not to burn them. (This procedure keeps the grains separate when they are cooked.)

3. Pour the water or broth into the skillet and cover. Steam over low heat for about 20 minutes, until all the water has been absorbed and the grain is tender. (Alternately, combine the pan-toasted kasha and boiling liquid in a casserole and bake, covered, in a preheated 350-degree oven for 20 minutes.)

4. Serve immediately, seasoned with freshly ground pepper and topped with sautéed onions, if desired. Or set aside and reheat in the oven. Kasha reheats perfectly in a covered casserole, though you may need to add a few additional tablespoons of liquid to keep it moist.

Microwave Method: Packages of kasha now give microwave directions, but they require more fussing than the conventional method and, to boot, take just as long.

Variation: Kasha is also delicious topped with sour cream or yogurt, and, if available, chopped scallions or chives.

Kasha Varnishkes

The ratio of kasha to bow tie egg noodles depends on taste and the amount of each available. I like more kasha than noodles, so, to the preceding recipe, I would not add more than 1 cup of cooked bow ties. You, however—especially in a pinch—may want the kasha simply to flavor your noodles, in which case you can stretch 2 cups of kasha for a pound of noodles. In any case, sautéed onions are an essential here, as many as you can manage.

Variations: Dried mushrooms are a superb addition to kasha varnishkes. Use the kind available in supermarkets, Polish mushrooms, or cêpes (or porcini; see page 168), and sauté the reconstituted mushrooms with the onions.

Ketchup

A condiment called "ketchup" or "catsup" was first made by the Chinese and called *ke-tsiap*. Made of brined fish or shellfish, it was introduced to the West by English seamen who discovered it in the late seventeenth century in Malaysia and Singapore. Imitating it back home was not so easy, however, and the English evolved condiments called "ketchap" made mainly with mushrooms and nuts. By 1748, Mrs. Harrison, in her *Housekeeper's Pocketbook,* warned the homemaker never to be without the pungent condiment, but it was tedious to make. In 1861, Isabella Beeton's *Book of Household Management* told readers that it is "one of the most useful sauces to the experienced cook, and no trouble should be spared in its preparation."

Americans followed that advice until 1876, when Henry Heinz introduced the first bottled tomato ketchup. I suppose we still do find it one of the "most useful sauces." Almost everyone has a bottle of tomato ketchup lurking in the back of the refrigerator, if not within handy reach on the refrigerator door. If you listen to the ketchup companies, it should be tossed out after about a year. But unofficially, as all infrequent ketchup users can attest, it keeps much longer than that. There is so much vinegar and sugar in ketchup that it is practically preserved for eternity. Just try to remember to wipe off the neck of the bottle after each use. More ketchup bottles get thrown out because of the darkening collection of ketchup on the neck than they do because the product in the bottle turned sour or moldy.

Red Salad Dressing

Old New York steak houses serve a dressing something like this, usually on a plate of thickly sliced beefsteak tomatoes and Bermuda onion, a standard salad appetizer. It's also right at home on a wedge or slice of iceberg lettuce.

Makes about ⅓ cup

¼ cup ketchup
2 tablespoons vegetable oil
1 tablespoon cider vinegar
¼ teaspoon sugar
1 clove garlic, cut in half

1. In a small bowl or cup, using a fork, beat the ketchup and oil together until well blended.

2. Beat in the vinegar and sugar.

3. Add the garlic and let stand as long as you can wait; you'll get a subtle garlic flavor after 30 minutes. Before serving, fish out the garlic with a toothpick.

Variation: If you want more garlic flavor or don't have time to let the dressing stand, smash garlic with the side of a broad-bladed knife. A few drops of Worcestershire and a couple drops of bottled hot sauce are to some people's taste.

Thousand Island or Russian Dressing

If there is any difference between Thousand Island and Russian Dressing, I dare you to name it. Consult cookbooks and you'll find the names are used interchangeably for the same combination of mayonnaise and ketchup with sweet pickle or relish.

Makes about ¾ cup

½ cup mayonnaise
¼ cup ketchup or chili sauce
2 tablespoons sweet pickle relish, or 1
*   medium sweet gherkin, minced*

1. In a small bowl or cup, blend the three ingredients together.

Variations: Add 2 tablespoons sour cream or yogurt and up to 1 tablespoon more ketchup. Some recipes include finely chopped hard-cooked egg white and/or minced pimento. You might also add minced pimento-stuffed olives.

Substitutions: Any kind of pickle—or no pickle—will do in a pinch. Instead of half the mayonnaise, use sour cream or yogurt.

A Fresh Touch: Chopped fresh chives are a classic addition; chopped fresh dill or tarragon are refreshingly different ones.

Lemons

So far as I'm concerned, there is no excuse for using bottled, reconstituted lemon juice or any other kind of lemon juice that doesn't come directly from a lemon. The convenience products are not only often bitter and metallic, they're not significantly more convenient than the fruit itself.

Their keeping ability isn't that much better either. Most produce guides tell us that lemons keep in a plastic bag in the refrigerator for several weeks. Would you believe several months? If growers and middlemen can keep them for 6 months in cold storage, then the only reason you can't is because they've done so already.

Aside from obvious dehydration, softness, or bad bruises, the only sure way to know you're buying a recently harvested lemon is the price. When they're a bargain it's because they are plentiful. All year, somewhere in the country lemons are being harvested, but only at certain times of the year—generally the winter months—is the supply so abundant and regular that they come to market immediately.

For the juiciest lemons, look for those with relatively thin, fine-grained skin. One lemon will give from 2 to 4 tablespoons of juice and any given lemon will give more juice when at room temperature than when cold.

Cut lemons also keep well if wrapped in plastic to prevent dehydration. If you really want to be frugal—as well as always prepared—use a swivel-bladed vegetable peeler and remove the yellow zest from lemons that are squeezed dry. It keeps, in a plastic bag in the refrigerator, for several weeks. I haven't had any success drying lemon peel, but the commercial product, available in the spice department of the supermarket, is much better than its juice relation.

There's certainly no need to extol the well-known virtues of lemons as a seasoning for food, but as a reminder to those who try to cut down on salt: Like salt, lemon juice works as a catalyst to heighten and accent other flavors.

Lemon Sponge Pudding

This is one of those magical recipes that delights children and skeptics. A pudding forms on the bottom of the pan while a frothy meringue surfaces from its depths.

Serves 4 to 8

2 eggs, separated
¾ cup sugar
Juice of 1 large lemon (about a scant
*   ¼ cup)*
1 teaspoon grated lemon peel
1 tablespoon melted butter
¼ cup flour
1 cup milk

1. Preheat the oven to 350 degrees.

2. In a mixing bowl, using a hand-held electric mixer or wire whisk, beat egg yolks until light. Add sugar ¼ cup at a time, blending each addition in well, then beating until the yolks are smooth and light in color.

3. Blend in the lemon juice, lemon peel, and melted butter.

4. Add the flour and milk. Beat well to make a smooth batter.

5. Rinse and dry beaters very well, then beat egg whites until stiff.

6. Fold beaten whites into the batter.

7. Pour the batter into an ungreased 8-inch-square baking dish (or similarly sized dish). Place in a larger pan (a roasting pan) and fill outer pan with boiling water to come up as far as the batter in the dish.

8. Bake for 45 minutes.

9. Let cool at least 5 minutes. Serve hot or warm, spooned into small bowls.

Substitutions: Using the same proportions, orange or grapefruit pudding is possible, but they're better if you add a squirt of lemon. For a coffee-flavored pudding, use a scant ¼ cup of strong black coffee fortified, if possible, with a few drops of vanilla.

Avgolemono

This is the most common Greek soup, and as these common national dishes go, there are almost as many recipes as commoners. They go from flour-thickened bouillons to smooth, egg-enriched stocks with a liaison of rice; the one constant is lots of lemon juice. This recipe is somewhere in between the richest and the most meager.

Serves 2

One 13¾-ounce can chicken broth
1 cup water
3 tablespoons white rice
2 eggs
3 or 4 tablespoons lemon juice
Freshly ground black pepper

1. In a small saucepan, combine the broth and water and bring to a boil.

2. Add the rice, cover the pot, and reduce heat to simmer the rice for 15 minutes.

3. In a small bowl, beat the eggs until well blended.

4. When the rice is tender, ladle a ½ cup or so of hot soup into the beaten eggs, stirring constantly as you add.

5. Pour egg mixture back into saucepan. Add lemon juice. Heat through but don't allow to boil.

6. Serve immediately.

Oriental Lemon Sauce for Noodles

Use spaghetti or Chinese egg noodles (mein), either hot or cold. The dressing is enough for 8 to 12 ounces.

Makes about ⅓ cup

¼ cup lemon juice
2 tablespoons soy sauce

1 or 2 teaspoons finely chopped fresh
   gingerroot
2 teaspoons sesame oil
1 clove garlic, finely chopped
   (optional)

1. In a small bowl or cup, beat all the ingredients together with a fork.

A Fresh Touch: Add chopped fresh coriander.

Lemon Curd

This is a traditional English filling for tarts and other pastries. As a dessert in a pinch, it is wonderful spread on matzoh, plain crackers, butter cookies, crisp amaretti and apple slices, and it is fabulously indulgent spread on hot toast or English muffins for breakfast. Use it as a fillip for ice cream, or fold it into sour cream or yogurt to make a faux fruit fool.

Makes about 2½ cups

4 eggs
1½ cups sugar
Grated zest and juice of 3 lemons (¾
   cup juice, 2 tablespoons zest)
4 tablespoons butter

1. In a large mixing bowl, whisk the eggs, gradually adding the sugar, until yolks are thick and lemon-colored.

2. With the whisk, blend in the grated lemon zest and juice, then pour into a small heavy-bottomed saucepan or double boiler. Place over medium heat, add a tablespoon of the butter and stir over medium heat until butter has melted.

3. Stir in the remaining butter, 1 tablespoon at a time, until each has melted. Continue stirring until the mixture has thickened—the pale foam on top will have dissolved and curd will be a uniform lemon color.

4. Let cool, then refrigerate in a jar.

Lettuce

There are innumerable varieties of lettuces and salad greens, but only iceberg lettuce—sometimes called head lettuce, technically known as crisphead, and still America's favorite—lasts and lasts and lasts. A well-chosen, well-stored head of iceberg will keep nicely for up to a month and no less than 2 weeks. Heads with a couple of fresh-looking, darker green outer leaves are best, but all iceberg should feel "springy-firm," in the words of the California Iceberg Lettuce Commission. Don't worry if the end of the core is brown, but don't buy heads with rust spots. The discolorations, a sign of overmaturity or improper storage or handling, are harmless but unappetizing and a signal that the lettuce is going to deteriorate more quickly. Spotted leaves mean the lettuce was improperly shipped with pears, apples, bananas, or tomatoes, which give off ethylene gas that do the damage. For the same reason, do not store lettuce in a crisper drawer with these fruits.

Use the crisp, juicy leaves of iceberg to add moisture and texture to sandwiches, shredded or chopped or cut into wedges for salad. It is particularly good as a receptacle for thick salad dressings, such as Thousand Island or Russian Dressing (see page 156).

Romaine lettuce also keeps fairly well, though not nearly so long as iceberg. Stored unwashed in the bottom of the refrigerator, its dark green, pear-shaped leaves will stay crisp for about 10 days.

Matzoh

I f matzoh doesn't exactly last forever, at least it lasts from one Passover to the next, which is about how often I buy it. To me, as a Jew, it's a seasonal food. And in the spring, when it's Passover, I can eat matzoh brei, matzoh meal pancakes, matzoh farfel kugel, matzoh everything and love it. Once the eight days of Passover are gone, however, the last open box of matzoh that's left just sits on the shelf until sometime in deep winter. I'll be cleaning out the cupboard some gloomy Sunday in February and discover three boards of matzoh, just enough to make a matzoh brei dinner for two. Sometimes, its last gasp is more divine than its first.

Keep matzoh on a dry shelf, and remember that it's a good bland cracker, not unlike the fancy English crackers called water biscuits. Dab it with jelly, smear it with cream cheese or peanut butter, butter it and sprinkle with salt, serve it with firm cheeses, or as something crunchy to go with a bowl of soup or chowder.

Matzoh Brei

My rule of thumb with this is one egg to each board of matzoh, but you can always use more eggs than matzoh; within reason, more eggs will make a better brei. To hold together a pancake omelet-style matzoh brei, as opposed to the following scrambled version, you will, in fact, need at least one egg more than matzoh boards. Some recipes call for soaking the matzoh, then squeezing it dry. I find that slowly pouring boiling water over the matzoh in a colander gives the texture I like, which is something like noodles.

Serves 2

3 matzoh boards
6 to 8 cups boiling water
3 eggs
¼ to ½ teaspoon salt
1½ to 2 tablespoons butter

1. Into a colander, break the matzoh into more or less 1-inch pieces.

2. Slowly pour the boiling water over the matzoh, wetting it down well, then leaving it to drain well.

3. In a mixing bowl, beat the eggs well with the salt.

4. Add the wet matzoh and mix well.

5. In an 8- to 10-inch skillet, over medium-high heat, melt the butter. When sizzling, add the egg-matzoh mixture. Immediately lower heat to medium; slowly cooking the eggs gives them a custardy consistency.

6. When the bottom starts to set, break up and turn the mixture gently. Cook 3 or 4 minutes, turning occasionally, until the matzoh brei cooks evenly and to the moistness (or dryness) you like.

7. Serve hot, with some freshly ground pepper, with preserves, or jam, or with sour cream.

Mayonnaise

Mayonnaise, like the other "aise" sauces, béarnaise and hollandaise, is an emulsion of a fat in egg yolks. In the case of mayonnaise the fat is oil. In the case of béarnaise and hollandaise, the fat is melted butter. Despite their reputations as tricky, they are not that difficult to make with the aid of an electric mixer or blender. Unfortunately, because of an increase in the incidence of salmonella contamination, raw egg yolks have become a health hazard in recent years and homemade "aise" sauces are now considered dangerous. Fortunately, there is Hellmann's (called Best Foods mayonnaise on the West Coast).

Hellmann's mayonnaise, which is subjected to heat processing that in effect cooks the egg yolks, was created in Hellmann's German-style delicatessen on the Upper West Side of Manhattan. Then, and as is sometimes the case now, New York German-style delicatessens specialized in homemade cole slaw, potato salad, and macaroni salad, as well as pickles, cooked dishes, and other salads that complemented the deli's stock in trade: cold cuts. There are, of course, other brands of mayonnaise and so-called "salad dressing." They all taste different, and you may prefer another, but, according to their cautious manufacturers, opened jars keep a minimum of a year in the refrigerator (or easily 6 months after any printed last date of sale), or a good 6 months to a year after that, if you ask me.

Salad Olivier

Outside the Soviet Union this gussied-up potato salad is known as "Russian salad," but the Russians call it by the name of a French chef, one M. Olivier who owned a restaurant called The Hermitage in Moscow in the 1860s. According to Anne Volokh in her book *The Art of Russian Cuisine,* the original salad was composed with bits of grouse, crayfish, and truffles. Nowadays in Russia, where the salad automatically appears as an appetizer on nearly every restaurant and hotel table, chicken is mixed with the cubed potatoes, diced pickles, onions, peas, and hard-boiled eggs. Russian salad is also very popular in Italy, where diced ham usually replaces the chicken. Whatever the specifics of the recipe, it is always bound with lots of mayonnaise.

Serves 4

1 pound potatoes, boiled and peeled
¼ cup diced pickle (any kind)
1 cup cooked frozen peas
1 small onion, finely chopped, or
  ⅓ cup finely chopped shallots
1 to 1½ cups mayonnaise
1 teaspoon dried dill (optional)
2 hard-boiled eggs, white and yolk
  separated

Olives (any kind, any color)
  (optional)

1. Dice the potato into approximately ⅓-inch cubes.

2. In a mixing bowl, combine the potatoes, pickle, peas, onion or shallots, mayonnaise, and dill, if using.

3. Dice the egg whites into ¼-inch pieces and add to the bowl. Mix to thoroughly blend.

4. Mound the salad on a serving plate and smooth the top. Press the egg yolk through a sieve and use to decorate the mound of salad. Decorate with olives, if desired.

Variations: Instead of all mayonnaise, use part sour cream or yogurt. Use ½ teaspoon dried tarragon instead of dried dill. Reseason the mayonnaise with additional lemon juice or wine vinegar, or with a tablespoon of prepared mustard, preferably Dijon or other sharp variety.

A Fresh Touch: Add 1 cup diced chicken, ham, shrimp, or flaked fish. Instead of a dried herb, use 1 tablespoon or more chopped fresh dill, parsley, basil, chervil, chives (or a combination), or 1½ teaspoons chopped fresh tarragon.

Tartar Sauce

A classic accompaniment to fried fish, tartar sauce can also be an emergency dressing for a cabbage or carrot slaw or a wedge of lettuce.

Makes about 1 cup

1 cup mayonnaise
¼ cup pickle relish or finely diced sweet or sour pickle
1 tablespoon lemon juice or vinegar

1. In a small bowl, blend the ingredients together.

Variations: Add up to 1 tablespoon finely chopped capers, 1 tablespoon grated onion, 1 tablespoon finely chopped shallots, ½ teaspoon crumbled dried tarragon, or 2 teaspoons dried dill or mint.

A Fresh Touch: Add up to 2 tablespoons finely chopped parsley, 1 teaspoon finely chopped fresh tarragon, or 1 tablespoon finely chopped fresh dill.

Other recipes featuring mayonnaise

All-American Cole Slaw (see page 70)
Thousand Island or Russian Dressing (see page 156)

Mushrooms *(Dried)*

Dried mushrooms have much more flavor than fresh mushrooms and a few slices or caps can go a long way in a soup or a stew; long enough, in fact, to make a large quantity of fresh mushrooms cooked with reconstituted dried wild mushrooms taste like fresh wild mushrooms; a nice trick to know.

Many kinds of wild mushrooms—porcini (cêpes), chanterelles, morels—are very expensive and found only in rarefied specialty food shops or ethnic markets, but any supermarket that caters to even a small Jewish or Eastern European clientele carries a variety of mild, less coveted wild mushrooms packaged in small plastic containers with snap-on plastic lids. You may find them in a special Polish or Jewish foods section, near the dried beans, or near the canned soups. They are generally very clean, white mushrooms, but with a distinctly wild flavor. Unlike dried morels, the dark Polish or Lithuanian mushrooms, or intense Italian porcini, they don't need long soaking, if any at all, and don't need to be rinsed after they are soaked. The plastic caps on most containers call them "imported," but who knows?

As expensive as they are, I find dried porcini—the Italian boletus mushroom—a good value, especially if bought in large quantity. The tiny bags of porcini that hold ½ ounce or less are the most expensive package. Bags holding about 8 ounces can cost half as much per ounce and will hold up well for several years if kept in a dark, dry place. Keep them in a tin, in a jar, or in a tightly closed plastic bag. If you keep them long enough—several years —eventually you will have to discard a few that develop a gray-white powder on the surface.

For most purposes, most dried mushrooms need to be soaked before they are added to a recipe. And because they sometimes contain some dirt or sand, their soaking water, which contains almost as much flavor as the mushrooms themselves, should be strained—I use a coffee filter but a strainer lined with cheesecloth is the more typical way—and used as well. If you have no immediate use for the mushroom water, store it in the freezer until you do. I've always found the supermarket "imported" mushrooms to be very clean, however, so I drop them into soups without reconstituting them. Other mushrooms will need from 30 minutes to 1 hour of previous soaking in hot tap water, depending on the type and how dry they are, and possibly a rinse under cold water after that, depending on how dirty they are.

Vegetarian Mushroom and Barley Pilaf

Note this recipe for when you can scrape together a carrot, an onion, and a couple of cloves of garlic, but not as much as a single bouillon cube for a base. There's a lot of meaty mushroom flavor in this.

Serves 2

1 small onion, chopped (about ¾ cup)
1½ tablespoons vegetable oil
1 medium carrot, peeled and cut into
    ¼-inch dice (about ½ cup)
1 or 2 cloves garlic, finely minced
    (about 1½ teaspoons)
½ ounce dried dark "Polish"
    mushrooms, soaked 20 minutes in
    hot tap water to cover and finely
    chopped (about ⅓ cup), or ½ ounce
    "imported dried" mushrooms
⅓ cup barley
½ teaspoon salt
Freshly ground black pepper

1. In a 3-quart saucepan, over medium-high heat, sauté the onion in the oil for 3 minutes.

2. Add the carrot and continue cooking, stirring frequently, until the onion begins to brown.

3. Add the garlic and mushrooms and sauté 1 more minute.

4. Strain the mushroom-soaking water into a 2-cup measure. Add enough hot water to make 2 cups. Add to the vegetables. Bring to a rolling boil.

5. Stir in the barley, salt, and pepper. Cover and lower heat so the liquid simmers briskly, not violently. Simmer 30 minutes, until barley is tender and has absorbed all the liquid.

6. Serve hot or at room temperature. Reheats very well, though you may have to add a few additional tablespoons of water.

Variations: Use this as a sauce for about ½ pound tubular macaroni. It's very filling. Add up to 1 cup diced potato (and an additional ¼ cup water) with the barley—also a worthy dish to put before a kingly appetite.

Mushroom Barley Soup I

Serves 4 to 6

½ ounce "imported dried"
mushrooms, or a lesser amount of
porcini or "Polish" black
mushrooms
3 tablespoons butter or vegetable oil
2 medium onions, chopped (1½ to
2 cups)
3 medium carrots, grated (about
1½ cups)
2 ribs celery, finely chopped (about
1 cup)
2 small potatoes, cut in ¼-inch dice
5 cups water (or combination 2 cups
beef broth and 1 cup water)
½ cup barley

1. In a small bowl or cup, combine the mushrooms with 1 cup boiling water and let soak until ready to add to soup. Or place mushrooms and tap water in a bowl or cup and microwave on HIGH for 1 minute.

2. In a large pot, over medium heat, melt the butter or heat oil and sauté onions for about 6 minutes, until tender.

3. Add the carrots, celery, and potatoes. Sauté another 5 minutes.

4. Add the water (or a combination of broth and water), the mushrooms and their soaking water, and the barley. Raise heat to high, cover, and bring to a simmer. Simmer, covered, for 1 hour.

5. Season to taste with salt and pepper. Serve very hot.

Mushroom Barley Soup II

Mixed bags of beans and barley with a packet of dehydrated seasonings are sold in the supermarket. Consider this the same, and just as easy to prepare. It's the kind of mushroom-barley soup that's often served in Jewish delicatessens and it's a meal unto itself.

Serves 8

4 tablespoons vegetable oil
2 cups finely chopped onions
    (2 medium)
2 cups shredded carrots (about
    6 medium)
6 cups beef broth
1¼ cups barley
½ cup green or yellow split peas
¼ cup dried baby lima beans
½ teaspoon freshly ground black
    pepper
½ ounce "imported dried"
    mushrooms

1. In a large pot, heat the oil over medium heat and sauté the onions and
carrots for 15 minutes, until very
tender.

2. Add all the remaining ingredients
and bring to a boil.

3. Lower heat and simmer gently,
partially covered, for 2 hours, until
the soup has become very thick. Add
more broth or water if necessary to
thin it to the texture you desire, then
check for salt and pepper.

4. Serve very hot. May be kept in the
refrigerator for several days, though
it will thicken and more liquid will
have to be added when it is reheated.

Omelet with Porcini and Croutons

This is more a lunch or supper omelet than a breakfast dish, especially if coupled with a vegetable,
such as peas or creamed spinach, and
a baked potato.

Serves 1

1 tablespoon olive oil
1 slice white bread, cut in ⅓-inch
    cubes
1 tablespoon butter or olive oil
1 clove garlic, finely chopped
¼ to ½ ounce dried porcini, soaked
    at least 2 hours in hot tap water to
    cover, drained
Salt and freshly ground pepper to
    taste
½ tablespoon butter
2 or 3 eggs

1. In an omelet pan or skillet, heat
the olive oil over high heat very hot
but not smoking: A test cube of bread
should sizzle immediately.

2. Add the bread cubes, reduce heat
slightly, and toss and turn until all

the cubes are browned and crisp. Set aside on a plate. (Or use Sautéed Bread Crumbs for Pasta, page 55.)

3. To the same pan or skillet, add butter or olive oil. Add the garlic and sauté 1 minute.

4. Add the mushrooms and sauté 2 or 3 more minutes, seasoning with a little salt and pepper. Set aside on the same plate as the croutons.

5. With the ½ tablespoon butter, make an omelet. Fill with the mushroom-crouton mixture.

6. Serve immediately.

Macaroni with Porcini and Hot Pepper

Serves 2

½ pound ziti, penne, or large elbow
  macaroni
3 tablespoons olive oil or butter
1 medium onion, finely chopped
6 or 8 pieces (about ⅜ ounce) dried
  porcini, soaked about an hour in 1
cup hot tap water and finely
  chopped
1 clove garlic, finely chopped
¼ teaspoon hot red pepper flakes
1 teaspoon flour
Freshly grated nutmeg
Salt and freshly ground pepper
Grated Parmesan cheese (optional)

1. Make the sauce while bringing the water to a boil and cooking the macaroni.

2. In a small saucepan or skillet, heat the oil or butter over medium heat and sauté the onion until tender, about 5 minutes.

3. Drain the mushrooms, reserving the liquid, and add the chopped porcini, garlic, and pepper flakes to the onion. Continue to cook about 2 minutes.

4. Stir in the flour until fully absorbed.

5. Pour in the mushroom soaking liquid, strained through a coffee filter, and bring to simmer. Simmer until slightly reduced and thickened. Add a few gratings of nutmeg, then salt and pepper.

6. Drain macaroni, and toss with the sauce.

7. Serve immediately, preferably with grated Parmesan cheese.

Nuts

Nuts are high in protein and unsaturated fat, which is why they are considered high-quality food, why they are fattening, and why they spoil—turn rancid—so quickly at room temperature or if exposed to air.

The nuts with the longest shelf life are nuts in their shells. They are also the least convenient to use. Depending on the oil content of the particular nut—almonds and walnuts are on the low end, pecans and pine nuts on the high—they can be kept from 3 months to 1 year in their shells at room temperature, from 3 months to 9 months, shelled and in a tightly closed container in the refrigerator, or from 9 months to 2 years in a container in the freezer. Though the freezer provides an optimum storage life for almonds, they lose their crispness there. For eating out of hand, recrisp them on a baking sheet in a 300-degree oven for at least 5 minutes.

Almond Tarator for Pasta or Vegetables

There's a walnut version of tarator on page 262, in the entry on yogurt, which is the main ingredient in the cold soup the tarator flavors. To what I said about this nut and garlic combination there, I should add here that it is most often thickened with soaked bread, making it a first cousin of gazpacho, which, in its most traditional form, is also thickened with dried bread rubbed with garlic. In fact, in *Mediterranean Cooking,* Paula Wolfert has a white gazpacho that is essentially this very tarator recipe with the addition of ½ cup bread, soaked in water and squeezed dry; 1½ teaspoons of wine vinegar, 3 cups of cold water (eliminate the boiling water, below), and a cup of seedless grapes for garnish. Try it on a hot summer night, very well chilled or made at the last minute and poured over ice in a glass.

Serves 2

½ cup blanched almonds (about 2 ounces)
2 medium cloves garlic (to equal the size of a walnut half), peeled
3 tablespoons olive oil
½ teaspoon salt
¼ cup boiling water, pasta cooking water, or vegetable cooking water

1. In a blender, combine the almonds, garlic, oil, and salt. Process until the mixture looks smooth. It won't be; it'll have minuscule bits of nut, but it'll look like mayonnaise.

2. Just before serving, whirl in the boiling liquid.

3. Use to sauce ½ pound spaghetti or macaroni, or a platter of boiled or steamed vegetables.

Other recipes featuring nuts

Thick Rice Soup (see page 222)
Curried Rice Salad or Pilaf (see page 220)
Microwave Brittle Candy (see page 119)
Bulgur Pilaf (see page 64)
Chocolate Brownies (see page 97)
Macaroni with Oranges, Nuts, and Black Pepper (see page 195)

Oatmeal

What I never understood about the oat bran craze of a few years ago was why people—for the benefit of reducing blood cholesterol—were not simply eating more oatmeal. Instead, they (and food manufacturers) put sawdust-like oat bran into all kinds of places it did not belong, including high-fat, high-calorie muffins that actually defeated the purpose of the oat bran altogether. I suppose preparing hot cereal for breakfast was too much trouble, and the taste of oatmeal was too much of a diet burden to bear. Steamed and rolled oats, the product Americans use to make breakfast cereal—porridge—takes 15 minutes to cook and is very bland and sort of gluey. And instant oatmeal (or "quick oats" as Quaker, our largest miller, calls them), which are oats rolled even thinner, haven't enhanced the reputation of oatmeal porridge either; though they certainly are more convenient and many products are presweetened and/or flavored.

On the other hand, travelers returning from Scotland and England often reminisce about the fabulous porridge they indulged in every morning. It is likely the double cream they poured on has something to do with the memory. But they are not mistaken: British oats have better flavor than ours. Now that I purchase tins of McCann's Irish oatmeal—a product Brits call "pinhead" oats, little pellets of cut, not rolled, oats—I am happy to eat oatmeal again—not just for good nutrition, but because it tastes so good. McCann's oatmeal can now be purchased in many supermarkets, in specialty food stores, and through some food and kitchenware mail-order houses. (It is always in the Williams-Sonoma catalog.) In about 30 minutes, it cooks up into a nutty tasting porridge with a slightly crunchy texture. Follow the cooking directions on the tin, or, for slightly quicker cooking and a slightly chewier effect, instead of adding the oats to boiling water, start them out in cold water and boil only for about 25 minutes. I eat oatmeal plain, with a little salt, even as a late-night snack. Most people prefer it with a little milk and sweetened with sugar, honey, or maple syrup. If you don't have the time to cook it up every morning, make enough for 3 or 4 days and keep it refrigerated, then spoon out a portion and reheat it in the microwave.

It may not be an exciting breakfast cereal, but for baking, and as the filler I prefer for meat loaf, I still keep a box of American oatmeal on hand. Rolled oats keep for at least a year in a closed container on a cupboard shelf.

Oatmeal Cookies

Chewy and homey, these are a classic American cookie, receptive to raisins, coconut, nuts, or chocolate chips. They keep very well but rarely stick around long enough to prove it.

Makes 4 to 5 dozen

12 tablespoons (1½ sticks) butter
¾ cup brown sugar (preferably dark)
¾ cup white sugar
1 egg
1 teaspoon vanilla extract
3 cups rolled oats
¾ cup flour
½ teaspoon baking soda
Big pinch salt

1. Preheat the oven to 350 degrees. Grease a cookie sheet.

2. In a large mixing bowl, cream together the butter, two sugars, egg, and vanilla.

3. Add the oats, flour, baking soda, and salt. Mix very well.

4. Drop the dough by very rounded teaspoonsful about 2 inches apart onto the cookie sheet.

5. Bake for 10 to 12 minutes, until lightly browned.

6. Cool on a rack.

Variations: For oatmeal-raisin, oatmeal-nut, oatmeal-coconut, oatmeal–chocolate chip, or some combination of the preceding, add about 1 cup of the additional ingredient after the dough is mixed.

Oatmeal Peanut Butter Bars

This is for kids—of all ages, as they say. It's more candy than cookie and more nutritious than most of either.

Makes 24 bars

2¼ cups old-fashioned or quick oats
¾ cup peanut butter, smooth or
    chunky
⅓ cup water
½ cup honey
½ cup nonfat dry milk
½ cup raisins, plumped in hot water
    if not fresh

1. Spread the oats on a baking sheet and bake in a preheated 350-degree oven for 20 to 25 minutes, turning and tossing twice with a broad spatula. Oats should be golden brown, a little darker at the edges.

2. Meanwhile, in a small saucepan, combine the peanut butter, water, honey, and dry milk. Stir over medium heat until mixture is smooth and comes to a full rolling boil.

3. Stir in the oats and raisins (well-drained, if plumped).

4. Press the mixture evenly into an 8-inch-square baking pan. Chill until firm, then cut into bars 1 inch wide and 3 inches long (three sections across one side of the pan, eight across the other). Keep refrigerated, but don't serve deep chilled.

5. Alternately, let the mixture cool enough to handle, then roll into balls. Warning: These are delicious eaten still warm, as you roll them.

Microwave Method: The oats must be toasted in a conventional oven, but the remaining ingredients (except raisins) can be combined in a 2-cup measuring cup or bowl. Mix well, then cover with plastic wrap. Microwave on HIGH about 3 minutes, stirring after 1 minute, until mixture comes to a full rolling boil.

Variation: If this is to be a strictly adult candy, substitute bourbon or Scotch whisky, or Cognac or other brandy for the water.

Microwave Flapjacks

I first encountered these candylike cookies in a tearoom in Southampton, England. Little did I know, they are a popular, very old-fashioned sweet. I asked for the recipe. The tearoom waitress looked at me as if I were mad. "They're nothing special. You can get a recipe in any cookbook," she said. Since I had read plenty of English cookbooks and never noticed flapjacks, I insisted I wanted that particular recipe. She then produced a cookbook from the English dairy council, or some such agency, and I copied the recipe on a paper napkin. As these things go, once you are aware of something—a word, a dish—it comes to your attention all the time. I've yet to be served flapjacks again at tea, but I have seen recipes in every English cookbook I've looked at since. This particular recipe is adapted from a baking book published by McVitie's, the English biscuit company.

Makes about 24 fingers or squares

4 tablespoons butter, cut into small
    pieces
2 tablespoons light brown sugar (or
    half dark brown, half white)
4 tablespoons corn syrup
2 cups rolled oats

1. Combine the butter and sugar in a microwave-safe bowl or pot. Microwave on HIGH for 90 seconds.

2. Add the corn syrup and oats and mix well.

3. Press the mixture into a greased 8-inch-square pan and, with a wet spatula, smooth the top.

4. Microwave on HIGH for 5 minutes.

5. Let rest for 5 minutes.

6. Score the top of the flapjacks into squares or fingers, then allow to cool thoroughly.

7. Cut pieces all the way through and serve. May be stored in a tin.

Honey Flapjacks

These remind me of a candy my maternal grandmother used to make for Passover, *einbelach,* which is matzoh farfel—little bits of matzoh—cooked in honey with ginger. Like she did with its cousin candy, *teiglach,* which is fried or baked dough balls treated the same way and made for Rosh Hashanah, the Jewish New Year, Elsie patted the hot *einbelach* into a thin layer with her bare, wet hands on a board sprinkled with sweet red wine. Then, before it cooled, she sprinkled ground ginger on top. If you love ginger, you might do the same with these.

Makes about 24 fingers or squares

5 tablespoons butter
6 tablespoons light brown sugar (or
    half dark brown, half white)
2 tablespoons honey
2 cups rolled oats
1/4 teaspoon ground ginger

1. Preheat the oven to 350 degrees. Grease an 8-inch-square pan.

2. In a saucepan, melt the butter over medium heat, then stir in the

sugar and honey until mixture is smooth.

3. Add the oats and ground ginger. Mix well.

4. Press the mixture into the pan and, with a wet spatula, smooth the top. Bake for 25 minutes.

5. Score the hot flapjacks into squares or fingers, then allow to cool thoroughly.

6. Cut pieces all the way through and serve. May be stored in a tin.

Olive Oil

Olive oil is an indispensable ingredient in a contemporary kitchen, especially one that assumes to be prepared for all contingencies. Besides its superior nutritional profile and qualities as a cooking oil and salad oil, virgin and extra-virgin olive oils have a longer shelf life than other vegetable oils. If kept away from light, an unopened bottle of olive oil will remain fresh for a minimum of a year, even in a typically overheated American kitchen. If kept in a cool place it will keep longer. Opened bottles can also have a year of shelf life, though 6 to 9 months is more likely.

It is unlikely, however, that such lengthy storage is necessary because olive oil has become a very popular cooking oil. As a mostly monounsaturated fat, it is said—and said over and over again—to reduce cholesterol. In moderation, that is. Olive oil doesn't have medicinal qualities. Fat is fat. Olive oil is simply a better fat than most.

Extra-virgin olive oils—the low acid, full-flavored, usually green or deep golden oil extracted by a first cold pressing—are inappropriate for general cooking, but they are the most desirable when you want the flavor of olive oil—as in salads, some soups, and very often on pasta or in its sauces. Light (and the new extra-light) "virgin" and "pure" olive oils, however, have so little flavor, you can generally use them instead of other light vegetable oils for sautéing and pan-frying.

You can now find olive oils from several countries in the

supermarket. Extra-virgin oils from Tuscany, Umbria, and Liguria in Italy are the most expensive—very expensive—but other green and fruity Italian extra-virgins are available at reasonable prices. More golden, slightly less assertive Spanish virgin and extra-virgin oils are also reasonably priced. Greek olive oils are even less expensive, but they are sometimes too strong for most American tastes. Which oil you use is up to your own budget and tastes. I keep a variety on the shelf, and use the one that seems to suit the dish being prepared. I always think olive oils carry the flavor of their homeland, so I'd use Italian oil for a pasta dish, but Spanish oil if, say, I was making a Spanish potato-and-onion omelet (see page 128).

Bagna Cauda

The name means "hot bath" in Piedmontese Italian dialect. And in the mountainous region where it was created by shepherds over their campfires—and is now served in fondue-type pots in fashionable ski resorts—the dish is prepared by numerous formulas. All, however, contain anchovies and garlic. Some are prepared with only olive oil, some use a combination of oil and butter. Some recipes even have cream. In all cases, the "hot bath" is a dip for raw vegetables. Carrot and celery sticks, crisp iceberg lettuce leaves, slices of firm-cooked potato, and slivers of raw, sweet onion are possibilities from your larder.

At a luncheon given by a Piedmontese family in their apartment in Milan, I learned about another bagna cauda tradition: When you are tired of dipping vegetables and there's a small amount of bagna cauda left in the pot, break eggs into the pot and either let them cook until the yolks are done to taste, or stir the eggs into the hot dip to make scrambled eggs.

With the rustic bread we had and the fruity red wine from their family vineyard, that could have been the whole lunch, but it wasn't. We sipped beef broth before the bagna cauda and ate the boiled beef after.

Use a chafing dish or fondue pot—preferably one of earthenware—if you have one. Otherwise, you'll have to prepare the bagna cauda in a saucepan and serve it in a bowl where it will not remain hot, though not necessarily less good.

Or, instead of serving the mixture as a hot dip, serve it as a hot, or even room-temperature, sauce: Arrange vegetables and hard-boiled eggs on a platter or individual plates, then drizzle on the bagna cauda. In this case, you may want to add a tablespoon or so of wine vinegar, or serve the vegetables with wedges of lemon.

For about 6 people

1 cup olive oil (or combination of
   olive oil and butter equaling 1 cup)
1 tablespoon finely chopped garlic
   (about 3 large cloves)
12 canned or jarred anchovy fillets
   (one 2-ounce can), or 6 whole
   salted anchovies, rinsed and
   filleted

1. In a fondue pot or small saucepan, over medium-low heat, combine the oil and garlic. (If using a combination of oil and butter, melt the butter into the oil first.) Cook gently for 10 minutes. Do not allow the garlic to color.

2. Add the anchovies, increase heat slightly, and stir until the anchovies have melted into the oil.

3. Serve immediately with vegetables for dipping, preferably keeping the mixture warm over a candle or alcohol lamp.

A Fresh Touch: The vegetable array for an authentic bagna cauda almost always includes raw cardoons —a bitter, celery look-alike that is related to artichokes and available in the United States only in late fall and only in Italian and specialty produce markets. Other vegetables you would not be likely to have in your refrigerator crisper are sweet red and green peppers, radishes, broccoli, mushrooms, and artichokes, which, when they are tiny and tender, can be eaten raw, too.

Aglio e Olio

Could 8 million Italians be wrong? This is the most likely contender for most popular pasta dish in Italy. You won't find it in most restaurants, but you will find it in just about every home. It is the ultimate Italian comfort, a national passion. Only the stubbornly helpless can't make "aglio olio." The amount of garlic and oil is, as these things go, a matter of personal preference. Forced to give a formula, I can live with the following, but you can vary these proportions—for instance, fat watchers may want to reduce the amount of oil to as little as two tablespoons, though I personally think less than three is pushing it. The important thing to keep in mind is to cook the garlic slowly and not to let it get dark brown: It'll turn bitter. What you want are tiny, crisped, barely tanned bits of garlic.

Serves 2

1 heaping tablespoon finely chopped
garlic, about 3 medium cloves
½ pound spaghetti
¼ cup olive oil
Hot red pepper flakes or freshly
ground black pepper

1. Bring a large pot of salted water to the boil while you peel and chop the garlic.

2. In a small skillet, combine the garlic and olive oil. Set over low heat and let sizzle gently while the spaghetti cooks. The garlic should become pale brown—the color of toasted almonds.

3. When the spaghetti is done to taste, drain well.

4. In a serving bowl, toss the hot spaghetti with the hot oil and garlic mixture. Season to taste with hot red pepper flakes or black pepper. Toss again.

5. Serve immediately, with or without grated cheese.

Variations: Some people like to cook the hot pepper (perhaps a whole chili) with the garlic: Make sure it doesn't brown either. I've also seen people eat this with a generous squeeze of lemon juice. With a can of whole baby clams (usually 10 ounces) or one of minced clams (usually 6½ ounces) you can turn this into a passable white clam sauce (see page 103).

Olives

One of the many gastronomic advantages I had growing up in an ethnic neighborhood in Brooklyn, New York, is that, at an early age, I was aware that not all olives were bland, black Colossals from California or the tiny pimento-stuffed olives that go in a martini. In fact, Greek Kalamata olives were the only thing that made what we Jews called "Greek salad" Greek—an oil-and-vinegar-dressed cabbage slaw with herring that is part of the Sunday morning lox-etc. ritual breakfast.

And my hospitable Italian neighbors always had big, split green olives on their tables; olives that they bought "raw" in late fall, cracked with a mallet, then soaked for 10 days in daily changes of water before putting them up in brine, sometimes marinating them in oil with hot peppers and garlic.

I knew about black, wrinkled, oil-cured olives, too, because there was an Arab neighborhood nearby and one of the wonders of those stores were (and still are) the barrelfuls of olives lurking under dark liquids.

Nowadays, we can buy those—as well as Niçoise, Gaeta, Picholine, Alfonso, and other imported olives—in jars in the supermarket, and loose (by the pound) in supermarket specialty sections and ethnic and fine-food markets. Unopened jars will keep on a cupboard shelf indefinitely—for several years, at any rate. Once opened, keep jars of brined or oil-cured olives in the refrigerator, still covered with brine if they have any. They still have years of life in them. Oil-cured olives will dry out eventually, but do not need brine or oil protection for long storage. Sometimes, even after short storage periods in the refrigerator, olives will develop a white film. This is salt crystallizing on the surface, not spoilage. A spoiled olive goes soft.

Any olives can also be stored in oil: Transfer them to a clean jar or canister and cover with olive oil, then cover with a cork or lid. A less expensive, light olive oil is fine because its flavor will become enhanced by the olives. As you eat the olives down, use the oil for salad dressing or in any pasta sauce or even plain on macaroni.

Along with nuts, olives of any kind are the ideal finger food to go with an alcoholic drink. They're vital to the Provençal spread called *tapenade* (see pages 188 and 229), are welcome whole or chopped in salads (see pages 89, 90, and 212), in rice or grain pilafs (see pages 64 and 65), to garnish bean dips (see page 243), Yogurt Cheese (see page 261), in omelets, or as the main feature of a pasta sauce (see page 247).

Spaghetti with Black Olives and Orange Peel

This is adapted from *The Renaissance of Italian Cooking* by Lorenza de Medici (Fawcett Columbine, 1989). There are many ways to combine olives and pasta, but the addition of orange peel is a brilliant stroke. Lemon peel adds the right bitter freshness, too.

Serves 2

½ pound spaghetti, linguine, or
  small macaroni
Peel of 1 orange
4 tablespoons olive oil
1 small onion, finely chopped
About 12 black olives, pitted and
  coarsely chopped

1. While the water comes to a boil and the pasta cooks, make the sauce.

2. Cut the orange peel into very thin strips and boil them for 2 minutes. Drain and set aside.

3. In a small saucepan or skillet, heat 2 tablespoons of the olive oil and sauté the onion over medium heat until tender, about 5 minutes.

4. Add the orange peel and olives and stir them into the onion and oil. Remove from heat.

5. Drain the pasta well and, in a serving bowl, toss with the olive mixture and the remaining 2 tablespoons olive oil.

6. Serve immediately, with or without cheese, or with toasted bread crumbs (see page 55).

Tapenade

(Olive Dip, Spread, or Sauce)

There are jarred versions of this available in Greek, Italian, and "gourmet" specialty stores, as well as in some supermarkets. It is indeed some trouble pitting enough olives to make a worthwhile amount of olive paste, but the result is very rewarding, less expensive than commercial products, and will keep in the refrigerator for months, ready when you are to serve with drinks—on crackers or croutons (page 54), as a dip for celery, or, thinned with a little more oil or butter or heavy cream, as a sauce for pasta.

Makes about ½ cup

*½ pound Kalamata, Gaeta, or
oil-cured olives, pitted
3 tablespoons olive oil
1 small clove garlic
¼ teaspoon dried thyme
½ teaspoon dried oregano
1 tablespoon red wine vinegar
2 or 3 teaspoons capers, drained and
rinsed (if salted, rinsed then
soaked in cold water)*

1. Combine all the ingredients in a blender jar and process to a fine paste on low speed. To accomplish this, keep turning the motor off and stirring and tamping the mixture down.

2. Pack into a 1-cup crock, canning jar, or small bowl, cover with plastic wrap, and let stand several hours before serving, if possible. The paste improves with a few days aging. Keep in the refrigerator.

Cocktail Olive Spread

I'm old enough to remember when this cracker spread was served seriously. It was made to go with a martini. Now it is made for that special retro taste—and a delicious laugh.

Makes about ½ cup

*½ cup green pimento-stuffed olives
(one 2-ounce jar)
1 3-ounce package cream cheese
6 to 8 drops Tabasco sauce (or to
taste)
1 teaspoon lemon juice (optional)*

1. In a food processor, chop the olives with three or four short pulses.

2. Add the cream cheese and pulse five or six times, until olives are finely chopped and well amalgamated with the cheese.

3. Scrape into a bowl and blend with the Tabasco and, if desired, the lemon juice.

4. Serve as a spread for crackers (see page 143), or even as a sandwich spread.

A Fresh Touch: Spread on slices of cucumber or dab onto endive leaves.

Onions

Real estate agents advise baking something with vanilla when prospective buyers come looking, but it's the aroma of onions cooking that would sell me on a house. It's that smell that often eggs me on to make dinner for myself when I need encouragement. Come home from work, put a chopped or sliced onion to sauté in a little butter or olive oil, and, even without an idea in your head about where to go from there, see if you're not inspired to cook up a bowl of something.

"Sauté an onion . . ." It's the first step in so many recipes. Fortunately, onions are easy to keep on hand. Stored at cool room temperature, preferably in a basket that allows air circulation, onions, and their first cousins, shallots—which have a sweeter flavor and a garlic undertone —should keep perfectly for a couple of months.

Multipurpose, brown-skinned Globe onions, the most piquant of onions, are sold mostly in net bags that make individual selection impossible. Still, make sure the brown skins are shiny and crisp, and squeeze several onions to see if they are hard. Soft or spongy spots indicate deterioration, which in storage will spread quickly from onion to onion. And check for sizes. Medium onions, generally defined as about three to a pound, are the ones most commonly called for in recipes in this book (and elsewhere), though a couple of large and several small onions are always handy, too. A black, powdery film on onions, often visible even through the papery skin, is a fungus that eventually causes deterioration. If you discover some under the skin of onions when you get them home, use these first, wiping off the black powder with a damp paper towel. As an onion sprouts it gets softer, but unless the onion has nearly collapsed, sprouted onions are often usable, too, and the green sprout itself can be a replacement for scallion greens, either cooked or as an herb garnish.

Sweet onions—the red or Italian onion, Bermuda or Spanish onion, not to mention the spring- and summer-season Vidalia, Walla Walla, and Maui—have a shorter shelf life than the common Globe onion. Like other onions, they can be refrigerated for longer keeping, but all onions must be kept isolated in a crisper drawer or they will perfume the rest of the contents of the refrigerator.

French Onion Soup

The secret to superb onion soup is superb beef stock, which is not what comes out of cans or from reconstituted bouillon cubes. Still, with plenty of onions and a touch of brandy or sherry as a distraction, this is an extremely fine onion soup. I give ingredients proportions for a large amount because I don't think it pays to make a little onion soup; it can be kept in the refrigerator for a week and freezes perfectly. The time-consuming part is cooking the onions and 2 or 3 cups of onions take just as long as 5 or 6. If you have only a few onions, however, go right ahead and halve this recipe. With my hat tipped to Julia Child for the basis of this recipe, this is the best onion soup I know.

Serves 6 to 8

3 tablespoons butter
1 tablespoon vegetable oil
5 to 6 cups thinly sliced onions (5
    medium onions, about 1½ pounds)
½ teaspoon sugar

3 tablespoons flour
Three 13¾-ounce cans beef broth
3 tablespoons dry sherry or brandy
Grated Parmesan cheese, or slices of
    toasted French or Italian bread
    topped with melted cheese

1. In a minimum 4-quart pot, melt the butter with the oil over medium heat.

2. Add the onions and toss well to coat them all with fat. Reduce heat to low, cover pot, and let cook for 15 minutes, until onions are quite wilted. There is no need to stir.

3. Uncover pot, increase heat to medium, and stir in the sugar. Let cook, stirring frequently, for about 40 minutes, until onions are deep brown.

4. Stir in flour and continue to cook until the flour turns the color of the onions, about 5 minutes.

5. Stir in the broth and 1 broth can full of water. Bring to a simmer and let simmer at least 20 minutes.

6. Stir in the sherry or brandy and simmer 5 minutes longer.

7. Serve very hot with grated Parmesan on the side. Or, on a baking sheet, toast 1-inch-thick slices cut from a long loaf, top with grated cheese, return to oven until the cheese melts, and put a slice of bread in each bowl.

Curried Onion Soup with Rice

This is a very easy recipe, but one for when you have a little time and want the smells of home cooking to pervade the kitchen—say a rainy Saturday afternoon. It's wonderful before lamb chops, or, in emergencies, can be followed by Scrambled Eggs (see page 126) and a baked potato (see page 210), Welsh Rabbit (see page 84); a can of sardines or tuna, sliced onion, and some bread; or Bulgur and Tuna Salad (see page 65).

Serves 2 or 3

¼ cup raw white rice
1 cup water
3 tablespoons butter
3 medium onions (about 1 pound),
    thinly sliced
2 teaspoons curry powder
⅛ teaspoon cayenne
One 13¾-ounce can chicken broth
    plus 1 cup water, or 2 chicken
    bouillon cubes dissolved in 2½
    cups water

½ cup yogurt, buttermilk, or soured
   milk
Salt
Optional garnish: Cracked or
   powdered coriander seeds

1. In a small saucepan, boil the rice in 1 cup water for 5 minutes. Drain and set aside.

2. In a 2- to 3-quart saucepan, melt the butter over medium heat and sauté the onions with the curry powder and cayenne for 2 to 3 minutes.

3. Reduce heat to low. Add the drained rice, cover, and let cook gently, stirring occasionally, until onions are very soft and rice has disintegrated, about 1½ hours.

4. Stir in the chicken broth and simmer, covered, for 15 minutes. (May be prepared ahead to this point.)

5. Just before serving, heat to just below a simmer, then stir in yogurt, buttermilk, or soured milk. Heat through to serving temperature without returning to a boil.

6. Serve very hot, garnished, if desired, with a pinch of coriander seed.

Roasted Onion Salad

If you want to turn a plain roasted onion into something slightly more elaborate, this is the way to go.

Serves 2

2 medium onions (red, white, or
   yellow)
2 tablespoons olive oil
2 tablespoons good-flavored vinegar
   (red wine, tarragon white wine,
   sherry, cider, malt, or Balsamic)
½ teaspoon salt
Freshly ground pepper

1. Roast the onions, unpeeled, in a 425-degree oven for about 1 hour. (There's no need to preheat the oven.)

2. Let them cool enough to handle, then peel and cut each onion into 6 or 8 wedges.

3. In a bowl, toss the onions with the remaining ingredients.

4. Serve warm.

Other recipes featuring onions

Orange and Onion Salad (see page 195)
Pissaladière (see page 134)
Eggs and Onions Salad (see page 127)

Oranges

It appears that oranges originated in China. It's known that they weren't planted in the New World until Columbus brought them here in 1493. They are now among the top three fruits consumed in the United States, just after bananas and about neck and neck with apples.

Oranges are available all year, but most abundant and well-priced during the winter months, just when you need their vitamin C the most to stave off colds. Nearly all the oranges sold in our supermarkets are grown in Florida and California, with Florida leading in the thin-skinned juice varieties, California in the thicker-skinned, more easily segmented eating varieties. Look for oranges that feel heavy for their size—indicating they are full of juice —and that have bright, relatively fine-textured skins. Oranges with soft spots should be avoided, but minor blemishes or brown mottling do not usually indicate deterioration. Areas of green on the skin can be ignored, too. Fully ripe fruit is often green and during certain times of the year mature fruit can undergo a process called "regreening."

Oranges can be kept at room temperature for at least 7 to 10 days, often as long as 2 weeks, but always with a loss of vitamin C. If kept in the refrigerator, however, they retain the vitamin longer and often remain viable for as long as 6 weeks to 2 months.

Macaroni with Oranges, Nuts, and Black Pepper

When she first saw a recipe for pasta with oranges on the back of a domestic pasta box, Anna Teresa Callen, the Italian cooking authority, called the combination a "pasta folly." I'm sure this recipe will correct her opinion. I saw the same box but thought the only thing wrong with the chef-created recipe was that it was too complicated. Here's my more primitive and I think delicious rendition.

Serves 2

½ pound ziti or penne, fusilli, wheels, or radiators
3 or 4 tablespoons butter
1 small onion, finely chopped (about ½ cup), or ⅓ cup finely chopped shallots
3 or 4 tablespoons coarsely chopped walnuts or pecans
2 eating oranges, peeled and divided into segments, each segment cut into 2 or 3 pieces (work over a bowl to catch any juice that may drip as you work)
1 teaspoon (or more) freshly ground coarse black pepper
Grated Parmesan cheese

1. Make the sauce while water comes to a boil and the macaroni cooks. In a medium skillet, heat the butter over medium-high heat and sauté onions until tender, about 5 minutes.

2. Add the nuts and continue to sauté 3 or 4 more minutes.

3. Add the orange segments and the pepper. Toss and stir until the oranges are heated through and exude some juice, about 2 minutes.

4. Toss with the drained macaroni.

5. Serve immediately with cheese on the side: the cheese really makes the dish.

Orange and Onion Salad

Besides that it's good to eat, this is a vitamin C powerhouse and a natural winter salad. On those days when you're stuffing yourself with C tablets, supplement them with this.

Serves 1

½ medium onion, preferably red
1 orange
⅛ to ¼ teaspoon salt
1 tablespoon olive oil
Freshly ground black pepper
2 to 4 black or purple olives

1. Cut the onion ¼-inch thick for an arranged salad, into chunks or half-moon slices for a tossed salad. If the onion is not a red one, or another kind of sweet onion, soak the onion in cold water for 20 minutes, then drain and pat dry.

2. Peel the orange and trim off the white pith. Cut the orange into ¼-inch slices for an arranged salad, into wedges for a tossed salad.

3. On a plate, either alternate the slices of orange and onion, or toss the orange wedges and onion slices together in a small salad bowl.

4. Sprinkle with salt, drizzle on the olive oil, grind on the pepper. Garnish with olives.

5. If possible, let stand about 30 minutes before eating.

Moroccan Sliced Oranges

The platter you use is important to this dish. If you serve sliced oranges on a plain plate, they'll be a plain dessert. If you arrange them in careful concentric circles on a pretty plate, and sieve on the sugar and cinnamon oh so creatively, you'll have a dramatic dessert. It's amazing how satisfying oranges can be when treated this way. If you happen to have orange flower water, as any Moroccan household would, sprinkle a few drops on the oranges before sweetening them with the sugar.

Oranges
Confectioners' sugar
Cinnamon

1. Peel oranges carefully, removing all the white pith.

2. Cut into ⅓-inch slices and arrange on a platter.

3. Using a fine sieve, sprinkle the oranges with confectioners' sugar.

4. Sprinkle on cinnamon lightly.

5. Serve immediately.

Mixed Fruit Salad

There are three fresh fruits in this salad, but this recipe is given here because oranges are the essential ingredient. You can make a two-fruit salad with oranges and bananas, or with oranges and apples, but without the oranges you don't get the juice and acid needed to marry two fruits into a salad. Of course, you can add more fruits to this recipe if you have them, or you can vary the salad with raisins or diced dried apricots, prunes, or figs.

Serves 2

3 oranges (preferably juice variety)
1 banana
1 apple
1 tablespoon sugar (optional)
1 or 2 tablespoons orange liqueur
    (optional)

1. Cut 2 of the oranges in half, pit them, then squeeze out the juice.

2. In a bowl, combine the orange juice, the remaining orange—peeled, pitted, and cut into segments—the banana—peeled and sliced—and the apple—peeled or not, cored, and cut into cubes. Toss and add sugar and/ or liqueur, if desired.

3. If possible, chill or let stand at room temperature at least 30 minutes before serving.

Other recipes with oranges

Carrot Ribbons with Orange Glaze (see page 76)
Carrot and Orange Soup (see page 75)

Pasta and Noodles

My feeling is, you have a box of spaghetti, you have dinner. You have nothing to worry about. You can feed anyone. Let a golden lump of butter melt over it and it's heaven. Pour on peppery, green olive oil and it's a plate to please the most critical connoisseur. A little grated cheese helps. A clove of garlic could come in handy. A sprinkle of hot pepper, a squeeze of lemon, some melted anchovies, a few chopped olives . . . you don't necessarily have to do much cooking to dress a bowl of spaghetti.

Pasta is the generic word for all Italian noodle products, both those made with eggs—fettuccine and company—and often called "homemade pasta," and those made of only semolina (the flour of hard durum wheat) and water—spaghetti and macaroni. The former are generally bought moist and flexible, though egg pasta can be dried. The latter should be made in a factory and is always purchased dried. If a restaurant or store advertises "homemade" or "fresh" spaghetti or macaroni, be suspicious. It is almost certainly gummy or soggy pasta, not firm and chewy like the best factory-made products.

The words "homemade" and "fresh" are no guarantee that egg pasta will be good egg pasta either. Egg pasta, no matter what shape, size, type, or flavor, should be thin and delicate, almost transparent before it is cooked. Commercially made "fresh pasta," which is what it is accurately called, is rarely thus. Shop around, wait to have it in a restaurant that does it well, or do without. If you do find a good source of egg pasta, even if it is not near home, buy as much as you can stock. After it is air-dried it will keep in a plastic bag, at room temperature, for at least a year. It takes slightly longer to cook than fresh "fresh pasta," but it is superior to "fresh pasta" that has been frozen.

Unfortunately, fresh pasta—that is egg pasta—has lately been marketed as superior to the eggless, factory-made dried macaroni products available in every super-market. It simply isn't so.

I think there are two firm rules about cooking pasta: Use at least 3 quarts of water for ½ pound of pasta, 5 quarts for 1 pound. And, though I know salt is a touchy subject these days, I use at least 1 heaping tablespoon of salt for every 3 quarts of water. I can eliminate salt from a sauce, but spaghetti and macaroni don't taste right without salt in the water.

There is no need to add oil to the water. You're just wasting oil. And Italian pasta should not be rinsed un-less you are precooking lasagna noodles or making an American-style pasta salad.

As soon as you add the pasta to the boiling water, stir it, then cover the pot to bring the water back to the boil quickly. As soon as the water is boiling hard again, stir and separate the pasta with a kitchen fork or wooden spoon. Most brands of regular spaghetti and smaller mac-aroni cook in 8 to 10 minutes, thin spaghetti requires less time, and big or heavy macaroni requires slightly more. Dried pasta that has been sitting on the shelf in an open box may require a minute or so more cooking time. The only way to know for sure if the pasta is done to your taste, to your bite, *al dente,* is to try a piece or strand.

Pasta will last a very long time—years—on the shelf,

but it doesn't last forever. Very old pasta will be so dry that even when it boils to an edible texture it becomes brittle and has a dead flavor—not the nutty grain flavor it should.

Most of the pasta we now make a regular part of our diet is Italian-style if not actually Italian-made. Domestic brands have improved in recent years and most are acceptable, though only a few compare favorably to pasta imported from Italy. First-quality Italian pasta not only tastes nuttier, but doesn't quickly go from underdone to overdone, as some domestic brands do. There is also inexpensive Italian-named pasta on the market that is made in Canada and Turkey. The Canadian pasta I've tried is the equal of most Italian pasta. The Turkish macaroni tastes good, but the spaghetti strands are short, and the macaroni shapes are unevenly extruded or cut.

There are Italian-style pasta recipes throughout this book. Look under the ingredient you have on hand. It's likely there's a pasta recipe featuring it.

Chow Mein

Dried Chinese egg noodles are now available in many supermarkets, usually in 12-ounce cellophane bags. Most bags contain three 4-ounce sheets of noodles curlicued over themselves, and each sheet cooks up to about 2 cups of noodles. Use about 3 unsalted quarts of water to cook the whole 12 ounces. They cook quickly, in about 3 minutes, but need constant attention: To prevent them from sticking together, jiggle and separate the noodles continually with a kitchen fork or chopstick. They are very starchy—a foam will form on the surface of the water—and unlike Italian pasta, should be rinsed immediately with cold water. Chinese noodles are served cold or reheated in a sauce, which is why many cookbooks and noodle packages instruct us to toss them with a little oil to prevent sticking before they meet their final destination. Cooked noodles will keep in the refrigerator, in a bowl covered with plastic, for about a week. These are the ideal noodles for a Szechuan peanut sauce (see page 203) or Oriental Noodle Soups (see page 61).

Rice Flour Noodles

Sometimes called "rice sticks," "long rice noodles," or Chinese vermicelli, rice noodles are easy to use in soups or as a replacement for a bed of boiled rice. I see mainly 7-ounce cellophane packages in better supermarkets, and that amount should be cooked in about 3 quarts of unsalted water for about 3 minutes. Or soak dried rice noodles in very hot tap water for 10 minutes before adding to a soup for a final 1 or 2 minutes of cooking. (See Oriental Noodle Soups, page 61). Dressed with a mixture of soy sauce and hot pepper, or soy sauce and Chinese mustard, they are a pleasant, simple snack.

Cellophane Noodles

Also called "transparent noodles," "bean thread," and "mung bean sticks," though they are often made from potato starch and green pea starch, they must be soaked in hot water for 10 minutes before being added to a soup or stir-fry dish, where they will need a final cooking of about 3 minutes. After they are soaked, cellophane noodles, which are sold dry in bags of 3 to 4 ounces, are often cut with scissors into small lengths because they are so slippery they are difficult to eat at their full length. Use them for Oriental Noodle Soups (see page 61).

Peanut Butter

Peanut butter is so beloved by Americans that a meal for some of us is simply sticking our finger in the peanut butter jar and licking it off. Or maybe you're a peanut butter and jelly on crackers snacker. Be it chunky, smooth, hydrogenated, sweetened, or natural, 85 percent of American households always have a jar of peanut butter on hand, according to the Peanut Advisory Board, which also calculates that in 1990—the one hundredth anniversary of peanut butter's creation by an unknown St. Louis physician—we ate 800 million pounds of peanut butter, enough to make 10 billion peanut butter and jelly sandwiches, or about 3.3 pounds of peanut butter per person.

With consumption figures like those it seems beside the point that an unopened jar of supermarket peanut butter will keep for 2 to 4 years at temperatures under 70 degrees, and once opened it easily has another 6 months to 1 year of life—longer if kept in the refrigerator. I've used, and enjoyed, opened peanut butter as long as 2 years after the label's expiration date, but that was when peanut butter always came in glass jars. In plastic jars, it turns rancid faster.

So-called old-fashioned or natural peanut butters, a growing segment of the peanut butter market, tend to separate, and the oil that rises to the top turns rancid rapidly, so if the peanut butter is not to be consumed quickly, keep it refrigerated and stir it occasionally.

Noodles with Spicy Peanut Butter Sauce

I break with a couple of Chinese traditions here: I use peanut butter instead of sesame paste, though I am certain many restaurants do, too. And I prefer the sauce on warm noodles rather than cold.

For 8 to 12 ounces Chinese noodles or spaghetti, serves 2 or 3

⅓ cup peanut butter
2 tablespoons vegetable oil
2 tablespoons soy sauce
½ teaspoon cayenne (or more to taste)
½ teaspoon sugar
1 tablespoon rice vinegar, distilled white vinegar, or white wine vinegar
1 large clove garlic, mashed or smashed and finely chopped (1 teaspoon)
8 to 12 ounces Chinese noodles or spaghetti, cooked

1. In a mixing bowl, combine all the ingredients except noodles. With a rubber spatula or a wooden spoon, work together until creamy and smooth.

2. If feasible, let stand for at least 4 hours, but don't worry if you can't.

3. Use to dress 8 to 12 ounces of cooked Chinese noodles or spaghetti, drained well.

Note: If serving noodles cold or at room temperature, toss while hot with 2 tablespoons vegetable oil.

Variations: Add ½ teaspoon very finely chopped gingerroot or crystallized ginger—its sweetness adds interesting contrast to the basically salty-spicy sauce. Garnish with grated or slivered carrots.

Substitutions: Use peanut oil instead of vegetable oil, or, even better, use toasted (Oriental) sesame oil. If you have hot chili oil, use some of it instead of the bland oil. If you have Szechuan peppercorns, use them instead of cayenne. Use egg noodles instead of Chinese noodles or spaghetti.

A Fresh Touch: Add finely chopped fresh scallion whites to sauce. Use chopped scallion greens as a garnish, top each serving with thin strips of peeled cucumber, and/or top each serving with chopped fresh coriander.

Peanut Butter Soup

There are two big myths about peanuts and peanut butter: (1) that the peanut comes from Africa and (2) that George Washington Carver invented peanut butter. Peanuts are native to South America and were introduced to Africa by the Spanish, and though the good Dr. Carver created more than 300 uses for peanuts, peanut butter wasn't one of them. The idea of using peanuts to flavor and thicken soup, however, may indeed be from Africa, where, it was reported by a missionary in the Congo in 1682, they extracted a "milk . . . like to that drawn from almonds." I believe this recipe is from Virginia, a state famous for ham made from peanut-fed hogs.

Serves 4

3 tablespoons butter or vegetable oil
1 small onion, finely chopped
1 small rib celery, finely chopped
3 tablespoons flour
1 quart chicken broth or bouillon
1 cup smooth peanut butter
1 cup milk
¼ teaspoon cayenne (or less, to taste)

1. In a 3-quart saucepan, melt the butter or heat the oil over medium-low heat and sauté onion and celery until soft but not browned, about 15 minutes.

2. Blend in the flour and continue to cook over medium heat about 5 minutes, or until flour is golden. Remove from heat and allow bubbling to subside.

3. Add the broth, stirring constantly with a wooden spoon or wire whisk. Place over high heat and, stirring constantly, bring to a boil. Lower heat and simmer gently for about a minute.

4. Stir in the peanut butter until completely dissolved. (At this point, if you want a very smooth texture, puree the soup in a food mill, blender, or food processor. Personally, I like the texture the bits of vegetable add.)

5. Stir in the milk, season with cayenne. Reheat to serving temperature. (May be made ahead.)

6. Serve very hot.

Substitution: Instead of onion, a couple cloves of minced garlic add good flavor.

A Fresh Touch: A sprinkling of finely chopped fresh coriander will be to some tastes. Heavy cream and half-and-half, rather than milk, makes an even richer soup.

Classic Crisp Peanut Butter Cookies

This is the peanut butter cookie I grew up with, a recipe that appeared on the Skippy peanut butter label in the early 1950s. It is still one of my favorite cookies, probably because other than some memorably green butter cookies we once pressed out on a rainy afternoon, these are the only cookies I ever remember my mother making. It's not that I had a cookie-deprived childhood, only that we had an excellent bakery right around the corner.

Makes about 5 dozen

2½ cups flour
1 teaspoon baking powder
1 teaspoon baking soda
1 teaspoon salt
1 cup butter or margarine
1 cup creamy or chunky peanut
  butter
1 cup sugar
1 cup firmly packed brown sugar
2 eggs, beaten
1 teaspoon vanilla extract

1. Preheat the oven to 375 degrees.

2. In a mixing bowl, stir together the flour, baking powder, baking soda, and salt.

3. In a large mixing bowl, using an electric mixer, beat together the butter or margarine and the peanut butter until well blended and smooth.

4. Beat in both the sugars until well blended.

5. Beat in the eggs and vanilla.

6. Add the flour mixture and beat until well blended.

7. Shape the dough into 1-inch balls and, as you roll them, place them on an ungreased cookie sheet about 2 inches apart. Flatten each ball with a fork, making a crosshatch pattern on the dough.

8. Bake for about 12 minutes, or until lightly browned.

9. Remove with a spatula and cool thoroughly on a wire rack. As good as the cookies are warm, they are even better (and gain crispness) when cooled. And they continue to improve for a few days. Store them in a tin.

Other recipes featuring peanut butter

Oatmeal Peanut Butter Bars (see page 178)

Peas *(Frozen)*

Fresh peas rarely please me. Like corn, as soon as they are picked their sugars start turning into starch. By the time they get to market they are inferior to the perfectly good frozen peas, the truly sweet peas, that are available all year in the supermarket.

Buying frozen peas can be almost as tricky as buying fresh, however. If thawed and refrozen they lose much of their flavor and crisp-skin texture. Look for boxes in which the peas still feel separate. Shake the box. If the peas rattle, chances are they remained frozen during their entire trip from processing plant to supermarket frozen food case. If peas have fused together into a frozen block, they probably defrosted at some point. Don't let this happen on the way home from the store, either. Make the frozen foods section your last stop at the supermarket before the checkout counter.

Unopened, a box or bag of peas should remain delicious for 6 months. If you use only a portion of a package for a recipe, replace the remainder in the freezer immediately, preferably wrapped in a tightly closed plastic bag to prevent the cold air from causing freezer burn, or dehydration.

Peas and Rice and Cheddar Cheese

If peas give you solace you will love this concoction. It can be fried or not; each way has its appeal. Tossed together and eaten as is, the mixture is creamy. And though I have found it impossible to get a neat rice pancake with a uniform crust (even with the addition of eggs), attempting to fry the rice into a pan-sized round creates lots of crusty bits I find irresistible.

Serves 1 or 2

2 cups hot cooked white rice
1½ cups (4 ounces) shredded or
   grated cheddar cheese
1 cup (one-half 10-ounce box) frozen
   green peas, cooked
Freshly ground pepper
2 tablespoons butter (optional)

1. For a creamy mixture, simply mix together the rice, cheese, and peas, season with salt and pepper, and eat.

2. For a mixture with crisped pieces, mix the ingredients together, then turn into a medium skillet with the butter sizzling over medium heat. With a spatula, flatten the rice into a pancake and let cook about 8 minutes, until the bottom is lightly browned. Turn the pancake in as large pieces as you can (it will not hold together) and continue cooking until there are enough crusty pieces to suit you. Eat immediately.

Pasta and Peas

Peas, cream, and Parmesan cheese are a classic topping for fresh egg pasta. A medium white sauce stands in very well for the cream, however, and spaghetti or macaroni is just as satisfying as fettuccine.

Serves 2

½ pound spaghetti, linguine, or
   macaroni
2 tablespoons butter
1 small onion, finely chopped
2 tablespoons flour
1¼ cups milk
Salt and freshly ground black pepper
⅛ teaspoon freshly grated nutmeg
2 cups (one 10-ounce box) frozen peas
½ cup grated Parmesan cheese

1. Make the sauce while bringing the pasta water to a boil and cooking the pasta.

2. In a small saucepan, over medium heat, heat the butter and sauté the onion until tender, about 5 minutes.

3. Blend in the flour and cook 2 or 3 minutes more, without coloring the flour.

4. Remove from heat and when the sizzling subsides, stir in the milk.

5. Return to heat and, stirring constantly, bring to a simmer. Season with salt, pepper, and nutmeg, then simmer gently 3 to 5 minutes.

6. Add the peas and return to a simmer. Cook until peas are just done, another 2 or 3 minutes.

7. Drain the pasta, toss in a bowl with the sauce and half the Parmesan cheese.

8. Serve immediately, sprinkling each portion with the remaining cheese.

Variation: Garnish with crumbled, crisp-cooked bacon.

A Fresh Touch: Diced ham or prosciutto, added with the peas, is always welcome.

Other recipes featuring peas

Thick Rice Soup (see page 222)
Risotto with peas (see pages 224–225)
Tuna, No Surprises (see page 255)

Potatoes

Potatoes should be smooth, relatively blemish-free, and rock hard when you buy them, but it is unlikely you have the storage conditions to keep them that way for long. For a vegetable (a tuber) that we consider pretty sturdy, potatoes have a relatively short usable life given the temperatures in most contemporary kitchens and cupboards. Unless kept in a dark, 45- to 50-degree spot, after 2 weeks or so they become soft or begin to sprout, an indication that they should be cooked as soon as possible. Keeping them in the crisper of the refrigerator gives them a longer lifespan, but the cold turns the potato's starch to sugar and they don't taste right unless allowed to sit several days at room temperature so the sugars can convert back.

After being disparaged for many affluent postwar years —attributable, I think, to the awfulness of dried, powdered, flaked, and frozen potatoes, plus the potato's erroneous reputation as a fattening food and not unwarranted reputation as poor man's food—potatoes are enjoying a renaissance. Growers have developed new varieties, and old varieties have been improved. Restaurants are again serving real, not instant, mashed potatoes, while the baked potato has been recognized as a nutritious, no-fat food for the weight- and cholesterol-conscious.

Baked Potatoes

Asked to define *gourmet,* James Beard answered, "A perfectly baked potato," by which he did not mean a microwaved potato. I've tried many different methods but have yet to make a potato cooked in a microwave oven taste as fine or be as fluffy as a potato baked in the dry heat of a conventional oven. And even if a microwaved potato doesn't turn out sodden—which it won't if you use a low-moisture, Idaho russet baking potato—the skin will not become crisp. It's like eating the dough of the bread without the crust.

Still, I microwave potatoes. A medium potato—one that is 7 or 8 ounces—takes about 6 minutes in the microwave, then about 2 minutes resting time, and it is certainly no less a good potato than if it were boiled or steamed. Baked by the conventional method, in, say, a 400-degree oven, that same potato will take 30 minutes or more. That time savings often seems vital when I walk into my kitchen hungry at the end of the day.

A really big potato, such as a 12-ounce, 15-minutes-in-the-microwave size, can easily be a whole meal with the right topping. I used to think caviar and sour cream (or crème fraîche) was the ultimate, until I heard that chef Daniel Boulud at Le Cirque was serving big bakers with butter and white truffles. They're not listed on the menu, but regulars know about the dish and, he confides, when someone orders one and he's not prepared, he even cooks the potato in the microwave.

To bake a potato in a conventional oven, scrub the potato (or potatoes) and dry it. Prick it in several places with the point of a sharp knife or fork. (Follow this procedure for microwaving, too.) Place it right on the rack in a cold or preheated oven set at from 375 to 425 degrees. Depending on size and temperature, the potato will take from 30 minutes to 1 hour to become soft at the center. Test it with a fork.

To serve the potato, microwaved or conventionally baked, hold it in a hand protected with a pot holder or oven mitt, and slit it open by poking a fork into it lengthwise and crosswise to form a cross. Then squeeze the potato to fluff out the flesh. Serve very hot.

Variations: Suggested potato toppings other than butter and sour cream: grated cheese of any kind, sautéed onions, cream cheese and chutney, Tuna, No Surprises (see page 255), Chili Beans (see page 39).

Garlic Mashed Potatoes

A couple of years ago a friend requested I make "Julia Child's garlic mashed potatoes" for his birthday dinner. Dutifully, I looked up the recipe, which I also remembered fondly and, way back when, had made many times. However, when I saw the instructions in *Mastering the Art of French Cooking,* Volume 1 (Knopf, 1966) I was appalled. Julia not only has us making a flour-thickened, milk-based white sauce to beat into the potatoes (starch on starch?), but instructs us to use a minimum of ¼ pound of butter plus 3 to 4 tablespoons of heavy cream—for a mere 2½ pounds of potatoes! I was prepared to indulge my friend, but I was not prepared for a coronary crisis. The following is, therefore, an update on Julia.

Serves 4 or 5

2 heads garlic, about 30 cloves
1 cup milk
2½ pounds potatoes (preferably russets), peeled and quartered
3 tablespoons butter
Salt and freshly ground pepper

1. Separate the garlic cloves and drop into a saucepan of boiling water. Boil 2 minutes. Drain, then peel.

2. In the same saucepan, combine the garlic cloves and the milk. Simmer very gently for 20 minutes, stirring frequently so that the milk does not scorch.

3. When the garlic is very soft, pour the milk and garlic into a blender or food processor and process to a smooth puree. (Can be made ahead. Reheat before adding to potatoes.)

4. Boil the potatoes until tender, then drain immediately.

5. Put the potatoes through a ricer, letting them fall back into the saucepan.

6. Place saucepan over low heat, then, with a wooden spoon, beat in the garlic milk, then the butter, salt, and pepper.

7. Serve very hot. (This can be kept hot for 30 minutes over very low heat, beating occasionally.)

Potato Soup

This is a very basic soup, the potato equivalent of spaghetti with oil and garlic. The liquid is merely water and the flavor of the soup depends entirely on the taste and quality of the potatoes and olive oil. Don't bother with this unless you have olive oil with a lot of flavor, though if you happen to have walnut or almond oil, they can carry the soup, too. You can, of course, use butter instead of oil, as most potato soup recipes do. But I think it's comforting to know that when there's no butter around, reliable, long-lived olive oil can be its equal, if not better.

Serves 2 or 3

3 tablespoons olive oil
1 medium onion, coarsely chopped
3 medium potatoes (about 1 pound),
    peeled and cut in rough ½-inch
    dice
2 cups water
¾ teaspoon salt

1. In a medium saucepan, combine the oil and onion and cook over medium heat until the onion is tender, about 6 minutes.

2. Add the potatoes and stir well to coat potatoes with the oil. Cook, stir-ring, about 3 minutes, until potatoes begin to sizzle.

3. Add the water and salt. Cover and bring to a simmer. Adjust heat and simmer briskly for about 10 minutes, until potatoes are very tender.

4. With a potato masher or the back of a wooden spoon, mash at least half of the potatoes, leaving the mixture lumpy and soupy.

5. Simmer another 1 or 2 minutes and serve very hot.

Potato Salad Becomes a Greek Meal

There are two ways to serve this: You can toss all the ingredients together and have an elaborate potato salad, but still really just potato salad. Or, for when you want to make almost nothing appear to be a little something, you can serve the dressed potatoes as one element and all the other ingredients separately on the side, to be added by each eater to taste.

Serves 2 or 3

*2 pounds all-purpose or boiling
    potatoes
2 medium onions, coarsely chopped
¼ cup olive oil
2 to 3 tablespoons wine vinegar
½ teaspoon dried oregano
¾ teaspoon salt
¼ teaspoon freshly ground pepper*

Suggested additions

*2 to 3 tablespoons capers
¼ to ⅓ cup pitted and sliced or
    chopped green Spanish, purple
    Greek, or oil-cured olives
6 to 12 anchovy fillets, cut into pieces,
    if desired
One or two 6½-ounce cans tuna,
    flaked into large pieces
About 4 ounces crumbled feta cheese
    (about ⅔ cup)*

1. Peel and boil the potatoes, or boil and peel the potatoes. It doesn't really matter.

2. Meanwhile, in a large skillet, over medium-high heat, sauté the onions in the oil until they are well browned, about 20 minutes.

3. When the potatoes are just tender, drain well. While still hot, cut into 1-inch chunks.

4. In a mixing bowl, combine the potatoes with the sautéed onions and all the oil in the skillet. Use a rubber spatula to get all the oil. With two spoons, gently toss to mix well.

5. Sprinkle on the vinegar, oregano, salt, and pepper. Toss again, trying not to break the potatoes too much.

6. Either toss in some or all of the suggested additions, or arrange potato salad on a platter and surround with piles of the different garnishes. Or serve the potato salad in a bowl and the garnishes in separate small bowls. An old-fashioned lazy susan is perfect for this and adds to the salad's amusement value—if amusement, in addition to nourishment, is what you're after here.

Curried Potatoes and Peas

This is far from an authentic Indian recipe, but it is one good way to fulfill that yen for curry that some of us get occasionally. An Indian cook would hardly take the shortcuts of using curry powder and tomato paste. The butter would be ghee (clarified butter), and, well, the dish would be a lot more complicated to make. This is a great side dish for scrambled eggs, or you might hard-boil some eggs and serve the curried vegetables with wedges or slices of the eggs. It's very colorful.

Serves 3 or 4

3 tablespoons butter or vegetable oil
1 tablespoon finely minced fresh
*   gingerroot (about a 1-inch piece,*
*   peeled)*
2 tablespoons curry powder
¼ teaspoon crushed red pepper
*   flakes, or ⅛ teaspoon cayenne*
2 heaping tablespoons tomato paste
1½ pounds all-purpose potatoes
*   (about 4 medium), peeled and cut*
*   into ½- to ¾-inch sticks*
One 10-ounce package frozen peas
*   (2 cups)*

1. In a 2- to 3-quart saucepan, over medium-high heat, heat the butter or oil. Stir in the ginger, then curry powder and pepper flakes. Let sizzle for 1 minute.

2. Add the tomato paste and 1½ cups of water. Stir well. Bring to a boil and stir again, until smooth. Simmer 1 minute.

3. Add the potatoes, cover, and lower heat to medium. Let simmer for 15 minutes, until potatoes are tender.

4. Add the frozen peas and stir well. Cover and return to a simmer. Cook until peas are crisp-tender, less than 1 minute.

5. Serve immediately or later at room temperature or reheated.

Variations: If you really like the taste of curry, the base sauce—the mixture of ginger, curry, hot pepper, tomato paste, and water—makes a very good sauce for spaghetti or boiled rice: leave out the potatoes, keep or don't keep the peas, and reduce the water to 1 cup. Or use the sauce (again, with or without the peas) to pour on baked potatoes, which you can then further embellish with a dollop of yogurt or sour cream.

A Fresh Touch: Add ¼ cup chopped fresh parsley or 2 tablespoons chopped fresh mint to the curried dish.

Potato Pancakes or Pudding

This potato mixture can be fried into thin, lacy-edged pancakes, the kind called *latkes* in Yiddish; the pancakes that are a Chanukkah treat for Eastern European Jews. Or it can also be poured into a baking dish to make a potato pudding, a *kugel* in Yiddish. The pancakes are generally served with sour cream or applesauce. The pudding stands alone—a masterpiece of Jewish starch cookery.

Serves 4 to 6

1 medium onion, peeled and cut into chunks
3 medium all-purpose or baking potatoes, about 1¼ pounds, peeled, cut into chunks, and kept white in cold water
2 eggs
1 teaspoon salt
¼ teaspoon pepper (preferably white)
3 to 6 tablespoons flour
Vegetable oil for frying
3 tablespoons vegetable oil (optional)

1. The potatoes and onions can be hand-grated, but it is far easier to use a food processor: Put the onion chunks in the work bowl fitted with the metal blade. Pulse on and off until very finely chopped, almost a puree. Scrape into a large mixing bowl.

2. About a potato at a time, process the potatoes with pulses, letting the processor run several seconds at the end, to make the pieces no larger than a match head. Scrape the potatoes into the bowl with the onion, stirring them together each time you add potato. (The acid in the onion helps keep the potatoes white.)

3. Deal in the eggs, salt, pepper, and some flour. The exact amount of flour depends on the moisture of the potatoes. The only way to know for certain if the amount is correct is to test a pancake; it should hold together but fry up with a lacy edge.

4. In a medium or large skillet, heat the oil over medium-high heat. The batter should sizzle when it hits the fat. Use a large kitchen spoon to measure out the batter and fry the resulting oval pancakes, without crowding the pan, until well-browned on the bottom. Turn and fry second side until brown, about 8 minutes all together.

5. To make batter into a potato kugel, add 3 tablespoons vegetable oil, pour into a greased 8-inch-square pan, and bake in a preheated 400-degree oven for 40 minutes.

Hungarian Potato and Egg Casserole

This is extremely nourishing, and though a fat-stripped formula, actually overnourishing. Hungarians serve it as a side dish. I'd rather wallow in it and eat it as a main course. It would be perfect with cucumber salad or a green salad or cole slaw (page 68). I first encountered it on a plate laden with stuffed cabbage in a Hungarian café in Manhattan's Yorkville section, the old Hungarian-German-Czech neighborhood where there are still Eastern European ethnic food stores and restaurants, holdouts amid the new high-rise apartment houses and upscale trattorias. At my request, the café proprietress talked me through the recipe, but with no great accuracy. Soon after, I coincidentally found the recipe on which the following is based in *Potato Cookery,* by the late Tom Hoge (Cornerstone Library, 1980). For many years, Hoge covered the U.N. for the Associated Press and occasionally wrote about food for the news service because he was a passionate eater and drinker. I know this because early in my career and late in his, we discovered each other and came to eat and drink passionately together several times. He might not approve that I have reduced by 6 tablespoons the amount of butter in his recipe, but so goes the world. Cholesterol watchers will cringe even at this.

Serves 4

1½ to 2 cups sour cream
1 small clove garlic, pressed or
   crushed
1 teaspoon salt

¼ teaspoon freshly ground black
   pepper
⅛ teaspoon cayenne (or few dashes
   Tabasco)
3 tablespoons butter
1½ to 2 pounds all-purpose potatoes
   (about 5 medium), peeled, cooked,
   and sliced ¼ to ⅓ inch thick
4 hard-boiled eggs, sliced (see Note)
½ cup fine dry bread crumbs
¾ teaspoon sweet paprika

1. Preheat the oven to 350 degrees.

2. In a small bowl, combine the sour cream, garlic, salt, pepper, and cayenne. Blend well.

3. With 1 tablespoon of butter, coat the inside of an 8-inch-square (or equivalent size) baking dish, then make a layer of about one-third the potatoes.

4. Arrange two of the sliced eggs on top of the potatoes. With a spatula, spread on about one-third of the sour cream mixture. Repeat the potato layer, the egg layer, and sour cream. Add a final layer of potatoes, then the final one-third of sour cream.

5. Sprinkle evenly with bread crumbs, dot with remaining 2 tablespoons butter, and sprinkle with paprika.

6. Bake for 30 minutes. Let stand 10 minutes before serving. (Can be reheated.)

Variations: Add a layer of chopped, sautéed onions or shallots and/or season with ¼ teaspoon coarsely crushed caraway seeds.

Substitutions: Use yogurt instead of sour cream for a lower-fat and tangier dish. The hard-boiled eggs are not essential; you can make the dish with potatoes only without changing the proportions.

Note: For the purposes of this recipe, and others where hard-boiled eggs are cooked again, place the eggs in boiling water and boil hard 5 minutes. Remove from heat and let stand 10 minutes. The yolks will be barely firm, so slice carefully.

Other recipes featuring potatoes

Mashed Potatoes and Onions (see Filling for Potato Blintzes, page 138)
Spanish Omelet (see page 128)
Chowders (see pages 103, 104, 107, and 256)

Rice

Rice, not wheat, is the staff of life for much of the world's population. More wheat than rice may be grown, but rice is the most revered plant on the planet. To cite only the most obvious, it is the main source of nourishment for the multitudinous Chinese, Japanese, and Southeast Asians, plus a good percentage of the peoples of the Indian subcontinent. Asians, however, do not have a monopoly on advanced rice cookery. Spanish paella is one of the world's great dishes. And the Italians are justly noted for risotto, their particular kind of round, short-grain rice braised in butter and broth. The Turks are known for fluffy pilafs, as are the Armenians, Georgians, and Greeks. And American Cajuns and Creoles are no slouches in the rice-cooking department, while Latin Americans happily and healthfully live on rice and beans, a classic example of the complementary plant protein theory that vegetarians espouse.

There are many different varieties of rice, but the most popular in American supermarkets—discounting those markets that cater to ethnic communities—is extra-long-grain white rice, an elegant rice that can be cooked up into separate grains. Until fairly recently, cooking sticky rice in America was a disgrace; hence the popularity of "converted rice," which is processed so it never clings, and instant cooking rice, which is in no way an equal to regular rice in either flavor or texture, but certainly cooks up separate.

Medium-grain rice, which is a decent substitute for Italian short-grain rice, is also sometimes available in mainstream markets. Short-grain rice, which is good for pudding, and both long- and medium-grain brown rice are also sold in supermarkets.

Specialty rices include basmati rice, which is a sweet, fragrant rice grown in the Himalayas; Texmati rice, a new hybrid grown in Texas that has some of the sweet fragrance of Himalayan-grown basmati rice; Watami rice, which is a brown rice with some basmatilike fragrance; and pecan rice, a white rice that has the faint flavor of nuts.

Brown rices have a shelf life of only about 6 months to a year because of the oil-rich bran layers left on the grain, but all kinds of white rice can be kept in a tightly covered jar at room temperature almost indefinitely.

Curried Rice Salad or Pilaf

S erve this hot or cold, as a side dish or as a lively bowl of supper for one very hungry person.

Serves 1 to 4

½ to 1 teaspoon salt
1 cup raw rice (to make 3 cups cooked)
⅓ cup raisins
1 tablespoon curry powder
3 tablespoons vegetable oil
3 tablespoons lemon juice
⅓ cup slivered or sliced almonds or coarsely chopped walnuts
¼ cup finely chopped onion, sliced onion greens, or scallion greens

1. In a small saucepan, bring 2 cups of water with ½ teaspoon salt to a boil. Stir in the rice, lower heat, cover, and simmer 12 to 15 minutes, until rice is tender and all the water has been absorbed. (If there is still a little water at the bottom of the pot when rice is tender, let cook, uncovered, 1 or 2 minutes, fluffing the rice with a fork.)

2. While the rice is cooking, plump raisins: Put in a cup or bowl and cover with very hot water.

3. Also while the rice is cooking, in a small skillet, over medium-low heat, toast the curry powder for a minute, until the aroma starts coming up. Stir in the oil and cook 3 minutes without burning the curry.

4. When the rice is cooked, turn it into a bowl and fluff it up with a fork while it's still hot. Pour on the curried oil and toss thoroughly.

5. Add lemon juice and toss again.

6. Add the drained, plumped raisins, the nuts, and the onion or greens. Toss again.

7. Serve warm, at room temperature, or chilled. (If serving cold, you may want to season, while still warm, with an additional ¼ to ½ teaspoon salt.)

Roots and Rice Supper

T his is a sweet, filling dish to set before yourself.

Serves 2

1 small to medium onion, sliced
2 tablespoons light vegetable oil or
   butter
A few center ribs of celery, cut into
   ½-inch pieces (about ½ cup,
   reserving leaves for garnish)
One 13¾-ounce can chicken broth
½ pound carrots, peeled and cut into
   ⅛-inch diagonal slices (1½ cups)
½ pound parsnips, peeled and cut
   into ½-inch cubes (1½ cups)
1½ cups water
½ cup white rice (any kind)

1. In a 2- to 3-quart saucepan, over medium heat, sauté the onion in vegetable oil or butter for about 5 minutes, until tender.

2. Add the celery and sauté another 2 to 3 minutes.

3. Add chicken broth, carrots, parsnips, and water. Increase heat, bring to a simmer, then adjust heat so soup cooks gently for about 10 minutes, until the carrots are just tender.

4. Add the rice, cover, and simmer another 15 to 20 minutes, until rice is tender.

Brown Rice and Lentil Stew

This is extremely nourishing and filling, and if you substitute water for the broth, a wonderful vegetarian dish even for those who think it's not dinner without meat.

Serves 3 or 4

¾ cup brown rice
½ cup lentils
1 small to medium onion, coarsely
   chopped (½ to 1 cup)
1 or 2 medium carrots, thinly sliced
   (½ to 1 cup)
1 or 2 ribs celery, sliced ¼-inch thick
   (½ to 1 cup)
1 clove garlic, minced
1 bay leaf
One 13¾-ounce can chicken or beef
   broth
One 14-ounce can plum tomatoes,
   chopped
1 teaspoon mixed dried herbs, such
   as "Italian seasoning," "herbs de
   Provence," "fine herbs," or a
   combination of your own

1. In a medium saucepan, combine all the ingredients plus 2½ cups water. Bring to a boil, reduce heat, cover, and let simmer gently for 45 minutes, until the rice is tender.

2. Before serving, remove and discard the bay leaf. May be served immediately, at room temperature, or it may be reheated on top of the stove or briefly in the microwave. When reheating, you want to add more broth to restore the stew texture. Otherwise it becomes more like a pilaf.

Thick Rice Soup

This is something like a Chinese congee, the rice gruel eaten for breakfast and restorative snacks. It's a good light meal unto itself, perfect for a nasty night when you just want to be cozy in front of the TV. It also serves well, however, as a first course soup-stew before a piece of broiled chicken or meat.

Serves 2 to 4

6 cups chicken broth or bouillon
1 cup rice
¼ teaspoon ground ginger, or ½
teaspoon finely chopped gingerroot

1 cup (one-half 10-ounce box) frozen
peas
One-half 10-ounce box frozen spinach
(chopped or whole leaf)
Salt
2 eggs

1. In a medium saucepan, bring the broth to a boil.

2. Add the rice and ginger, cover, and simmer 30 minutes, or until the rice has just about disintegrated.

3. Stir in the peas, spinach, and salt (amount depends on saltiness of broth). Return to a boil.

4. In a small bowl or cup, beat the eggs very well, then drizzle them a little at a time into the boiling soup. Do not stir, but let the soup simmer another 4 or 5 minutes.

Substitution: Use brown rice instead of white, but the soup will take more than 1 hour to cook, and the rice will not make as thick a soup.

A Fresh Touch: Scallions, sliced thin and including the greens, are a delicious garnish on each portion, or use the greens from a sprouted onion.

Armenian Pilaf

You can look at this as a way to extend a little rice, or a way to use up the end of a box of spaghetti. In any case, it was the inspiration for Rice-a-Roni, "The San Francisco Treat," as the TV commercials used to say.

Serves 4

2 tablespoons butter
½ cup raw spaghetti, broken into
    ½-inch pieces
¾ cup white rice
2 cups chicken, beef, or vegetable
    broth or bouillon
1 small clove garlic, pressed or
    smashed
½ to ¾ teaspoon salt
Freshly ground pepper

1. In a 2- to 3-quart saucepan, over medium-high heat, melt butter and sauté the broken spaghetti for about 3 minutes, until the spaghetti is getting tinged with color.

2. Add the rice and stir to coat with butter. Stirring frequently, sauté the rice and spaghetti about 3 minutes, until spaghetti is mostly nutty brown.

3. Add the broth, garlic, and salt. Cover; simmer over low heat for 18 to 20 minutes, stirring a few times.

4. Stir in a few twists of the peppermill and serve immediately.

Variations: Stir in separately cooked onions fried in butter or oil to a deep brown—even slightly burned. Add pine nuts or slivered almonds that have been toasted or sautéed with the spaghetti. In any case, the dish is good topped with a dollop of yogurt.

Basic White Risotto

They might (and do) charge $15 or more a plate for something like this in a nice Italian restaurant, and it wouldn't be as good as when you make it yourself. Risotto (pronounced reez-oat-toe, accent on the oat) is braised rice—it's first cooked in a little fat, then in liquid—and it can be elegant. Add asparagus or seafood or truffles and anything is elegant. But I think of risotto more as a comfort food. I like to wallow in risotto and eat enough of it to fill me up without having to save room for anything else. I used to think that Italian short-grain rice, principally Arborio type, which is the most available in this country (there are others), was the only rice good for risotto. At the urging of the Rice Council of America, however, I have tried making risotto with American-grown medium-grain rice. It is not exactly right, but it is very, very good —like Italian rice, the medium grains can be cooked so they form a creamy liaison yet remain individual and slightly chewy or *al dente*. From my experience, American medium-grain rice requires at least ½ cup more liquid than Arborio, perhaps even more than that, and it should be pulled off the heat when the grains are not quite fully tender, then left to stand, with a cover, for 5 to 8 minutes before serving. If you cook it fully, it turns out mushy.

Serves 2

1 small onion, finely chopped
2 tablespoons butter or olive oil, or 1
    tablespoon of each
2 cups (approximately) chicken broth
    (1 can of broth plus water to make
    2 cups)
1 cup Arborio rice
¼ cup dry white vermouth or white
    wine (optional)
Freshly ground pepper
1 tablespoon butter (optional)
⅓ cup (or more) grated Parmesan
    cheese

1. In a medium saucepan, over medium heat, sauté the onion in the butter until golden, about 5 minutes.

2. Meanwhile, in a small saucepan, bring the broth to a very gentle simmer.

3. Add the rice to the onion and fat, and stir to coat all the grains with fat. Stir for about 3 minutes.

4. Add the vermouth or white wine and stir. The liquid will evaporate almost immediately.

5. Add enough broth to barely cover rice. Stir frequently, if not continuously, and continue to add broth about ½ cup at a time, always keeping the rice barely covered with liquid and bubbling briskly.

6. After the last ½ cup of broth has been added, taste a few grains of rice. If the liquid is almost gone and the rice is still hard in the center (not just firm, as it should be), add water by tablespoonfuls until rice is cooked through and there is a creamy emulsion holding the grains together. The rice should be neither soft nor soupy.

7. Take the rice off the heat and stir in the optional butter and very necessary Parmesan cheese.

8. Serve immediately, with extra grated cheese on the side if possible.

Variations: For spinach risotto, follow the above directions and with the last ½ cup of liquid, add one-half 10-ounce box of frozen chopped spinach, cut into cubes and barely thawed, plus a few gratings of nutmeg. For risotto with peas, add one-half 10-

ounce box of peas (about 1 cup), still frozen, at the same point. For saffron risotto, add a big pinch (or several threads) of saffron to the heated broth. For wild mushroom risotto, add up to ½ ounce dried mushrooms that have been reconstituted, and use the filtered mushroom water (see page 169) for part of the liquid; beef broth instead of chicken broth would not be inappropriate.

A Fresh Touch: Risotto can be made with almost anything, and is. There was a period when fruit risottos were fashionable in Italy, and I once had a strawberry risotto and a curry risotto with coconut in what was considered one of the Verona area's best and not necessarily avant-garde restaurants. I'll stick to mainly vegetables and seafood now.

Turkish Rice Pudding (Sutlac)

The Turks have a passion for pudding and they make many kinds, as well as special tin-lined copper bowls used exclusively for baking and serving pudding. The following recipe is from a Turkish grill in New York called Marti Kebab. It is extremely simple and, in fact, has the same ingredients and proportions as old-fashioned New England–style rice pudding. The big difference is that the New England pudding is cooked in the oven for about 3 hours, where it develops a brown crust; this one is cooked on top of the stove in about 1 hour and turns out snowy white.

Serves 4 to 6

¼ cup white rice
1 quart milk
¾ to 1 cup sugar
Grated peel of ½ to 1 lemon,
*   or ½ orange*
Cinnamon (optional)

1. In a saucepan, combine the rice and milk. Bring to a boil, stirring frequently.

2. Adjust heat so that milk simmers gently, stir in ¾ cup of the sugar, and cook, stirring frequently, for about 45 minutes.

3. Stir in citrus peel, taste for sugar and add more if desired, then simmer about 15 minutes longer, or until pudding is fairly thick.

4. Pour into dessert cups and chill well. Sprinkle tops with cinnamon, if desired.

Other recipes featuring rice

Peas and Rice and Cheddar Cheese (see page 207)
Triple Tomato and Cheddar Soup (see page 249)
Chick-pea and Rice Soup (see page 41)

Sardines *(Canned)*

The sardine, since it has no head,
Is frequently encountered dead.
　　　　　　　—HOWARD SPOERL, *Finlandia*

A can of beer, a can of sardines, sliced raw onion, some dense bread, and a little mustard—I can always scrape them together and be happy for it. Americans simply don't take sardines seriously enough. All 260 million of us eat only 40,000 cans a day, while the population of Scandinavia—a total of 18 million people—eats 46,000 cans a day. And the French, who consider sardines a noble hors d'oeuvre, actually age sardines in the can for as long as a dozen years. Just remember that when you find a forgotten tin lurking in the back of the cupboard!

All sardines, and there are many different kinds, are technically different herrings that are called sardines because they were first fished off Sardinia—so some sources say—or something like that. The world of little fish is extremely confusing. But all you need to know is this:

Most of the imported sardines sold in the United States are the small and fatty Norwegian bristling sardines, which are naturally smoked, unlike Portuguese sardines and Maine and Nova Scotia sardines, the bristling's chief competitors. Portuguese sardines, which are larger and leaner and no less a delicacy than bristlings, are packed skinned and deboned and are not smoked. North American sardines, bristlings, or a tiny variety called slids, which have the potential to compete with the best Norwegian sardines, are unfortunately often flavored with liquid smoke and packed in oils not quite up to the olive's.

For my taste, and for one or two servings, I find ideal either the familiar 3¾-ounce can of about 8 skinless and boneless Portuguese sardines or the same-sized can of 18 to 22 bristlings packed in "two layers," in olive oil, in the distinctive square can with a key. For salt and fat watchers, bristlings are now also packed without salt and in water. Watch what you buy because all the products are packed in the same can, called a "Dingley can" in the trade. It might also contain "one layer" with 8 to 12 larger sardines, or 28 to 32 tiny fish packed "crossback," or sardines in tomato sauce, or sardines in mustard sauce, etc.

Incidentally, a well-drained can of oil-packed sardines contains 260 calories and 5.1 grams of Omega-3 fatty acids, making sardines the best food source of fish oil, an acknowledged cholesterol cutter.

Sardines Susan

Just a change of pace from plain sardines.

Serves 1 or 2

One 3¾-ounce can sardines
1 teaspoon lemon juice, or cider or
  wine vinegar
2 tablespoons prepared mustard (any
  kind, but a strong one like Dijon is
  preferable)
1½ tablespoons bread crumbs
  (unseasoned or seasoned)
1 teaspoon butter or reserved sardine
  oil

1. Preheat the broiler.

2. Drain the sardines, reserving the oil if desired. Turn sardines out of their can onto an ovenproof plate. Keep them arranged neatly. Sprinkle with lemon juice or vinegar.

3. Spread the mustard evenly over the sardines, then sprinkle with the bread crumbs.

4. Place the sardines about 5 inches under the broiler and cook until the crumbs are browned, just 2 or 3 minutes.

5. Serve immediately.

Variations: Tarragon vinegar or a pinch of dried tarragon crumbled into the mustard is a refreshing addition. The sharpness of horseradish, about 1 teaspoon mixed into the mustard, is also good against the unctuous sardines.

Sardines Rockefeller

There's enough added fat here to counteract any nutritional benefit of eating sardines. This is rich food for a very indulgent day.

Serves 1 or 2

One 3¾-ounce can sardines
1 tablespoon prepared mustard (any kind)
2 tablespoons mayonnaise

1 ounce cheddar, Swiss, jack, Gruyère, or other good melting cheese, diced or shredded

1. Preheat the oven to 350 degrees.

2. Drain the sardines, reserving the oil if desired. Turn sardines out of their can onto an ovenproof plate.

3. In a small bowl or cup, blend the mustard and mayonnaise together. Stir in the cheese.

4. Spread topping mixture evenly over sardines. Bake for about 15 minutes, until topping is lightly browned. Serve immediately.

Variation: A teaspoon of horseradish is a good addition to the topping mixture.

Sardine Tapenade

There are many, many recipes for this specialty of southern France, which is served as an appetizer spread or dip for raw vegetables, crackers, and bread, as well as with boiled potatoes and hard-boiled eggs for a fuller meal. Most recipes are anchovy-based, some include tuna. Olives are a constant. Capers should be essential, since the word *tapenade* comes from *tapeno,* the word for capers in Provençal dialect, but not all recipes contain them, as this one does not. Paula Wolfert has a marvelous, silken-textured version in *The Cooking of Southwest France* (Harper Perennial, 1985) that uses egg yolks, mayonnaise-style, to bind the large quantity of oil she uses. This version has no egg yolks (also not nearly as much oil), so you may find some oil oozes. Simply stir it back in before serving. The mixture will keep for several weeks in a tightly closed jar in the refrigerator.

Makes about ½ cup, 2 to 4 servings as an appetizer spread or dip

¼ cup oil-cured olives, pitted
1 small to medium clove garlic, cut in
    a few pieces
1 tablespoon olive oil
1½ to 2 tablespoons lemon juice (½
    lemon)
1 teaspoon Dijon mustard
¼ teaspoon ground hot pepper
    (cayenne or hot paprika)
One 3¾-ounce can sardines in olive
    oil

1. In a blender jar or small food processor bowl, combine the pitted olives, garlic, olive oil, lemon juice, mustard, hot pepper, and any oil you can drain off the can of sardines. Process until olives and garlic are a fine paste.

2. Add the sardines and process again, turning the motor on and off a few times, and, if necessary, tamping the mixture down, until you have a fine paste.

3. Scrape into a small bowl and taste for lemon and hot pepper.

4. Serve at room temperature.

Variation: You might stir in 1 tablespoon of brandy.

Another recipe with sardines

Cream Cheese and Sardine Spread (see page 87)

Sauerkraut

Salting is an ancient method of preserving food, and despite sauerkraut's sour taste, which gives our taste buds the impression that it is put up in vinegar, sauerkraut is simply salted cabbage. A natural fermentation of the cabbage's sugars is what creates the acidity, which varies depending on the length of fermentation.

So-called "fresh" sauerkraut is crisp, has a low acidity, and is sold in jars in refrigerated cases in supermarkets, sometimes near the dairy, sometimes near the meats it goes with so well—bacon, sausage, ham, and other pork products. It keeps well only for a week or two.

Strong, fully fermented sauerkraut is sold in vacuum bags, which also need to be kept refrigerated, or in cans. Canned sauerkraut can be kept on the shelf for about 6 months, but it has a tinny taste. Vacuum-bagged sauerkraut, which can be as crisp and clean-tasting as kraut right out of the barrel, has held up smelling and tasting perfect after a year in my refrigerator, though the sauerkraut companies recommend it be used within a few weeks of purchase.

Sauerkraut Potato Cakes with Dill

I could eat these for lunch or supper any day, in which case I'd want four. Or I could proudly serve them to friends alongside a simple grilled something and a salad, in which case two per person are plenty.

Serves 2 to 4

1 pound potatoes (2 large), preferably baking potatoes
1 medium onion, finely chopped
1 tablespoon butter or vegetable oil
1 pound sauerkraut, drained
1 tablespoon dried dillweed
1 egg, beaten
½ teaspoon salt
¼ teaspoon freshly ground pepper
Flour or cracker crumbs to dredge cakes
Vegetable oil (plus butter, if desired), for frying

Possible garnishes

Sour cream
Horseradish
Sour cream and horseradish mixed together
Applesauce or apple butter

1. Peel the potatoes, cut them in quarters, and cook in unsalted water to cover until tender.

2. Meanwhile, in a medium skillet, over medium heat, sauté onion in butter until tender, about 5 minutes.

3. While the onion is cooking, take small handfuls of drained sauerkraut and squeeze out any remaining moisture. Chop coarsely.

4. When the onion is tender, add sauerkraut and dill to skillet and, with a fork, separate the sauerkraut, mix well, and sauté lightly, for about 2 minutes. Set aside.

5. Put the potatoes through a ricer into a large mixing bowl. Or mash the potatoes as smooth as you can with a hand masher or hand-held electric mixer.

6. Add the sauerkraut mixture and mix well.

7. Add the beaten egg, salt, and pepper. Mix well again.

8. Shape the mixture into eight 3-inch-wide cakes. As you go, dredge each one in flour or cracker crumbs, patting off excess.

9. In a medium to large skillet, heat about ¼ inch of vegetable oil over medium-high heat. (For flavor, the oil can be supplemented with 1 or 2 tablespoons of butter.) Fry patties four at a time for 4 to 5 minutes a side, until well-browned.

10. Serve with any or all of the garnishes on the side.

A Fresh Touch: Use fresh dill instead of dried.

Sour Cream

Like yogurt, sour cream is a cultured product. A benign bacteria, Streptococcus lactis, is added to homogenized, pasteurized cream, and its metabolism creates what the scientists call an "acid gel product." The acidity (about 0.5 percent) is what gives sour cream its tart flavor. A minimum of 18 percent butterfat is what gives it its richness.

Also like yogurt, sour cream has a very long shelf life, though not as long. Fresh containers from the supermarket usually have a last date of sale that is about 2 months ahead. Once opened, that container, if kept tightly covered and promptly returned to the refrigerator after each use, will still be good another month after that. If mold forms on top, skim it off and use what remains immediately.

After butter, sour cream is the most popular topping for a baked potato (see page 210), and a traditional topping for blintzes (page 137) and potato pancakes (*latkes*, page 214; Sauerkraut Potato Cakes with Dill, page 232). My mother's favorite dish for her son when he was recuperating from an illness was boiled potatoes with a good dollop of sour cream, so I have a particular affection for that combination, mashed together in the bowl with lots of freshly ground pepper. Other classic combinations are sour cream with sliced bananas and a sprinkling of sugar (white or brown), and sour cream with berries of any kind, also with a little sugar, preferably brown. Sour cream blended with some horseradish makes a terrific sauce for fish, and there are too many sour cream–chip dip combinations to even consider. Use your imagination with whatever seasonings seem appropriate and available: garlic, dried herbs (well pulverized), capers, anchovies, caramelized grated onion, etc.

Sour Cream Coffee Cake

My sister, Andrea Alexander, a chocoholic, is always prepared with the ingredients in this rich cake, and insists so is everyone she knows. She admits that the cake actually tastes better after resting about 6 hours, but that doesn't stop her from eating it as soon as it cools. I've included the crumb topping she puts on it, which certainly does enhance the cake, but it is not necessary. If you are short on ingredients or time, leave it off.

Serves 8 to 10

For crumb topping

4 tablespoons butter
½ cup flour
½ cup brown sugar
1½ teaspoons cocoa
½ cup chopped walnuts

For cake

1 cup sugar
8 tablespoons (1 stick) butter, at cool room temperature
1 cup sour cream
2 eggs
2 cups flour
1 teaspoon baking powder
1 teaspoon baking soda
1 teaspoon vanilla extract
6 ounces chocolate chips or chopped semisweet chocolate squares (optional), and/or ½ cup walnuts, chopped

1. Preheat the oven to 350 degrees. Butter a 9-inch tube pan, preferably

one with a removable bottom. Set aside.

2. If using crumb topping, prepare it first: In a small mixing bowl, combine all the topping ingredients, except the walnuts. Blend together with a pastry cutter, with 2 table knives, or with the tips of your fingers. Mixture should be a combination of tiny and up to ¼-inch crumbs. Mix in the nuts.

3. To prepare the cake: In a large mixing bowl, using a hand-held electric mixer (or standing mixer), cream together the sugar and butter.

4. Beat in the sour cream and eggs just until mixture is smooth.

5. Add the flour, baking powder, baking soda, and vanilla extract. Beat together on low to medium speed, until well mixed. Then beat on medium to high speed a full 3 minutes.

6. Stir in the chocolate and/or chopped walnuts

7. Scrape batter into pan and smooth top. If using the topping, sprinkle on the crumbs.

8. Bake for 55 to 60 minutes, until cake tests done with a skewer.

9. Let cool about 15 minutes on a rack, then remove from pan and let cool thoroughly before slicing. Cake doesn't really come into its own for 6 to 8 hours. Until it has cooled thoroughly, it will be particularly light and difficult to slice.

Other recipes with sour cream

Cabbage and Noodle Kugel (see page 69)
Hungarian Potato and Egg Casserole (see page 215)
Spinach Dip (see page 240)

Spinach *(Frozen)*

As a man who is willing to make few culinary compromises it took me a while to admit that frozen spinach, if handled correctly, can taste almost as good as fresh. And it doesn't have to be cleaned in three changes of water. What I mean by "correctly" is: Don't overcook it. Any spinach becomes bitter and metallic when cooked too long. Frozen spinach, which is blanched before it is turned into a solid icy block, can turn bitter and metallic in no time at all when you go to cook it again.

Also try to be careful about which packages you take from the supermarket freezer. Feel the box. If the spinach appears to have shifted so that more is in one end of the box and the other end feels empty, the spinach has likely thawed and been refrozen somewhere on its travels from the processor to your hand: not good. To ensure maximum quality and storage time—for spinach, about a year under optimum conditions—all frozen products must be kept frozen until they are used. For that reason, always remember to make the frozen food section your last stop at the supermarket.

Actually, for some recipes that call for cooked spinach, it is better to just thaw spinach, not boil it, so it doesn't have to be cooked a third time. For example, there is no need to boil spinach if it is going to be sautéed.

Creamed Spinach

This is creamed spinach without cream but you wouldn't know it. I love it with a plate of scrambled eggs and some toast—the spinach is delicious smeared on an occasional bite of the toast—or use it as a bed for baked eggs (opposite), as an omelet or crêpe filling (see page 137), or as a topping for boiled rice or boiled or baked potatoes.

Serves 2 or 3

*One 10-ounce box frozen chopped
  spinach
2 tablespoons finely chopped shallot
  (about 2)
1½ tablespoons butter
2 tablespoons flour
1¼ cups milk
Scant ½ teaspoon salt
Freshly grated nutmeg*

1. In a small saucepan, combine the frozen block of spinach with ¼ cup water. Cover and bring to a boil over high heat.

2. As soon as water comes to the boil, break up the frozen spinach with a fork, cover again, and let cook 1 or 2 minutes more, until the spinach has completely thawed. Remove from heat, drain immediately and well, and set aside.

3. In a small saucepan, over medium heat, sauté the shallots in butter for 2 minutes.

4. Stir in the flour and, stirring constantly, cook the flour for 2 minutes. Remove from heat.

5. As soon as the flour mixture stops bubbling, stir in the milk. Make sure the flour is completely dissolved.

6. Return to medium heat and, stirring constantly, bring to a boil. Reduce heat and simmer gently for 2 minutes.

7. Add the drained spinach and stir to blend it evenly into the sauce.

8. Season with salt and a few gratings of nutmeg. (May be made ahead and gently reheated—you may want or need to thin it out with 1 or 2 tablespoons milk.

9. Serve very hot.

Sautéed Spinach with Garlic

This doesn't have to be a mere side dish—not to say it doesn't make a good one. With leftover corn bread as a starch base, I can make a meal of greens cooked like this. All I do is add a little chicken broth to make the spinach wet, as wet as it needs to be to soften the day-old, or perhaps several days-old corn bread.

Serves 2

2 tablespoons olive oil
2 large cloves garlic, finely chopped
One 10-ounce box frozen leaf or
    chopped spinach, defrosted
Salt and freshly ground pepper

1. In a small skillet, heat the olive oil over medium heat and sauté the garlic until very lightly browned, the color of almonds.

2. Add the defrosted spinach and toss with the oil and garlic until coated. Continue cooking about 3 minutes.

3. Season with salt and pepper.

4. Serve hot or at room temperature.

Variation: To give the greens a Mexican flavor, especially good on the corn bread, add to the oil, along with the garlic, about ½ teaspoon finely chopped dried chilies of any kind.

Eggs in Creamed Spinach

Whether made on top of the stove or in the oven, this is a fine light supper dish even when prepared with plain spinach, instead of creamed or sautéed with garlic. Simply cook the frozen vegetable until it is fully thawed, drain well, then, if you can spare the calories, toss with butter or olive oil.

Serves 1 or 2

1 recipe Creamed Spinach (opposite)
    or Sautéed Spinach with Garlic
    (above)
2 to 4 eggs
Grated Parmesan cheese (optional)

1. Arrange a layer of spinach in the bottom of a small saucepan or skillet with a cover (or in a small lightly buttered casserole, or 2 lightly buttered single-serving baking dishes).

2. With the back of a spoon, make as many indentations in the spinach as you have eggs. Break the eggs into the indentations.

3. Cover the saucepan or skillet and cook over low heat for about 15 minutes, or until the eggs are set as desired. Or bake, uncovered, for 10 to 12 minutes in a preheated 400-degree oven.

4. Serve immediately, with grated cheese, if you have it on hand.

Spinach Dip

The Middle Eastern flavors here, especially if you make the dip with yogurt, call out for pita crisps (page 55) as a dipper. Raw vegetables are virtuous. Potato chips are indulgent. I draw the line at corn chips.

Makes about 2 cups

One 10-ounce box frozen leaf or chopped spinach

1 small to large clove garlic (to taste), pressed or smashed
1 tablespoon lemon juice or wine vinegar
1 rounded teaspoon dried mint
1½ cups yogurt or sour cream
Cayenne or freshly ground black pepper

1. In a small saucepan, combine the frozen block of spinach with ¼ cup water. Cover and bring to a boil over high heat.

2. As soon as water comes to a boil, break up the frozen spinach with a fork, cover again, and let cook 1 or 2 minutes more, until spinach has completely thawed. Drain immediately and let cool enough to handle.

3. Drain spinach again by squeezing it in handfuls.

4. Chop the spinach very fine; even if you are using chopped spinach, it should be finer.

5. While the spinach is cooking, then cooling, in a small bowl, combine the garlic, lemon juice or vinegar, and dried mint.

6. Add the spinach to the seasoning mixture and blend well.

7. Stir in the yogurt or sour cream.

8. Serve slightly chilled, if there is time.

Other recipes featuring spinach

Lentils and Rice (see page 45)
Eggs in Creamed Spinach (see page 239)
Thick Rice Soup (see page 222)

Tahini

Tahini is sesame seed paste, ground raw sesame seeds, or sesame butter, to put it in American terms. It is a Middle Eastern product, though the Chinese also use sesame paste made from toasted seeds. Tahini is no longer only an ethnic food, and it appears to be available nationwide, in any supermarket. The nutrition/health-food movement has seen to that. It is now widely used as a high-protein (and non-dairy vegetarian) salad dressing substitute for conventional oil-based and cream-based dressings. I must say, it does a good job of it. Flavored with lemon juice and thinned out with water, it's a wonderful medium for anyone's imagination. Use yours.

Tahini comes in jars and cans (often with plastic lids). Unopened, most products have a shelf life of at least 1 year. Once opened, keep the container tightly covered and in the refrigerator. It should hold several, if not many months. Tahini separates, so don't be alarmed if an oil layer forms on top—in a newly opened can or jar or in a long-stored one. Take a sturdy spoon and stir the paste and oil together again. I say a sturdy spoon, because tahini can be stubborn and you often have to be tough and strong to get it smooth and silky again.

Tahini Cream

A magic moment in cookery: Add the lemon juice and the sesame paste tightens. Add water and it not only thins out, it turns white. Kids love it. You will, too.

Makes about ½ cup

¼ cup tahini
2 tablespoons lemon juice
3 to 6 tablespoons cold water

1. In a small bowl, blend the tahini with the lemon juice.

2. Add water to achieve the consistency you desire. The lesser amount makes it thick enough to use as a dip for pita or pita crisps (page 55), crackers, or raw vegetables. The larger amount thins it to a pourable salad dressing.

Variations: As either a dip or salad dressing, add ground hot pepper, a tiny crushed clove of garlic, dried mint, or oregano.

To garnish as a dip, spread the tahini cream on a small plate and surround or decorate with olives. And/or sprinkle the center with a little hot or sweet paprika or ground cumin, then drizzle a tablespoon of olive oil over the spice. Or sizzle a ½ tablespoon of dried mint with a tablespoon of olive oil, then pour on top.

A Fresh Touch: Chopped fresh parsley, dill, or mint can be an additional or substitute garnish.

Hummus with Tahini

T here is hummus without tahini, but the more familiar form of this Middle Eastern chick-pea dip is blended with anywhere from a very little sesame seed paste to as much as half tahini. In almost all parts of the Middle East this is daily food. Even here in New York, it is extremely popular. Arab restaurants introduced it many years ago. Then Israeli immigrants, who love the stuff as much as Arabs, opened pizza and felafel stands to cater to the kosher community. Now it is served on every third street corner in parts of Midtown and in the kosher and Arab neighborhoods of Brooklyn and New Jersey. It's a terrific snack and party food. Scoop it up with pita or raw vegetables, or spread it on crackers.

Serves 4 to 6

One 19-ounce can chick-peas,
drained (reserve liquid)

*1 or 2 medium to large cloves garlic,
    each cut in a few pieces*
½ cup tahini
2 to 3 tablespoons lemon juice

Suggested garnishes

Ground cumin, paprika, or cayenne
Olive oil
Black or purple olives

1. In a food processor fitted with the steel blade, combine the chick-peas and garlic. Turn on and off a few times to puree the chick-peas and garlic.

2. Add the tahini. Process a few seconds again.

3. Add the lemon juice. Process again.

4. If the puree is too thick, add a few tablespoons of the reserved chick-pea liquid.

5. To serve, spread it on a platter, mounding it up in the center and making a sort of moat between the center and a raised edge. Sprinkle the center mound with ground cumin or a little paprika or cayenne, then drizzle a little olive oil over the spice so some of the oil, colored by the spice, drizzles down into the moat. Black or purple olives are another (or additional) garnish.

Tomatoes *(Canned)*

Canned tomatoes should be a staple on every cupboard shelf. Except when fresh tomatoes are at their local peak, the canned varieties—Italian-style plum tomatoes; round, sweet California tomatoes; and crushed tomatoes—are always better than anything the vegetable market has to offer. For cooking, that is. For salads and sandwiches, you have to compromise with fresh or do without during the off-season months.

There are definite quality differences among brands of tomatoes, but with so many domestic and imported brands available you should have no trouble finding one that consistently packs a well-colored, full-flavored product. Some are packed in juice, which is generally rich enough to offer flavor to soups and stews, and some are packed in puree, which is thick and flavorful enough to use as a base for a sauce.

To bolster the flavor of canned tomato sauces and soups —and for occasionally giving a boost or some color to other dishes—tomato paste is also valuable to have on hand. I find tomato paste in tubes a big convenience. It may be more expensive than paste in cans, but paste left over from a can is difficult to store and inevitably spoils, while the tube keeps the paste perfectly.

Unopened cans of tomatoes have a shorter shelf life than some other canned goods. Some authorities advise allowing them as little as 6 months on the shelf. I've had no problems with cans that have gotten lost at the back of a cupboard for as long as a year, though this is generally a product that turns over so quickly in my house, I usually pick up a few cans every time I do a major marketing.

Spicy Tomato Jam

Fat-free, cholesterol-free, and salt-free, as well as a laser beam of flavor, this condiment (or dip or spread) is always the life of a party. With drinks, it's something to smear on bread or toasts, or to scoop up with a vegetable. On the table, it can be a relish for roasted or broiled anything, including vegetables, particularly eggplant, zucchini, and sweet peppers. And yes, it's good with baked or microwaved potatoes, and roasted or microwaved onions. It can also top tubular macaroni or a bowl of boiled rice.

Makes about 1½ cups

One 28-ounce can Italian-style plum tomatoes, drained
3 or 4 cloves garlic, sliced very thinly or minced

½ teaspoon hot red pepper flakes, or more to taste
2 to 4 tablespoons honey

1. In a medium saucepan, combine the tomatoes and garlic. With the side of a wooden spoon, break up the tomatoes. Place over medium-high heat and simmer briskly, stirring often, until tomatoes are reduced to a chunky, thick sauce.

2. Add the hot pepper flakes and 2 tablespoons of the honey. Continue to cook briskly until the mixture is reduced to jam consistency.

3. Taste and adjust honey and pepper to taste. (You can add salt, but I find it unnecessary—this is primarily a hot and sweet condiment and the canned tomatoes already have some salt.)

4. Cool. Serve at room temperature or chilled.

Sweet, Smooth Tomato Sauce

The freshest tasting of spaghetti sauces, this recipe requires a food mill to give it the right texture. A blender or food processor can be used, but it's not quite as good.

Makes about 2 cups, for ¾ to 1 pound spaghetti or macaroni

One 28-ounce can Italian-style plum
   tomatoes, with juice
1 carrot, peeled and cut into 4 hunks
1 small onion, peeled and cut
   halfway through with an X
2 tablespoons butter or olive oil
¾ teaspoon sugar
¾ teaspoon salt
½ teaspoon dried marjoram or
   oregano

1. With a food mill, puree tomatoes directly into a 2-quart saucepan. (If you don't have a food mill, use a blender, but you may have to add another ¼ teaspoon or so sugar to compensate for the bitterness of the seeds ground into the sauce.)

2. Add remaining ingredients and simmer gently but steadily for 40 minutes, occasionally stirring and scraping down the sides of the pot.

3. Discard vegetables and serve.

Tomato Sauce with Olives and Capers

This sauce offers big flavor with little work and in no time.

Makes about 1¼ cups

3 medium cloves garlic, sliced thin
   (about 1 tablespoon)
2 tablespoons olive oil
One 14- or 16-ounce can Italian-style
   plum tomatoes, drained (1¾ to
   2 cups)
8 oil-cured olives, pitted and cut into
   strips (about 2 rounded
   tablespoons)
2 teaspoons capers, drained and
   rinsed
One 1-inch strip orange peel
   (optional)
Pinch dried oregano or marjoram
Freshly ground black pepper

1. In a medium skillet, over medium heat, sauté garlic in olive oil until beginning to turn nutty colored, about 3 minutes.

2. Add tomatoes and break them up with the side of a wooden spoon. Increase heat and simmer briskly until tomatoes are reduced to pulp, about 5 minutes.

3. Add olives, capers, and optional orange peel. Simmer another 3 to 4 minutes. Serve immediately. (If macaroni is not yet cooked, set aside and reheat rather than keeping sauce on heat.) No salt is necessary because the capers and olives add enough.

Variations: A 6½-ounce can of tuna can be flaked into and heated in the sauce at the last moment, making this a much more substantial dish. Or, for flavor only, add a few chopped anchovies. The anchovies make it one of many versions of puttanesca, the sauce attributed to *le puttane,* the prostitutes of Italy, because, as one theory goes, it can be made as quickly as "slam, bam, thank you, ma'am."

Coarse Tomato Sauce with Onion and Hot Pepper

Here's a zesty marinara-style sauce that proves tomato sauce doesn't have to be cooked a long time to be thick and rich.

Makes about 1½ cups

1 medium onion
2 cloves garlic, minced
2 tablespoons olive oil
One 28-ounce can plum tomatoes,
    drained (3½ cups)
½ teaspoon salt
Big pinch sugar, if necessary
¼ teaspoon hot red pepper flakes (or
    other hot pepper)

1. Peel onion and cut about ¼ inch off the root end. Slice onion through the root end, to form long slivers.

2. In a medium skillet, over medium heat, sauté onion and garlic in olive oil until onion is wilted, about 3 minutes.

3. Add tomatoes and break them up with the side of a wooden spoon. Add salt, sugar, and hot pepper.

4. Stir well, increase heat, and simmer briskly 10 to 15 minutes, until most of the liquid has evaporated.

5. Serve immediately.

Sugo Finto

I never knew this sauce had a name until Anna Teresa Callen, a New York–based Italian cooking teacher, gave me the one above. It means "fake sauce," meaning fake *meat* sauce; except for the fact that it has no meat, you make it as you would a meat sauce.

Makes about 1½ cups

*1 medium onion, finely chopped
   (about 1 cup)
1 medium carrot, finely chopped
   (about ⅓ cup)
1 medium rib celery, finely chopped
   (about ⅓ cup)
2 to 3 tablespoons olive oil
One 14- or 16-ounce can Italian-style
   plum tomatoes, with juice (1¾ to
   2 cups)
½ teaspoon salt
Freshly ground pepper
Big pinch of sugar, if necessary*

1. In a medium saucepan, over medium heat, sauté the onion, carrot, and celery in olive oil until onion is translucent, about 5 minutes.

2. Add tomatoes and break up with the back of a wooden spoon. Simmer briskly for about 15 minutes. Season with salt and 5 to 8 twists of the peppermill. Add sugar if sauce is a little acidic.

Triple Tomato and Cheddar Soup

Condensed tomato soup is so much sweetened pap next to this almost as convenient restorative. For a substantial and enticing looking meal in a bowl, mound plain boiled white rice in the center of the bowl, ladle the soup around it so a peak of white shows through, then scatter strips or shreds of cheese on top. Incidentally, this started out as a recipe from a family friend, Joan Krantz, a vegetarian who makes her own vegetable stock—no doubt an improvement over a cube or can.

Serves 4 to 6

*2 cups Knorr vegetable bouillon or
    diluted canned chicken or beef
    broth*
*One 28-ounce can crushed tomatoes
    (3½ cups)*
12 ounces V-8 juice (1½ cups)
*One 14-ounce can Italian-style plum
    tomatoes (1½ cups), coarsely
    chopped and including juice*
1 large clove garlic, crushed
2 teaspoons sugar
Freshly ground pepper
*8 to 10 ounces sharp cheddar cheese
    (preferably white), shredded or cut
    into fine strips (about 3 cups,
    loosely packed)*

1. In a 3-quart saucepan, combine all the ingredients except the cheese. Simmer gently, uncovered, for 20 minutes.

2. Serve very hot, each portion topped with grated or slivered cheese. Or follow the tomato soup and rice instructions above.

Variations: You can turn this into a chili-style dish by adding chili powder or your choice of chopped dried chilies—chipotle add a haunting smoky flavor. Instead of rice, strips of cornmeal tortilla add substance. Or serve the soup with corn chips. Or add small pasta, such as tubettini, farfallini, or tiny elbows, in which case you want to use grated Parmesan or Romano instead of cheddar.

A Fresh Touch: Chopped fresh parsley, basil, dill, or coriander are all good additions. Chunks of avocado are thematic and a good bland contrast if you decide to zip up the soup with chilies.

Other recipes with tomatoes
Spaghetti all'Amatriciana (see page 25)
Tomato Bulgur (see page 65)
Manhattan Clam Chowder (see page 103)

Tortillas

Packages of tortillas always say they are "baked daily," a freshness claim that is reduced to absurdity as the tortillas sit in a plastic bag in my refrigerator for months. I suppose there is a difference between freshly baked tortillas and not freshly baked tortillas, but I find that unless they have something growing on them I can always manage to revive the old ones so that they taste quite fresh enough.

The same revival techniques go for both corn and flour tortillas: They can be softened by heating them in a dry, hot skillet, by wrapping in paper towel and microwaving several seconds, by wrapping them in foil and heating them in the oven, or by frying in a pan glazed with oil or in a more significant amount of oil, depending on the desired effect. A small amount of oil will make them crisp. Frying in about ⅛ inch of very hot oil will make them puff up.

Quesadillas

Corn or flour tortillas
José's Black Bean Spread or Bean
  Cream (see pages 34 and 38)
Shredded cheese
Butter or oil (optional)

Any kind of turnover is a quesadilla, says Josefina Howard, proprietor of Rosa Mexicano restaurant and one of New York's resident Mexican food experts. "In most parts of Mexico, you make a special dough for quesadillas and they have nothing to do with tortillas. Only in the north do they make quesadillas with turned tortillas, which is how it comes to Tex-Mex food and what Americans think of as quesadillas." Loosely translated, the word *quesadillas* means "little cheese things," but they are actually filled with almost anything—refried beans, guacamole, sausage, shredded beef or chicken, mushrooms, even, according to Josefina, sweet fillings. I stick with cheese and beans, alone or together, and include hot peppers—fresh and diced or strips of canned green ones, depending on what's available.

Quesadillas are a great snack or appetizer—what Mexicans call an *antojo,* a craving or whim. But, especially filled with both beans and cheese, a large portion of quesadillas can be a whole meal. In either case, they can be topped with a dab of sour cream or salsa.

1. Simple quesadillas are more method than recipe. They can be made with either corn or flour tortillas, in a dry skillet or sautéed in a small amount of butter or vegetable oil. Either way, get the skillet very hot, but not hot enough to make the butter or oil burn or smoke if you are using one or the other.

2. Spread a tortilla with bean spread or bean cream and/or shredded cheese (almost anything but Parmesan). Put the tortilla, filling side up, in the hot skillet. Top with another tortilla. Cook about 1 minute, then, with a wide spatula, turn the quesadilla and cook another minute.

(If you have only 1 tortilla and want to make a snack, put the filling on one-half of the tortilla, then fold the other half over the filling when it becomes soft enough to do so.)

3. Cut into wedges with a serrated or very sharp knife and serve immediately.

A Fresh Touch: A dab of guacamole on each wedge is always welcome. Whole leaves of fresh coriander, sandwiched in the tortillas with cheese alone, makes an interesting quesadilla.

Tortillas for Soup

Fried corn tortilla strips are often used in Mexican soups in the same way noodles are elsewhere. Cut the tortillas in half, then into ½-inch wide strips. Heat about ¼ inch of vegetable oil in a heavy skillet until very hot—until a strip of tortilla sizzles and puffs immediately. Fry the strips on both sides, drain on a paper towel, and stir into broth the last minute. As additional substance, try strips of canned green chilies, diced canned tomato, and diced raw onion.

Tuna *(Canned)*

No one in America ate fresh tuna until recently. I'm still not sure why we do. Unless it is nearly raw—a way few people like it—fresh tuna is a dry, coarse fish. The Japanese have it right. Fresh tuna is best eaten completely raw. But young American chefs, who undoubtedly grew up eating what they must consider plebian white bread sandwiches of canned tuna mashed with mayonnaise, love to cook fresh tuna.

Canned tuna is another story, if not exactly a totally different fish. It may not have a reputation as a delicacy in America, but in the south of France and in Italy, where canned tuna is always dark pink and wonderfully moist, it is considered a highly worthy food. Canned tuna is fresh tuna that has been steamed, salted, and vacuum packed, either with vegetable oil, olive oil, or water. Personally, I prefer what is called "chunk light" tuna to the more popular "solid white" tuna. Light tuna is more like European tuna but much less expensive than the imported brands that can cost triple the price of the domestically canned product. It is also sufficiently moist to be palatable even when packed in water.

So far as I can determine, canned tuna will hold up for many years on the cupboard shelf, a good reason to stock up when the price cycle regularly hits bottom.

Tuna Sandwiches

If the tuna sandwich is not an art form it is at least high craft. My most basic tuna salad—for a sandwich or otherwise—is a well-drained can of tuna with a heaping tablespoon of mayonnaise, blended together with a fork until shredded but not mushy. From there, it depends.

You might add a few drops of lemon juice or vinegar. Chopped celery is standard. On a sandwich, preferably on rye bread, thin slices of cucumber are refreshing. Thin slices of raw onion are bracing. Both together are better than either alone.

Sliced pimento-stuffed Spanish olives not mixed in but arranged neatly over the tuna, itself neatly forked onto white bread toast, give me a lot of pleasure—the making of it as well as the eating of it. A layer of sliced dill pickle or sweet gherkin does the same.

I would only bother with sliced tomato when tomatoes are at their local peak, but the crunch and moisture of iceberg lettuce is always welcome.

Tuna, No Surprises

Snivel, and call it tuna à la king if you must. It's a comfort food for some of us. Personally, I like it on a baked potato, but use it as a sauce for egg noodles or macaroni or try it on rice; yes, even on toast.

Serves 2

1 medium onion, finely chopped
2 tablespoons butter
2 tablespoons flour
1½ cups milk
1 cup frozen peas (half 10-ounce box)
One 6½-ounce can tuna, drained
*   well*
2 or 3 tablespoons freshly grated
*   Parmesan*
¾ teaspoon salt
Freshly ground black pepper

1. In a small saucepan, over medium heat, sauté onion in butter until golden, about 8 minutes. Add flour. Stir well and continue stirring 2 more minutes. Remove from heat and let cool a few seconds.

2. Add milk, stirring continuously. Return to medium heat and bring to a simmer, still stirring. Let simmer gently 2 minutes.

3. Add peas and bring back to a simmer, cooking until peas are just done, about 2 minutes. Stir in tuna, then cheese. Season with salt and pepper.

Tuna Chowder

What's the difference between chowder and soup? Very little, except that chowder is made with potatoes, the fat is usually salt pork or bacon, and most chowders are made with milk or cream. This is meant to be a quickie supper, but if you let it stand awhile—even refrigerate it overnight—the potatoes thicken the liquid even more and make the chowder even more comforting.

Serves 2

2 tablespoons butter
1 medium onion, chopped (¾ to 1 cup)
8 ounces all-purpose or new potatoes, peeled (if thick-skinned), cut into ½-inch dice (about 1½ cups)
1 cup milk
One 6½-ounce can tuna (chunk white or light, in oil or water), drained
¼ teaspoon salt

1. In a small saucepan, over medium heat, melt butter and sauté onion for about 8 minutes, until golden.

2. Add the diced potatoes and milk. Bring to a simmer and cook about 10 minutes, until potatoes are very tender.

3. Add tuna and salt. Stir and heat through.

4. Serve very hot.

Tuna-Noodle Casserole

I totally agree with Nika Hazelton, whose definitive recipe this is: "When well made, this is a very good dish, bearing little resemblance to what school and college cafeterias serve. Increase the noodles or macaroni only if you absolutely must."

Serves 4

3 tablespoons butter
3 tablespoons flour
2 cups milk
¾ cup shredded Swiss or cheddar cheese
Salt
Freshly ground pepper
One 13-ounce can (or two 6½-ounce cans) white meat tuna, drained and flaked

4 ounces medium noodles or elbow
macaroni, cooked al dente and
drained
3 tablespoons finely chopped pitted
black or green olives or minced
parsley
½ cup fine, dry bread crumbs
blended with 2 tablespoons butter,
melted

1. Preheat the oven to 350 degrees. Butter a 2-quart casserole.

2. In a heavy saucepan, over low heat, melt the butter, stir in the flour, and cook, stirring constantly, for 1 minute.

3. Whisk in the milk and cook, stirring constantly, for 4 to 5 minutes, or until the sauce simmers and becomes smooth and thick.

4. Add the cheese and stir until just melted. Season with salt and pepper. Remove from heat.

5. In a large bowl, combine the tuna, noodles, olives or parsley, and cheese sauce. With two forks, toss together.

6. Spoon lightly into the casserole. Top with buttered bread crumbs.

7. Bake for 20 to 30 minutes, or until golden brown and bubbly. Serve very hot.

Variations: Use a slightly larger casserole and add as much as 1 cup chopped cooked ham and/or ½ to 1 cup cooked peas.

Quick Macaroni with Tuna

If some night all you can bear to do is boil water and open a can, this is your dish. Use white tuna packed in water, if you must, but it'll taste much better with drained, oil-packed tuna, preferably light, not white.

Serves 2

½ pound ziti, penne, shells, or other
macaroni
¼ cup olive oil
One 6½-ounce can tuna, drained
¼ teaspoon hot red pepper flakes (or
more to taste)
Salt

1. Boil the macaroni. Drain well and, in a serving bowl, toss with the olive oil.

2. Add the tuna, hot pepper, and salt. Toss again.

3. Serve immediately, though it's a good macaroni salad when cool.

Variation: You have to ask? Of course you can add garlic, crushed or finely chopped, raw or cooked in the oil.

A Fresh Touch: Some diced fresh tomato would be fabulous.

Tuna and Caponata

I have been eating this regularly for more than 20 years now. I eat it so often that I rarely buy a can of tuna without one of caponata. Caponata is an Italian vegetable dish—mainly eggplant, but also onions, celery, capers, and olives—and I find that canned caponata, I don't care which brand, is almost always better than the caponata served in restaurants or that I find in fancy takeout stores. American cooks don't seem to understand that the eggplant is supposed to be soft, not firm; that the chunky mixture should hold together, not fall into separate vegetable pieces.

A 7½-ounce can of caponata blended, gently with a fork, into a 6½-ounce can of tuna is a perfect proportion, though you could stretch the can of caponata to season 2 cans of tuna. A possible addition is about ½ cup chopped red onion, and/or lemon juice, wine, or balsamic vinegar. A fresh touch would be ¼ to ½ cup finely diced red or green sweet pepper.

Tuna and Beans

This is a popular antipasto and lunch salad in Italy, though lately, in restaurants, it has been superseded by shrimp and beans, which may be more luxurious than canned tuna, but not necessarily more delicious.

Serves 2 for a light meal, 4 as an appetizer

One 6½-ounce can tuna (preferably light, not white), drained
One 16-ounce can cannellini beans, drained
1 small onion or 2 shallots, finely chopped (optional)
1 small rib celery, finely chopped (optional)
1 to 2 tablespoons lemon juice or red wine vinegar
1 or 2 tablespoons olive oil
Freshly ground black pepper

1. In a small mixing bowl, using a fork, gently blend all the ingredients together, being careful not to mash the beans.

2. May be served immediately or chilled before serving.

A Fresh Touch: Finely chopped fresh basil, mint, or parsley is always welcome.

Other recipes featuring tuna

Cream Cheese and Tuna Spread (see page 87)
Spaghetti with Tuna Sauce (see page 247)

Sweet- and-Sour Tuna Toss

Raisins and pine nuts are a traditional pairing in Italian sweet-and-sour dishes. Along those lines, this is a concoction for a quick supper.

Serves 1

2 tablespoons raisins
3 tablespoons red wine or Balsamic vinegar
1 medium onion, cut in half and very finely sliced (about 1 cup)
2 tablespoons olive oil
1 rounded tablespoon pine nuts
1 6½-ounce can tuna, drained

1. Combine the raisins and vinegar and set aside so raisins will plump up.

2. In a skillet, over medium-high heat, sauté the onion in oil for about 3 minutes, until wilted.

3. Add the pine nuts and sauté another 3 to 5 minutes, until nuts have colored lightly.

4. Add the plumped raisins and all the vinegar. Toss with the onions a few seconds, then add the tuna and toss again.

5. Serve immediately or at room temperature.

Yogurt

Yogurt is a naturally preserved food. It is meant to hang around the back of your refrigerator until needed. It is intentionally soured, acidified, or "cultured" by the metabolic action of two benign bacteria—Lactobacillus bulgaricus and Streptococcus thermophilus—which, in effect, keep it safe from other, unwanted invisible creatures that would make it sickening instead of delicious and wholesome.

Different yogurt cultures (that is, colonies of bacteria) have idiosyncrasies that produce different-tasting yogurts with different textures. The flavor and fat content of the milk from which the yogurt was made also have an impact on its personality. Every supermarket now carries many brands and kinds of yogurt. The recipes here are concerned only with unflavored yogurt, of which you have a choice between no-fat (under 0.5 percent), low fat (between 0.5 percent and 2 percent, the most popular kind), whole milk (at least 3.25 percent), or one of the extra-rich yogurts, sometimes called "farm style," which have a layer of heavy yogurt cream on the top (well over 3.25 percent).

Making Yogurt

If you do not have enough yogurt for a recipe (or eating for its own sake) in the refrigerator, and have the time to let some culture, it is very easy to do. Use any kind of milk as a base—even reconstituted nonfat dry milk—and heat it to just under a simmer. Let cool until it feels slightly warmer than body temperature, then stir in 1 rounded tablespoon of yogurt. Wrap the container in a towel to retain heat and let stand until thickened, several hours or overnight, depending on the temperature and the culture.

Yogurt Cheese

(Strained Yogurt)

This isn't really cheese (because it isn't curdled by enzyme action). It's low-moisture yogurt with the consistency of cream cheese, though it's possible to make a looser spread, more the consistency of, well, very thick yogurt. To keep the yogurt cheese mild let it drain in the refrigerator. At room temperature (cer-

tainly in the summer) it becomes stronger tasting as it sits and drips and its colony of bacteria continues to grow. There are lots of uses for yogurt cheese, but my favorite is as an appetizer spread, drizzled with a little olive oil, perhaps a sprinkling of hot paprika or other red pepper, or crumbled dry mint and surrounded by black olives. Hot pita is the ideal bread on which to spread it. Yogurt cheese is delicious spread on cucumber slices or as part of any salad—use it as goat cheese has come to be used, spread on croutons (possibly rubbed with garlic) as an added attraction to a plate of salad greens.

1. Take any amount of yogurt and put it in a strainer lined with cheesecloth or a coffee filter.

2. Put the strainer over a bowl to drain.

3. When the yogurt has thickened to the consistency you want, turn it into a crock and keep refrigerated.

Turkish Yogurt Soup

It seems as if every restaurant in Turkey that isn't a mere kebab shop has this soup on the menu. Honestly, it's rarely as good as this recipe, even though this one is prepared with diluted canned broth. The mint butter is a great fillip—and pretty—but so is a little hot paprika.

Serves 2 or 3

One 13¾-ounce can chicken broth
2 tablespoons white rice
½ cup yogurt
2 tablespoons flour
1 egg yolk
1 tablespoon butter (optional)
½ teaspoon dried mint (optional)

1. In a small saucepan, combine the broth, 1 broth can of water, and the rice. Cover and bring to a boil. Reduce heat and simmer, covered, for 12 minutes, or until the rice is just tender.

2. Meanwhile, in a medium bowl, stir together the yogurt, flour, and egg yolk.

3. When the rice is tender, pour the broth into the yogurt mixture, beating steadily with a wooden spoon or wire whisk.

4. Pour soup back into the saucepan and simmer 5 minutes.

5. To make the mint butter, melt the butter in a butter warmer or small skillet, then let mint sizzle in the butter for about 30 seconds, being careful not to burn it.

6. Drizzle a little flavored butter over each portion of soup in its bowl and serve very hot.

Cold Tarator Yogurt Soup

The combination of pulverized nuts and garlic is common in the cooking of the Mediterranean and Caucasus. From Spain and Greece, through the Levant, and on to Soviet Georgia and Azerbaijan, wherever the Arabs traveled, they left a love for this potent paste. It is lavished on fish, poultry, and vegetables, or, as here, it is used as a flavoring for a cold yogurt soup or dip, depending on the thickness of the yogurt.

Serves 3 or 4

¼ cup shelled walnuts
2 cloves garlic (to equal the size of a
  walnut half), cut into several
  pieces
2 tablespoons olive oil
½ teaspoon salt
1 tablespoon vinegar (preferably
  wine) or lemon juice
3 cups plain yogurt
1 cup milk or water

1. In a blender jar, combine the walnuts, garlic, olive oil, salt, and vinegar. Turning the motor on and off a couple of times, process until the walnuts and garlic are finely ground.

2. Add 1 cup of the yogurt and process another few seconds to blend well.

3. Pour into a bowl and blend in remaining yogurt, and the milk or water.

4. Chill well before serving.

Cold Tomato-Yogurt Soup

The idea for this refreshing soup came from Lillian and Miles Cahn, owners of The Coach Farm, goat cheese and yogurt producers in Columbia County, New York, only two hours north of Manhattan. The Cahns use their own incomparable Yo-Goat, a liquid yogurt culture, but the soup is delicious with any plain yogurt.

Serves 1

¾ cup tomato juice
½ cup yogurt
1 tiny clove garlic
Big pinch dried dill or mint
Pinch salt (if necessary)
Freshly ground pepper

1. In a small bowl, with a wire whisk, beat together the tomato juice and yogurt.

2. Crush the garlic through a press into the liquid or smash it with the side of a wide-bladed knife and add to the liquid.

3. Rub the pinch of herb between your fingers and add to liquid. Stir in, adding a little salt, if desired, and a turn of the peppermill.

4. Chill well before serving.

A Fresh Touch: About ⅓ cup diced cucumber is an ideal addition. Of course, fresh dill or mint is superior to dried.

Spaghetti with Onions and Yogurt

The inspiration for this recipe comes from an Afghan restaurant in New York, once called Khyber Pass, now known as Café Kabul. The noodles prepared at this restaurant are prepared like Italian egg pasta, except that they are rolled out with a heavy metal bar that gives them their characteristically slick finish. Spaghetti and linguine are good substitutes. Packaged egg noodles will do, too, though I like the longer strands of Italian pasta.

Serves 4

1 pound spaghetti or linguine, or 12
    ounces to 1 pound medium or wide
    egg noodles
6 tablespoons butter
1 medium-large onion, coarsely
    grated
½ teaspoon salt
2 cloves garlic, finely chopped
1½ cups plain yogurt, at room
    temperature
1 to 2 teaspoons dried dill
Freshly ground black pepper

1. Bring salted water to a boil and cook spaghetti or egg noodles.

2. Meanwhile, in a medium skillet, heat 4 tablespoons of the butter over medium-high heat and as soon as it begins to sizzle, add the grated onion. Season with salt, and sauté, stirring constantly, until the onion begins to brown, about 10 minutes.

3. Add the garlic and cook another 4 or 5 minutes, until the onion is well browned and the garlic is lightly colored.

4. Remove from the heat and add the remaining butter; let melt.

5. Drain spaghetti.

6. In a serving bowl, toss the spaghetti with the yogurt, then the onion and garlic butter, dill, and pepper.

7. Serve immediately.

Index